I0795918

IMAGES
of America

SOUTH MILWAUKEE

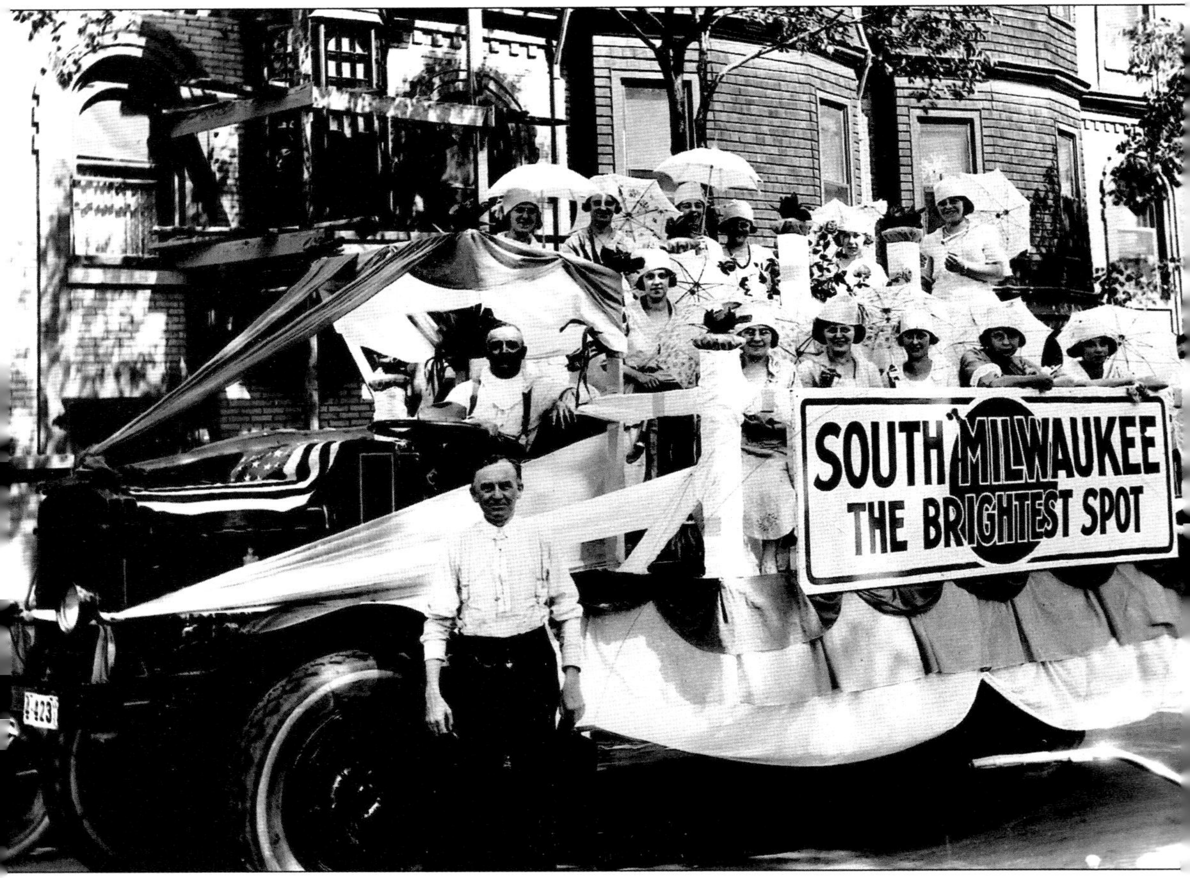
SOUTH MILWAUKEE
THE BRIGHTEST SPOT

IMAGES
of America

SOUTH MILWAUKEE

Nels J. Monson and Dean Marlowe Jr.

ARCADIA
PUBLISHING

ISBN 978-0-7385-3349-0

Published by Arcadia Publishing
Charleston, South Carolina

Printed in the United States of America

Library of Congress Catalog Card Number: 2004111998

For all general information contact Arcadia Publishing at:
Telephone 843-853-2070
Fax 843-853-0044
E-mail sales@arcadiapublishing.com
For customer service and orders:
Toll-Free 1-888-313-2665

Visit us on the Internet at www.arcadiapublishing.com

This book is dedicated to my parents.

Nels J. Monson

Contents

Acknowledgments

I would like to thank the City of South Milwaukee as well as the officers and the board of directors of the South Milwaukee Historical Society for helping make this book a reality. Special thanks go out to Historical Society President JB Bulley and Past President Don Bulley for their unwavering support of this project. Special mention goes to the late Gertrude Endthoff, for her 50-plus years of research in, and promotion of, South Milwaukee's history.

I would also like to acknowledge the contributions of all those individuals who have, over the years, donated their photographs to the historical society. Without these, this humble book could not have been possible. Thanks to Joe Szatmary, Beverly Rayeske, Walter Shelenske, Joe Hosmanek, Mary Nelson, Edie Ottman, Fred Mitchell, and Pete Brunner for access to their photographic collections.

A special thank you is in order to Judy Balestrieri, a descendant of the venerable old Fowle family, who was very helpful in "filling in the gaps." Lastly, I would like to thank my dear wife Julie and daughters Erika and Monika for putting up with me all this time.

A genuine and sincere effort was made in preparing as accurate a portrayal of South Milwaukee's history as possible. Any omissions or errors are the fault of the author. Unless otherwise noted, all photographs are from the archives of the South Milwaukee Historical Society.

Proceeds from the sale of this book will benefit the South Milwaukee Historical Society.

Introduction

South Milwaukee, Wisconsin, has always offered a fascinating blend of independence, industry, rustic charm, and natural beauty. The city is located near the highest point on the western shores of Lake Michigan, where the meandering Oak Creek empties into that great lake. First settled in the spring of 1835 by New England Yankees and English immigrants, the area quickly became a focal point in the Township of Oak Creek, which in 1841 became the seventh and final original Milwaukee county township. The name had been chosen by these early pioneers because of the dense woodlots of white oak trees that lined the creek. By the 1850s, this rural hamlet had blossomed into a small community of businesses and dwellings situated along the old Chicago Road and Hawthorne Avenue.

In 1891, fate took a hand in the matter, when a small group of dedicated businessmen and capitalists began securing land options on nearly 1,000 acres of farmland in the northeast corner of the township. The intention of this newly formed "South Milwaukee Company" was to create and develop a substantial new industrial suburb, one to perhaps rival Milwaukee itself. In 1892, the Village of South Milwaukee incorporated, officially separating itself from the Township of Oak Creek.

The South Milwaukee Company successfully attracted nearly a dozen new "manufactories" to the area, most notably the Bucyrus Steam Shovel & Dredge Company, which was relocated from Ohio and remains a South Milwaukee fixture to this day. Also taking an important role in the development of this new community was the Chicago & Northwestern Railroad, which ran spur lines to all major plant sites, as well as one to the new harbor area on Lake Michigan. A beautiful new railroad depot was built, designed by the noted architect Charles Sumner Frost.

Workers were needed for these new factories, and by 1897 thousands of new arrivals, including many German and Polish immigrants, flooded into the community. South Milwaukee was quick to respond to the needs of its residents. Along Milwaukee Avenue, which was the heart of a new downtown shopping district, many new businesses sprang up. Also, a burgeoning tavern scene was sure to slake the thirst of even the most rapacious factory worker.

Working class roots aside, South Milwaukeeans have always found time to enjoy the more leisurely pursuits in life. Athletics were always a popular pastime, and a community baseball team was formed as early as 1893. Originally, there was even an opera house in the works. In 1911, Grant Park was established. This 400-acre gem lies along the wooded bluffs of Lake Michigan. Grant Park would eventually boast of a lush network of walking and bridal paths, an

18-hole golf course, a mile-long beach with bathhouse, pavilions, picnic groves, athletic fields, and a campground.

Over the coming decades, South Milwaukee flourished, its fortunes tied closely to the expansion of the post-World War II economy.

We invite the reader to sit back and enjoy this glimpse into South Milwaukee's past. Whether the images contained herein evoke memories of a bygone age to some or bring a sense of discovery and enlightenment to others, we sincerely hope the experience will be a pleasant one.

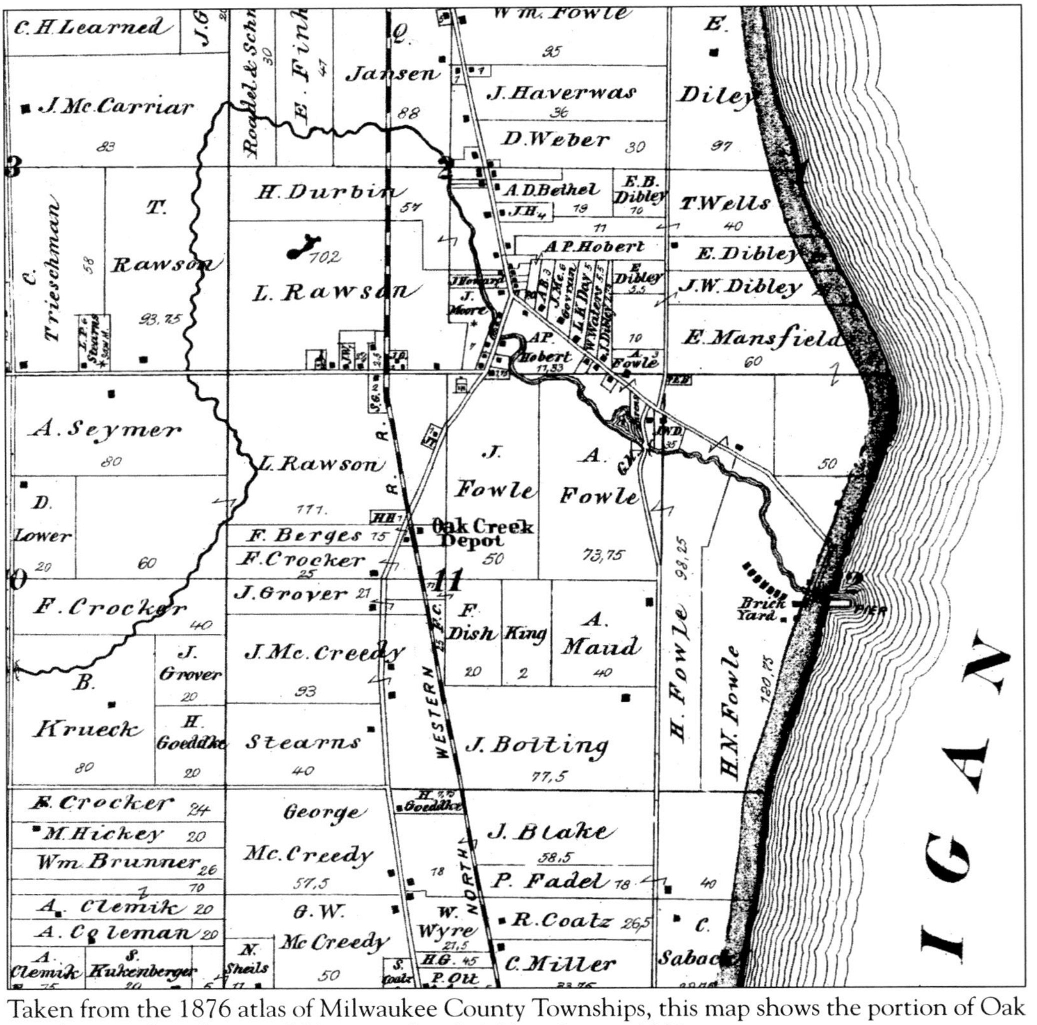

Taken from the 1876 atlas of Milwaukee County Townships, this map shows the portion of Oak Creek Township that would become South Milwaukee in 1892.

One

Oak Creek Township

Elihu Higgins is credited as being the first settler to arrive in what is now South Milwaukee. Higgins, from Buckland, Massachusetts, came to the area in the spring of 1835. Struck by the beauty and potential of the area, Higgins wrote back home to his wife Eliza and urged her to bring their small daughter and join him at once. Accompanied by her brother, Moses Rawson, Mrs. Higgins made the trek in a wagon pulled by a yoke of oxen. When he arrived to reunite the Higgins family, Moses Rawson was impressed by what he saw. Upon his return to Massachusetts, he convinced his father, Oliver Rawson, to move his family to this "new and promising land."

While the Rawsons were in transit, the families of John Fowle and Joseph Dibley, recently arrived from England, settled in the area. Soon afterwards, they would be joined by the Jesse Baldwin family and the McCreedy brothers from New York. These and other families would form the nucleus of what would in 1841 become Oak Creek Township.

By 1840, both Higgins and John Fowle had built sawmills on Oak Creek. Fowle would later add a gristmill, the first such mill in Milwaukee County. Around 1844, Fowle built a new and improved flour and gristmill further upstream. This mill would come to be known as one of South Milwaukee's most famous early landmarks.

A school and church were soon established. John Grover built the first basket factory in Wisconsin in 1855. It was located east of the Chicago Road, just south of Hawthorne Avenue. There were also brickyards that produced the coveted "Cream City" bricks. Other settlers dabbled in shipbuilding. These early enterprises brought commerce to Oak Creek. But it was just the beginning . . .

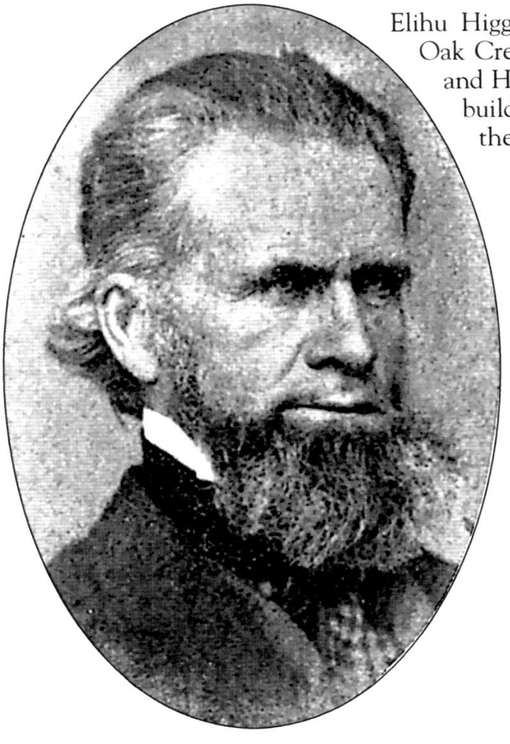

Elihu Higgins (1808–1875) built the first log cabin in Oak Creek near the intersection of the Chicago Road and Hawthorne Avenue. He would later convert this building to an inn. This intersection would become the community's commerce center.

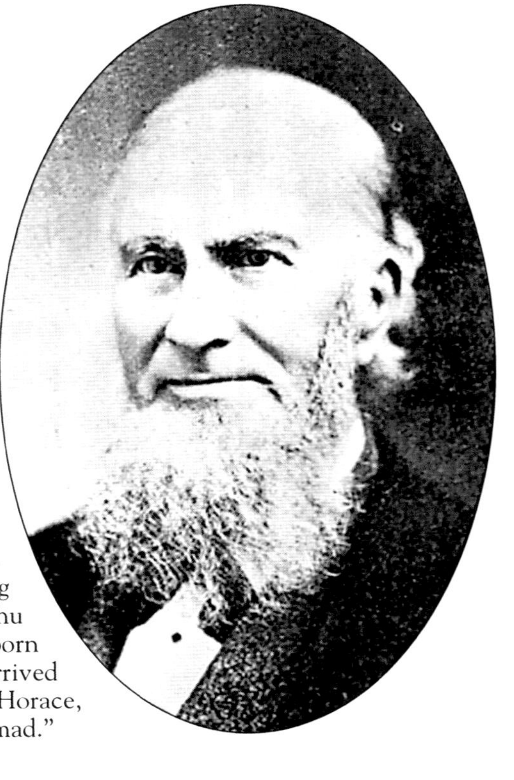

Born in Sussex, England, John Fowle (1796–1887) arrived in the area in June 1835 with his wife and nine children. Fowle would quickly establish himself as one of the leading figures in this new community. He and Elihu Higgins vied to father the first "white child" born in Oak Creek. When Mary Augusta Higgins arrived on February 22, 1837, four days before his son Horace, the elder Fowle was reported as being "plenty mad."

Oliver Rawson (1781–1868) came from one of New England's most distinguished families. His father, Moses Rawson, spent four years fighting in the American Revolutionary War. After his arrival in Oak Creek in 1836, Oliver and his son Luther purchased 320 acres of land straddling the road that now bears his name.

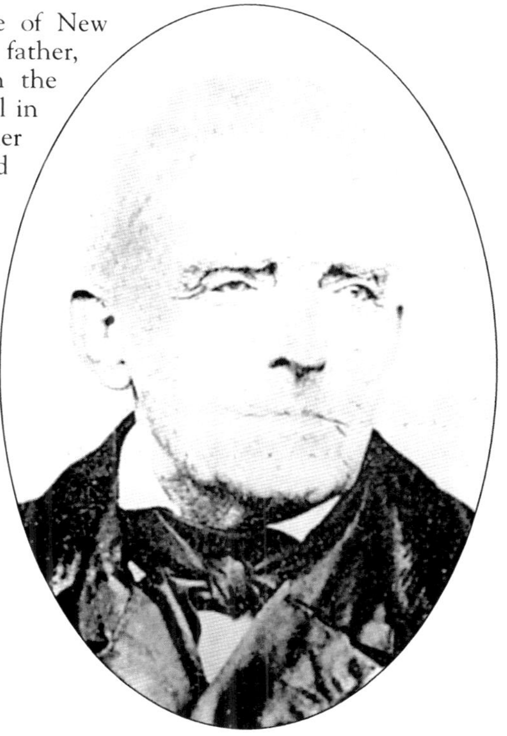

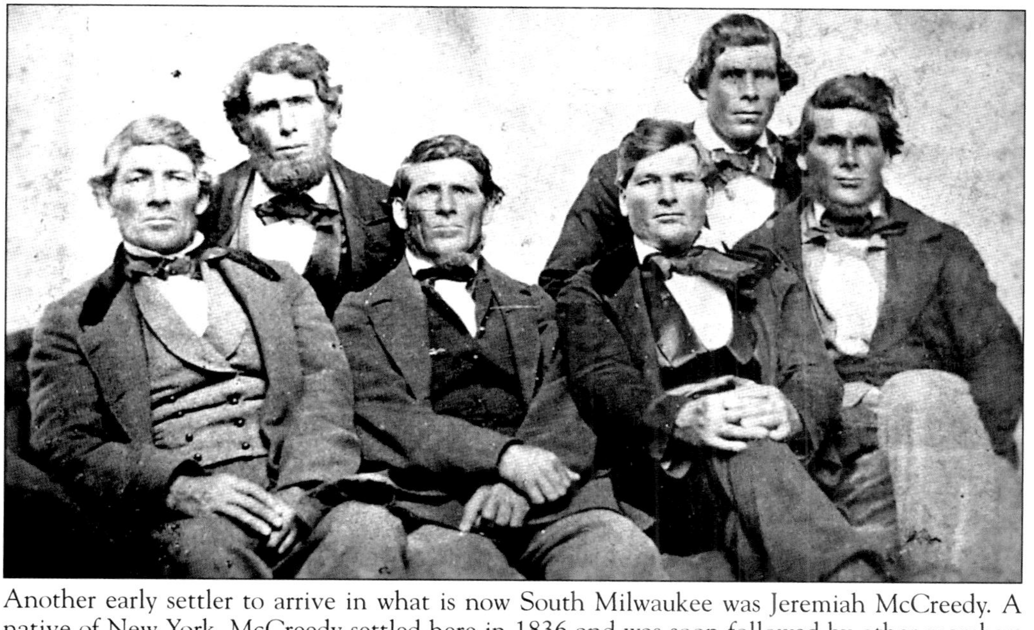

Another early settler to arrive in what is now South Milwaukee was Jeremiah McCreedy. A native of New York, McCreedy settled here in 1836 and was soon followed by other members of his family. In this undated photo, Jeremiah is seen on the left along with his brothers George, James, Sidney, Asa, and Nathan

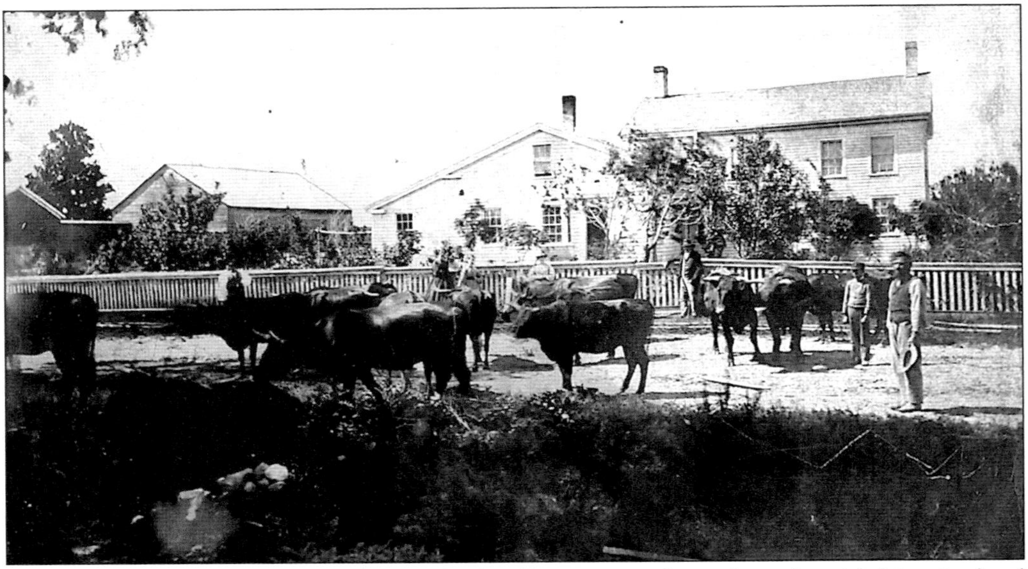

In this photograph, taken around 1861, Luther Rawson stands on the right with his prize herd of red Devon cattle. His son, Edward is standing next to him. Oliver Rawson, Luther's father, is standing along the fence. The others in the photo are unidentified, though they are probably family members. The building is Luther's home, which stood on Rawson Avenue. Reputedly, part of this structure still stands today at 707 Monroe Avenue.

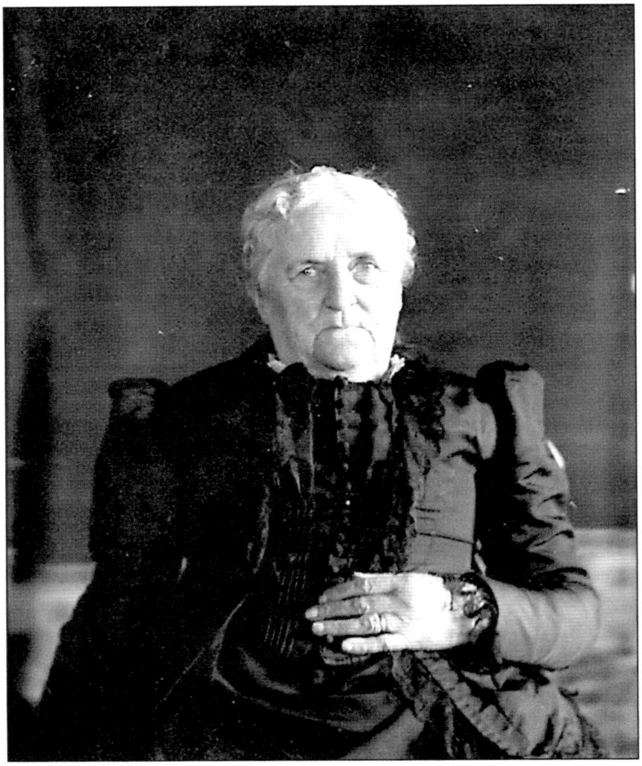

Electa Rawson, born in 1823, was the daughter of Oliver Rawson. She made the trip from Massachusetts to Oak Creek with her family in 1836. She married Frederick Fowle, son of pioneer John Fowle, in 1842. Frederick died of typhoid fever just five weeks after their wedding. In June 1846, Electa would become Mrs. Farrier Mansfield.

This portrait is believed to be Erv McClay, Company K, 24th Wisconsin Volunteer Infantry Regiment. When the 24th was organized in August 1862, 37 Oak Creek lads were assigned to Company K. Known as the "Milwaukee Regiment," the 24th would be commanded by Lt. Col. Arthur MacArthur. Though MacArthur would win the Medal of Honor for his actions at the Battle of Missionary Ridge in 1863, his son Douglas would gain even greater military renown.

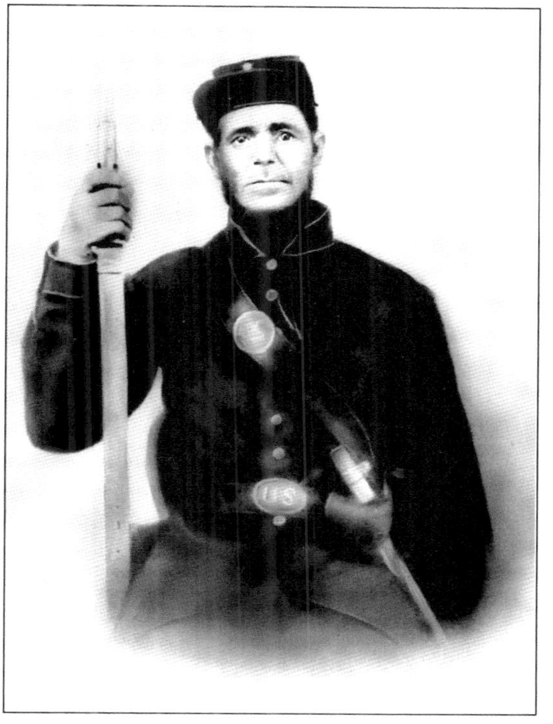

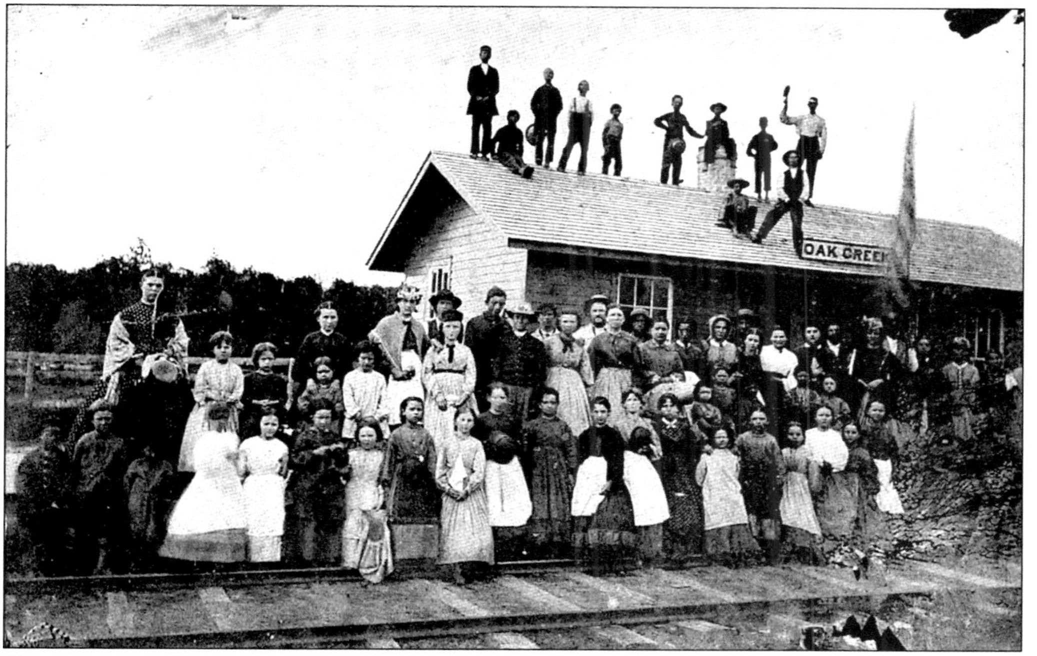

This rare photograph, taken in July 1865, shows the Oak Creek townsfolk awaiting the return of the 24th Wisconsin. Period accounts relate the frustration of the soldiers as they passed through their town on the way to Milwaukee, where they were mustered out a few days later. This depot was located on the same site as the one built in 1893.

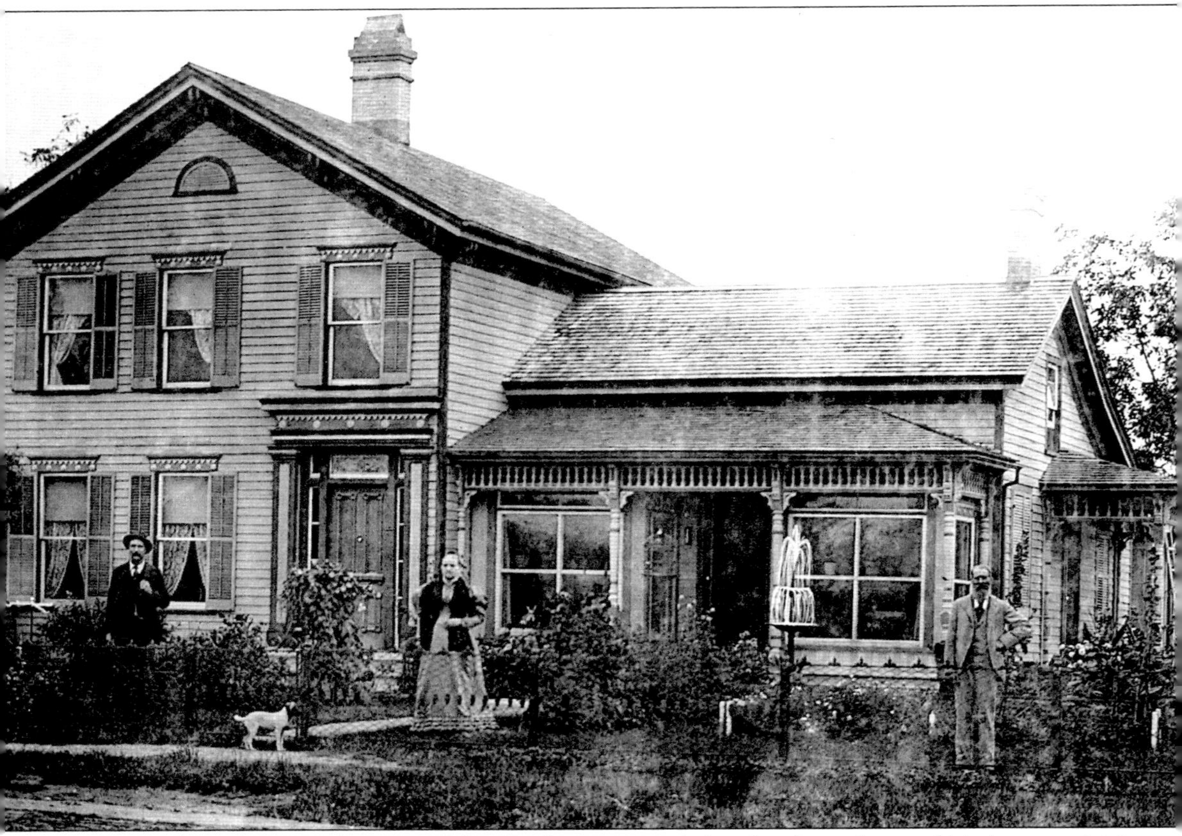

Alfred Fowle, son of pioneer John Fowle, poses with his family in front of his home, which still stands at 626 Hawthorne Avenue. It was noted that Alfred's "love of flowers was one of his chief characteristics, the lovely display in his garden and conservatory giving pleasure to all who chanced to pass his home." Taken *c.* 1895, the photo shows, from right to left: Alfred, his wife Mary Jane (nee Baldwin), and son Francis. Notice the water fountain and the family pet, "Polly." Built around 1848, it was in this house that Alfred would die of pneumonia on December 22, 1904, at age 83. (Courtesy of Judy Balestrieri.)

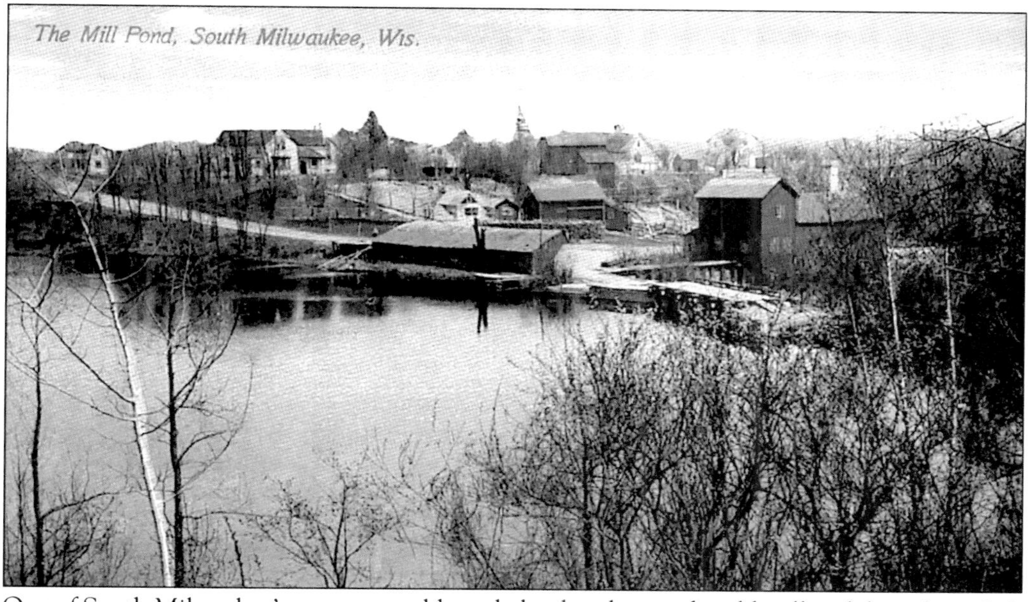

One of South Milwaukee's most venerable early landmarks was the old mill and dam along Oak Creek. Built around 1844 by John Fowle, the mill can be seen at right center in this c. 1910 photograph. In the center of the photo are the sheds where farmers would rest their horses while waiting for their wheat to be ground. Also seen in this view is the home of then owner John Ahrens, which sits on the hill overlooking the mill and dam.

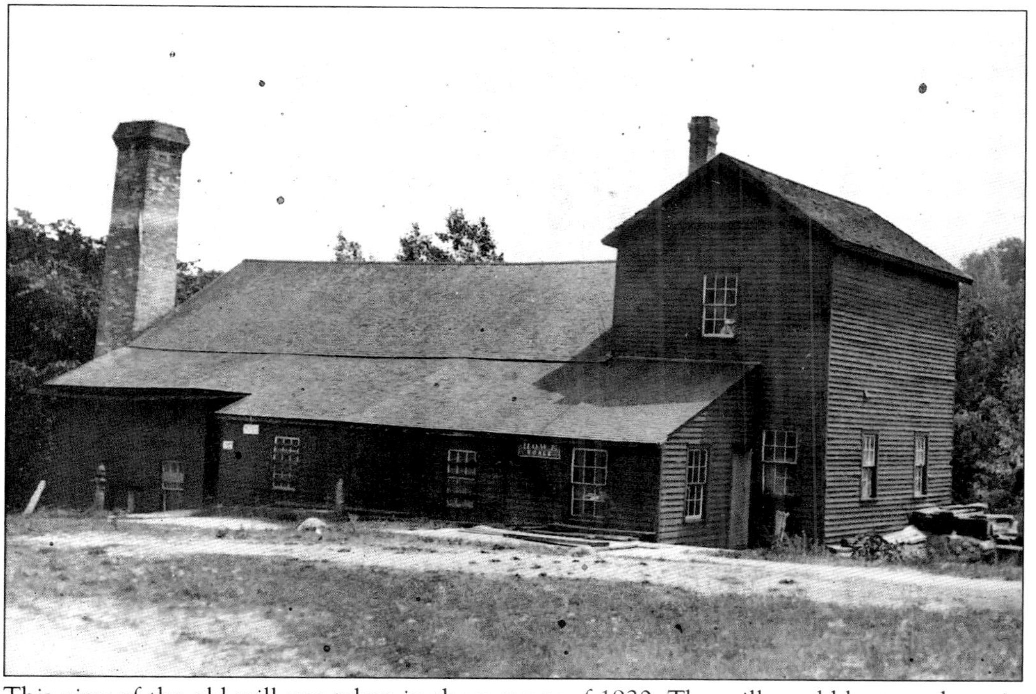

This view of the old mill was taken in the summer of 1920. The mill would be torn down in 1933, after the land was sold to the Milwaukee County Park system.

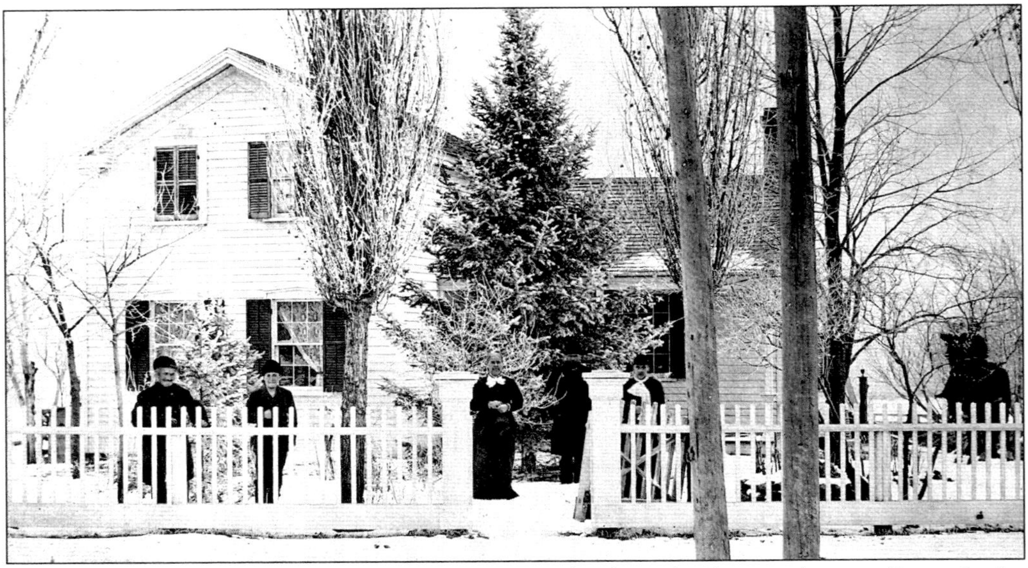

The William Wyre house was located on the east side of South Chicago Avenue (formerly the old Chicago Road), near the intersection with Columbia Avenue. A Civil War veteran, Wyre was one of the original Company K "boys" from Oak Creek. In this *c.* 1880 photograph, Wyre can be seen in the center with his wife Sarah. Also included are his father-in-law Duncan Sovey, son George, and daughter Rosetta.

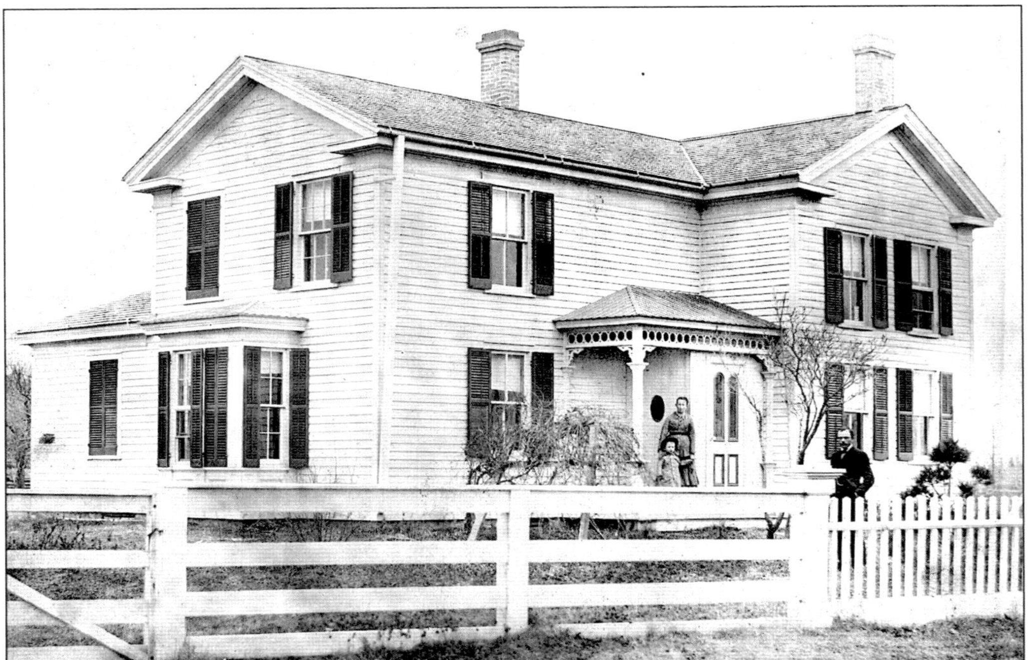

Though commonly identified as the George Hook house, research indicates that this *c.* 1895 photo was more likely the home of Elsworth S. Cook. The house was located at 1102 Rawson Avenue.

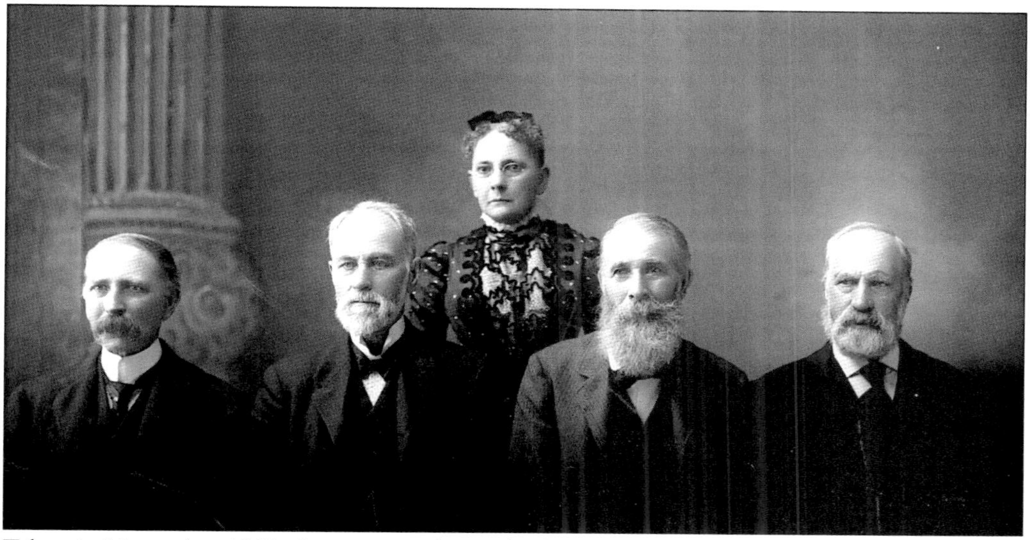

Taken in November 1901, this portrait shows the five surviving children of Oak Creek pioneer John Fowle. Pictured from left to right are Horace, Henry, Charity Jane, Alfred, and William. (Courtesy of Judy Balestrieri.)

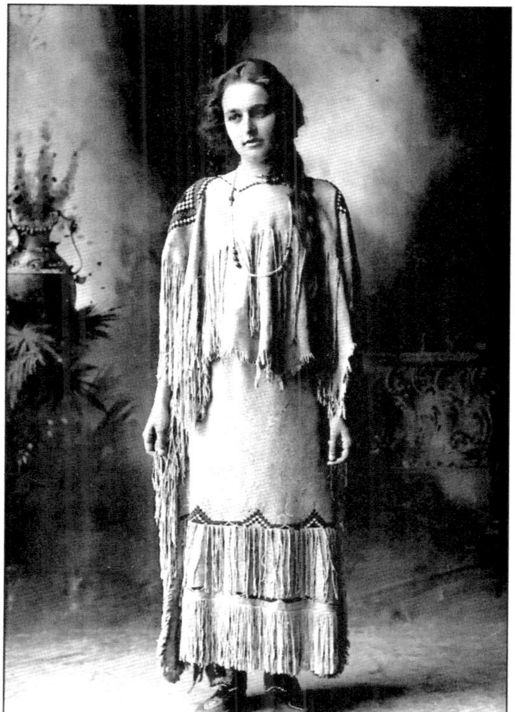

Miss Jessie Rundle, great-great-granddaughter of John Fowle, appears in native-American dress in this c. 1900 photograph. (Courtesy of Judy Balestrieri.)

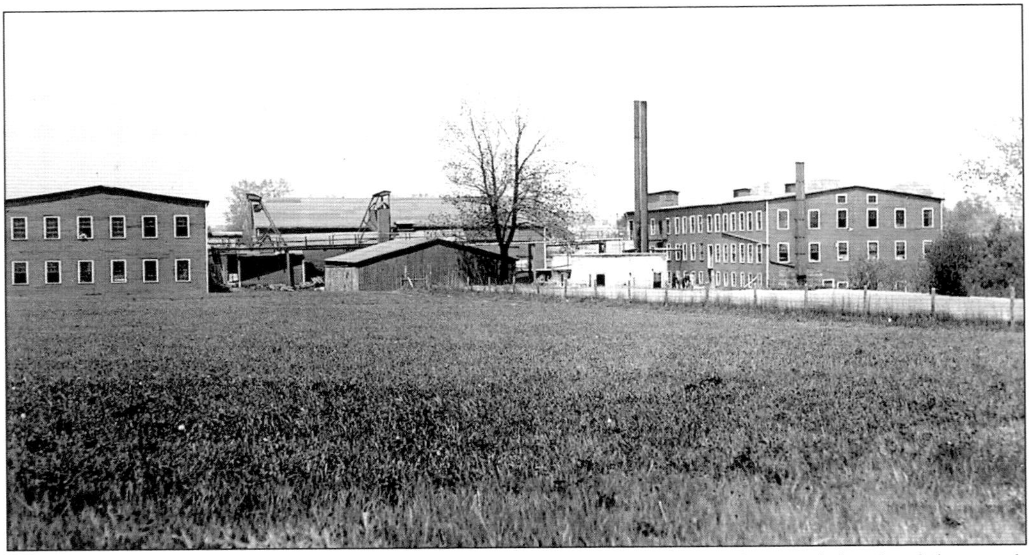

The Moore Basket Works were established in 1872. Located along the south bank of the creek west of the Chicago Road, this company would change owners several times before closing down in 1925. Later, the land would be sold to Milwaukee County. Today the area is heavily wooded and little evidence of the factory remains.

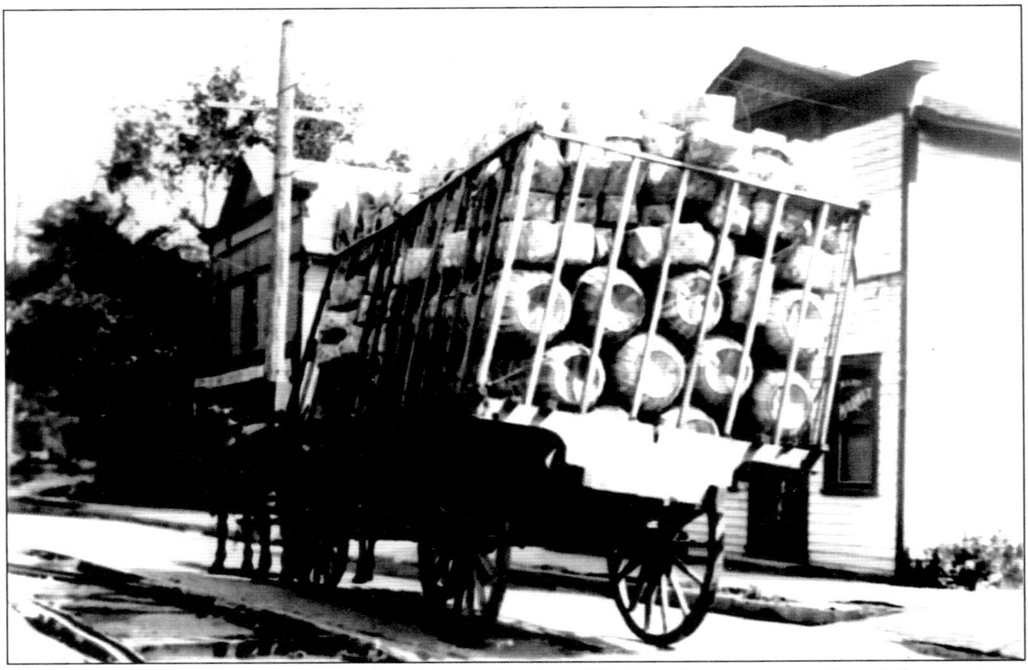

A wagonload of product from the nearby Basket Works tilts precariously while awaiting delivery to Milwaukee. This photo, *c.* 1910, was taken on North Chicago Avenue just north of Hawthorne and shows McCreedy's "pioneer grocery" store in the left center background.

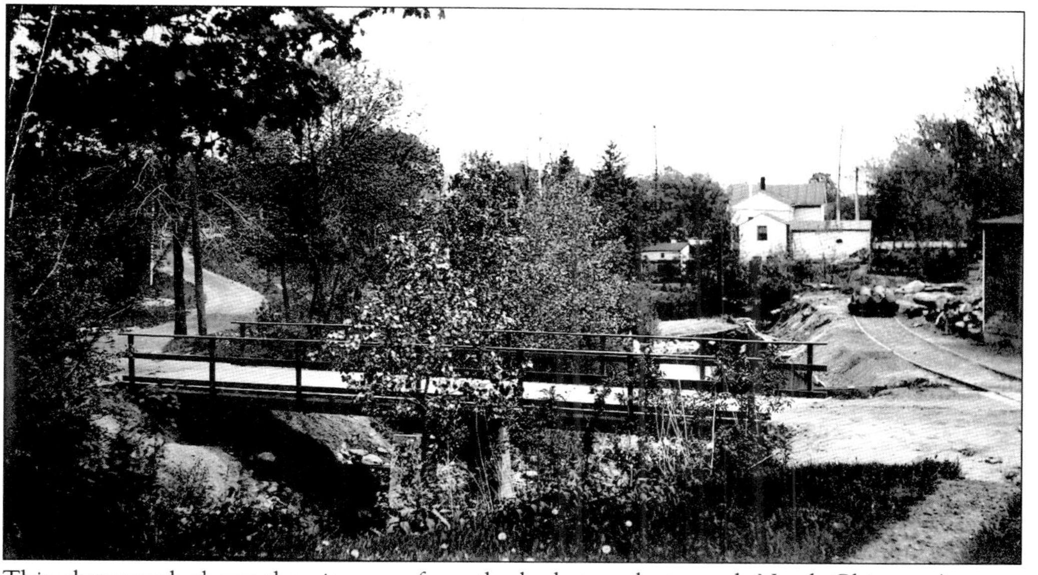

This photograph shows the view east from the basket works towards North Chicago Avenue. The bridge across the creek was used by the wagon drivers to reach the road. Today, remnants of the bridge's concrete supports are about all that remains of this once active site.

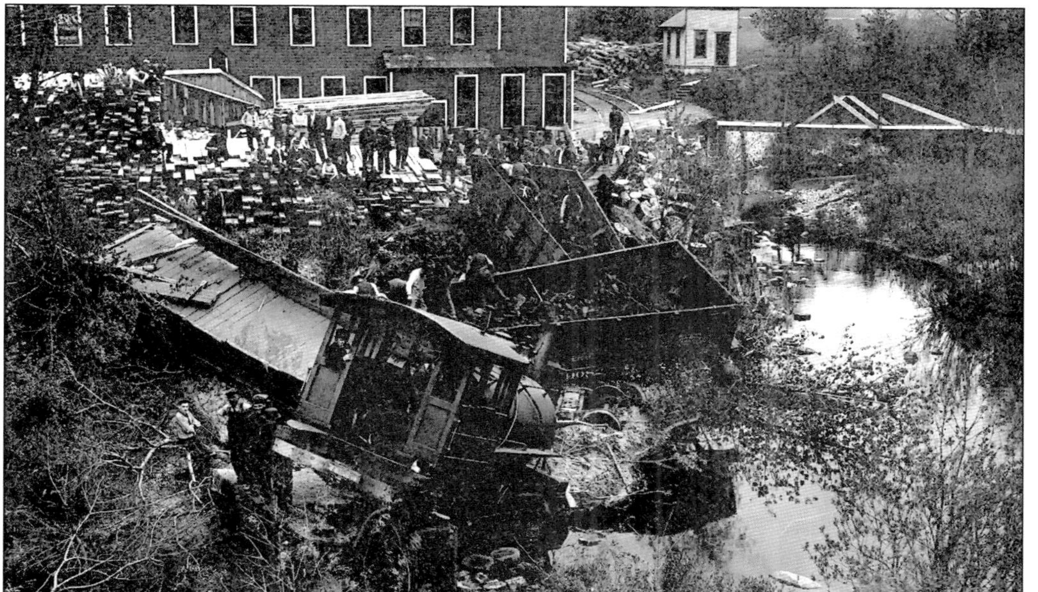

This view shows the 1910 wreck of the "Dinky," a small train used by the basket factory to haul coal. The Dinky jumped its tracks and plunged into the creek. The basket factory's office can be seen above the bridge.

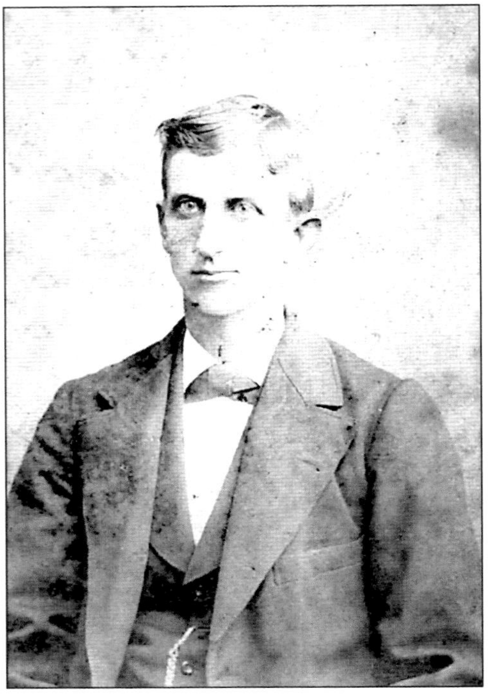

Born in 1851, Edward L. Rawson was the grandson of early pioneer Oliver Rawson.

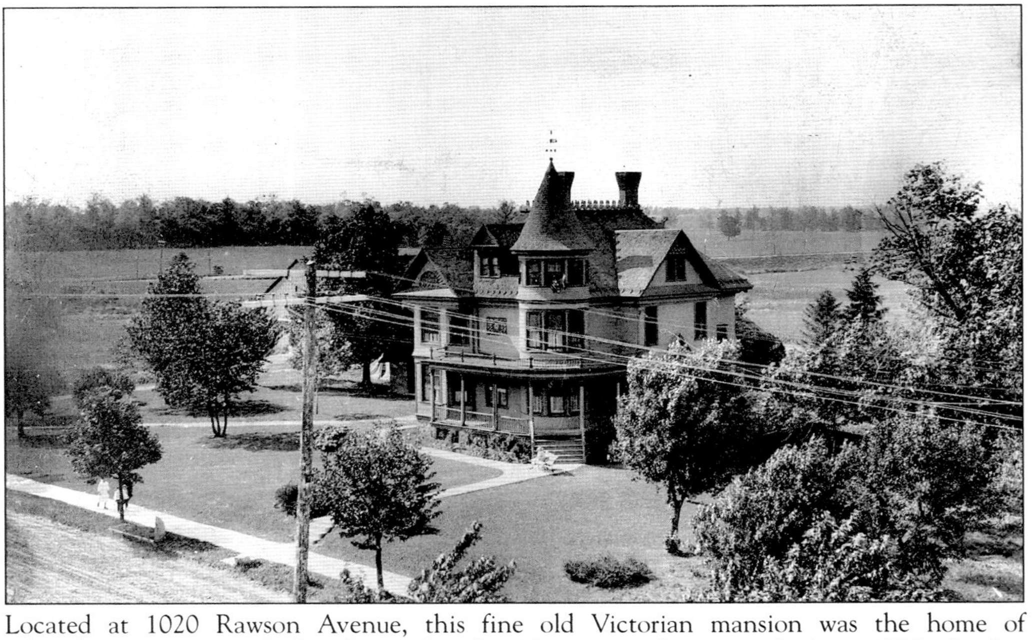

Located at 1020 Rawson Avenue, this fine old Victorian mansion was the home of Edward L. Rawson. Pinkish-red in color, the 12-room residence was built in 1893 after his marriage to Ida Fowle. This view, dated around 1900, faces northwest and was taken from the upper level of the high school at Tenth and Rawson Avenues. Sadly, the beautiful dwelling was purchased by Bucyrus in 1981 and immediately razed.

Two

The South Milwaukee Company

It was in the spring of 1891 that the makeup of Oak Creek Township began a significant transformation. William M. Williams and his brother in-law Frederick C. Mansfield started securing land options on nearly 1,000 acres in the northeast corner of the township. Aided in this venture by prominent Milwaukee capitalist Fred W. Rogers and other men of vision, this newly formed "South Milwaukee Company" would seek to develop the area into a powerful new industrial suburb.

The South Milwaukee Company quickly attracted businesses to the area. A new business district was created along Milwaukee Avenue. In 1891–92, the Schutz Brothers Furniture Company built the first factory. The imposing new South Milwaukee (or Koch's) Hotel, on the northeast corner of Eleventh and Milwaukee was the first public building to be erected. When the Bucyrus Steam Shovel & Dredge Company began operations in its new factory in April 1893, it quickly became the cornerstone of the new community. Aided by the support of the Chicago & Northwestern Railroad, a beautiful new railroad depot was opened in December 1893.

With the changes brought about by the South Milwaukee Company, the stage was set for greater things yet to come. . . .

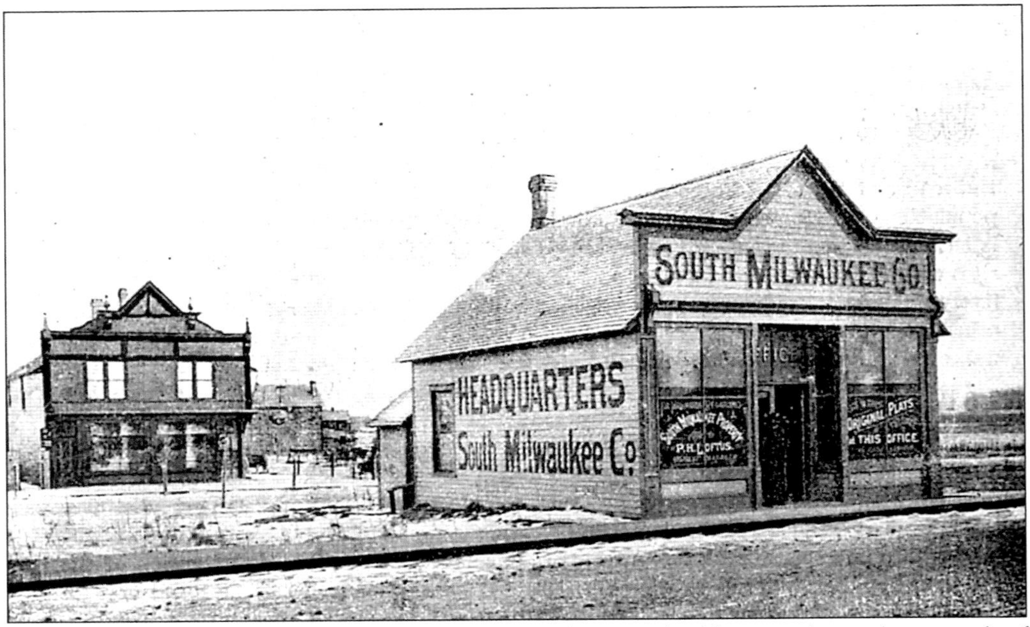

In early 189, the South Milwaukee Company's headquarters building was located just south of the depot. The building in the left background still stands on the northeast corner of Eleventh and Madison.

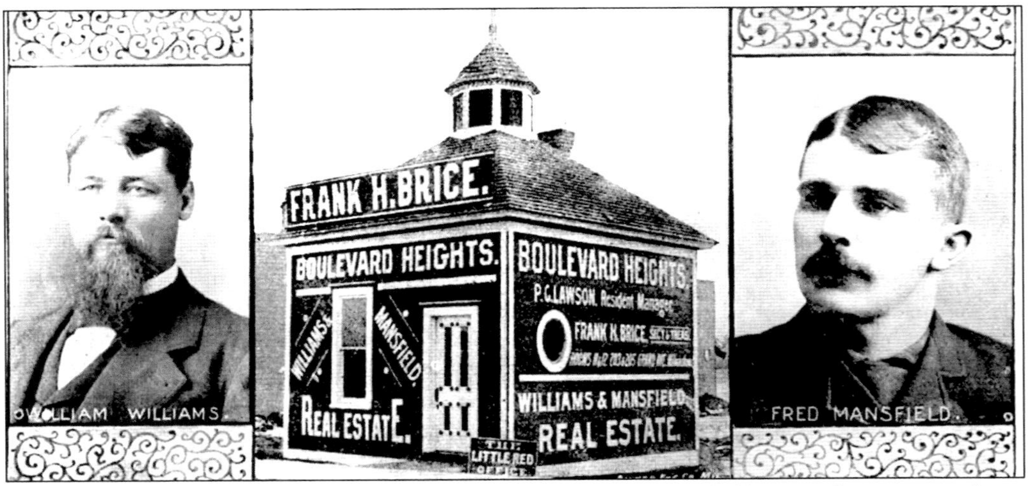

William M. Williams (left) and his brother in-law Fred E. Mansfield secured options on large tracts of farmland in the northeast corner of Oak Creek Township; they then approached wealthy Milwaukee capitalist Fred W. Rogers to help support the creation of a new town. These land options were then transferred to Rogers and the newly formed South Milwaukee Company was incorporated on June 20, 1891. Fred Rogers would come to be known as the "Father of South Milwaukee."

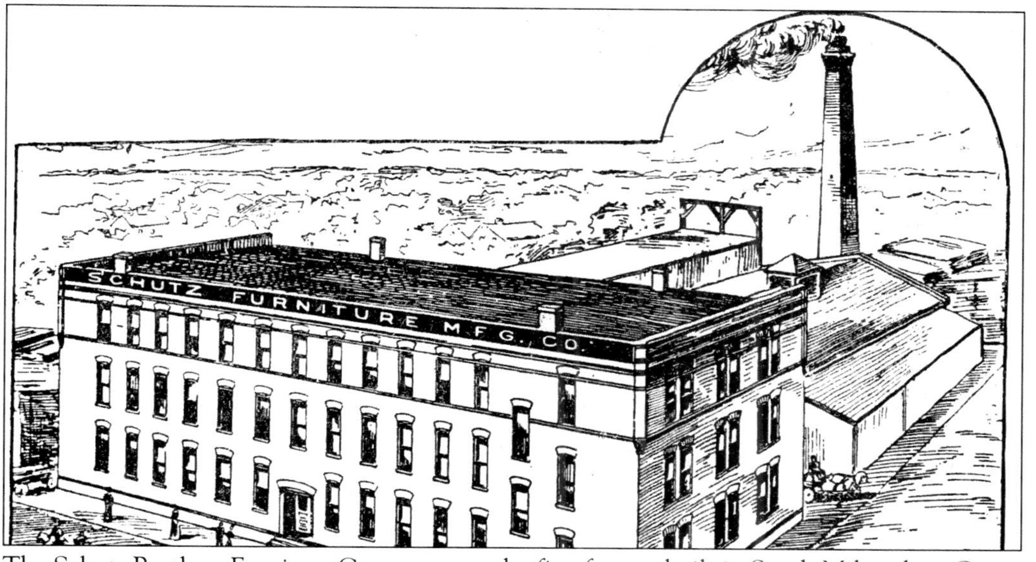

The Schutz Brothers Furniture Company was the first factory built in South Milwaukee. Going into operation in October 1892, the company specialized in making tables. The company lasted about 10 years before being bought out by the Racine Fire Engine & Motor Company, which held on to it for only a few years. Afterwards, it was purchased by Bucyrus. Since 1996, it has been the home of the South Milwaukee Community Center.

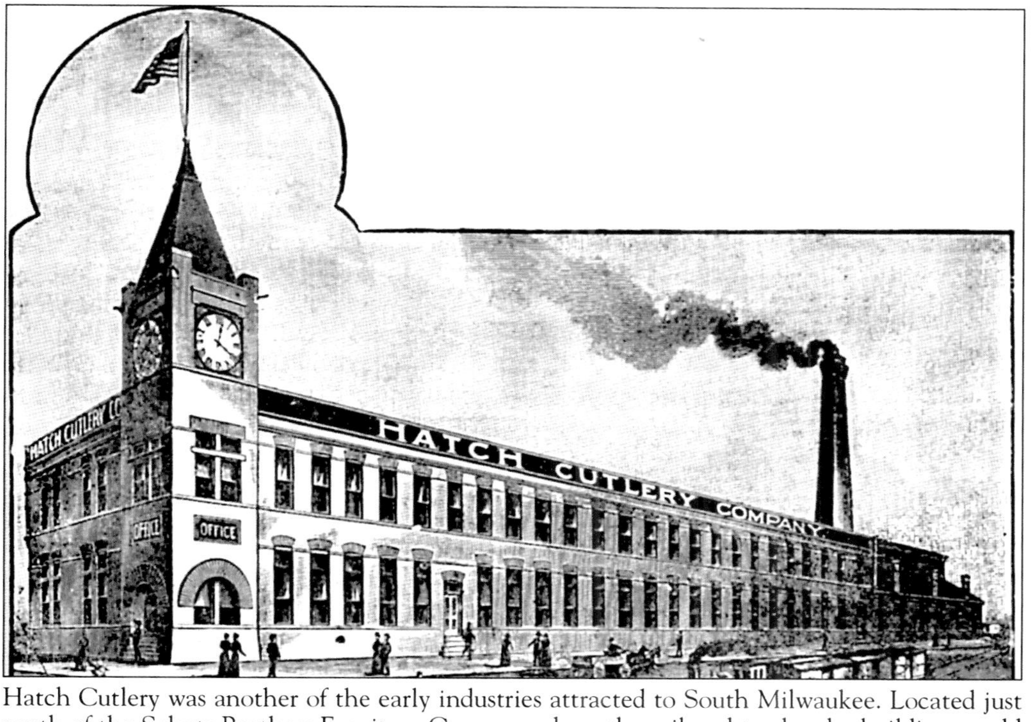

Hatch Cutlery was another of the early industries attracted to South Milwaukee. Located just north of the Schutz Brothers Furniture Company along the railroad tracks, the building would be destroyed by fire some time around 1894. Rather than rebuilding in South Milwaukee, the company was moved to Pennsylvania.

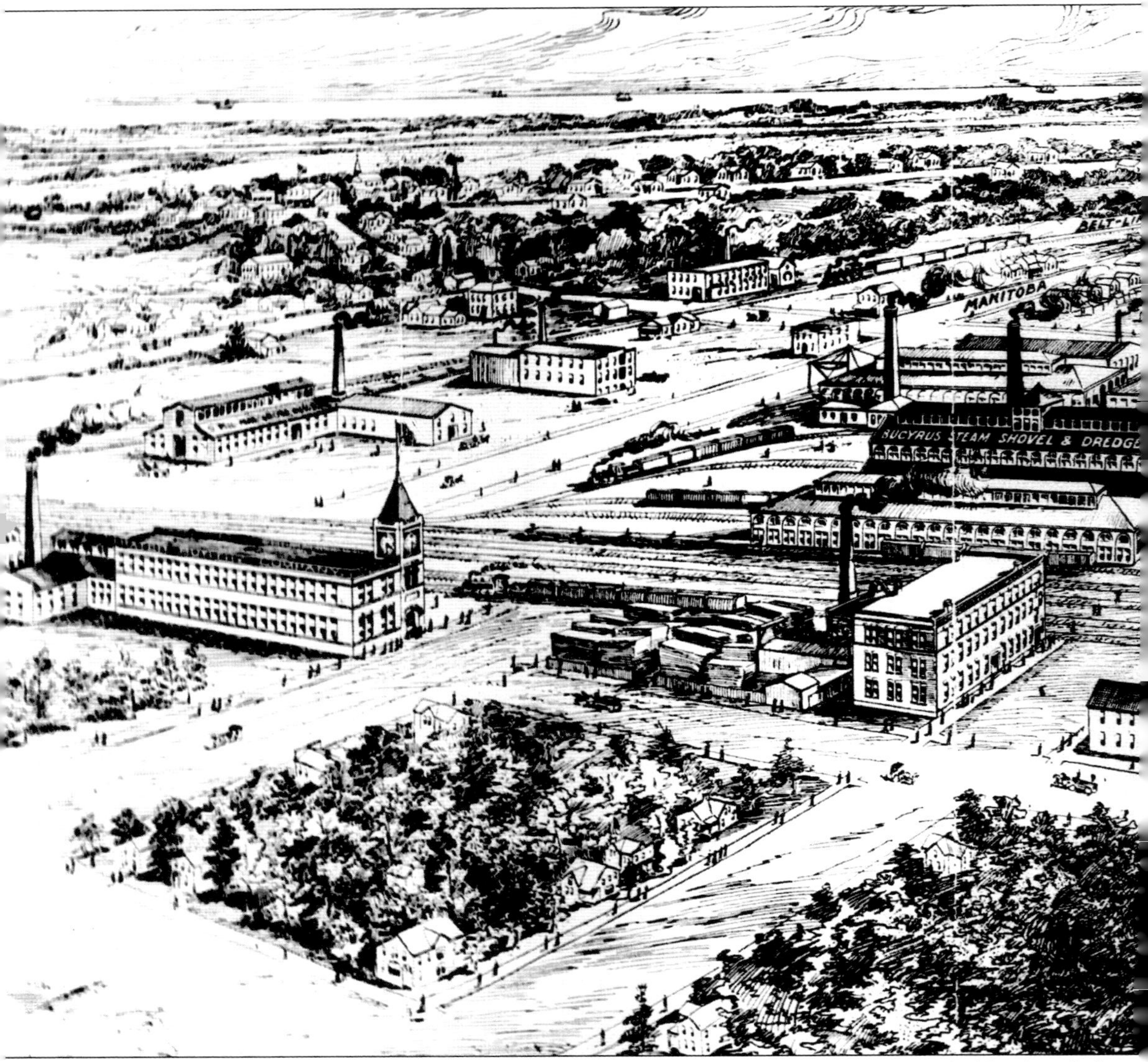

A bird's-eye view of South Milwaukee as it appeared in 1893, this remarkably detailed illustration was produced by the South Milwaukee Company and designed as an advertisement to attract new business to the area. Many of South Milwaukee's most prominent buildings can be seen here. Visible near the bottom center edge is the elegantly appointed Lake View Club House, which was built as the new city's recreation center and described as being "an ornament

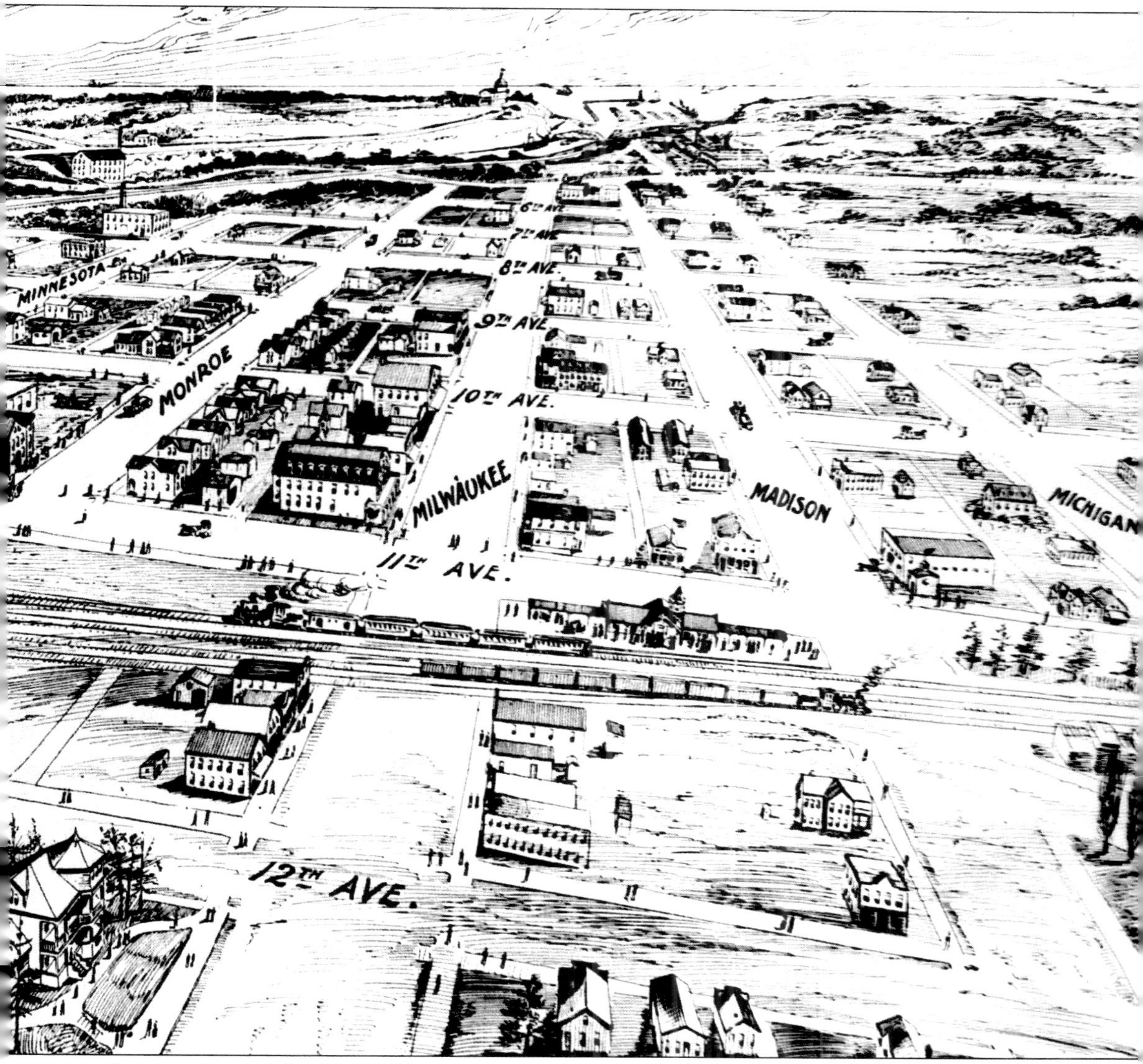

as well as a substantial edifice." Due to the depression of 1892–93, the clubhouse became a financial failure and was purchased by Mr. W.P. Hatch of Hatch Cutlery for use as a private residence. Because this building burned to the ground in March 1893, very few images of it are known to exist.

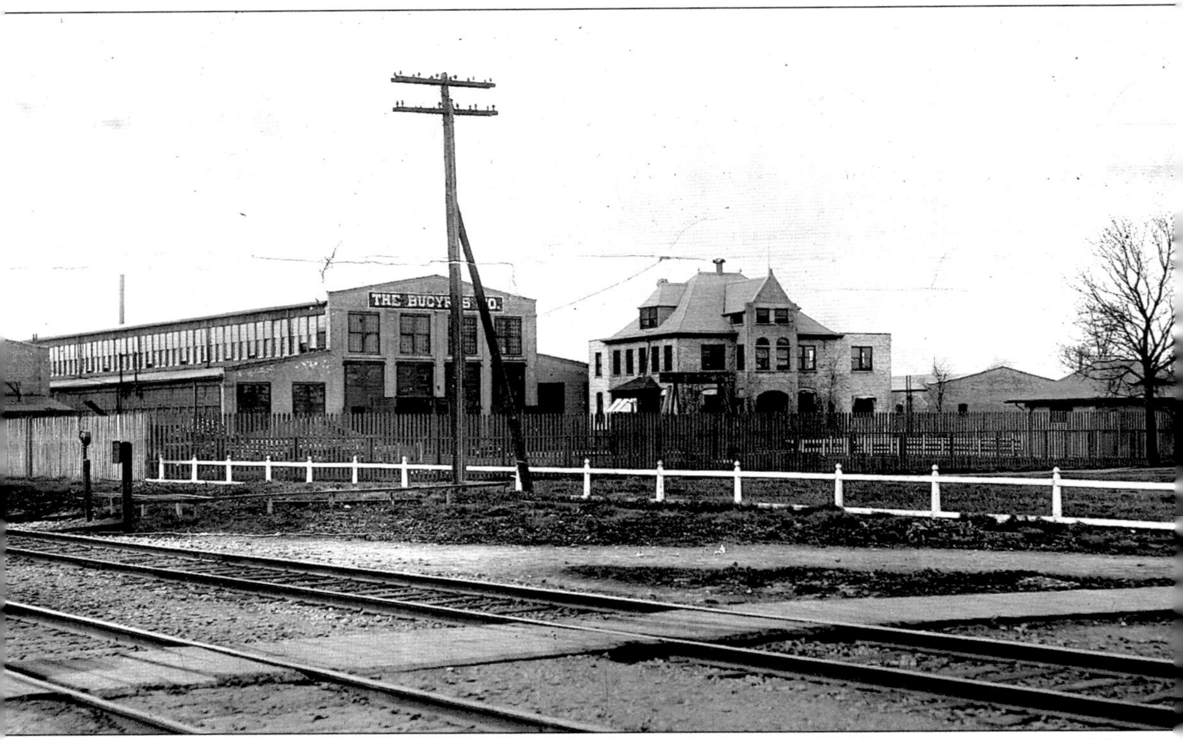

The old Bucyrus Gate House as viewed from the railroad tracks at Milwaukee Avenue *c.* 1895. One of the first industries to relocate to South Milwaukee, the Bucyrus Steam Shovel & Dredge Company moved here from Ohio in 1892. The deal was finalized when the South Milwaukee Company offered Bucyrus 15 acres of land and $50,000 towards the construction of a new plant. The Gate House was torn down in the 1970s to make room for a new Bucyrus office building.

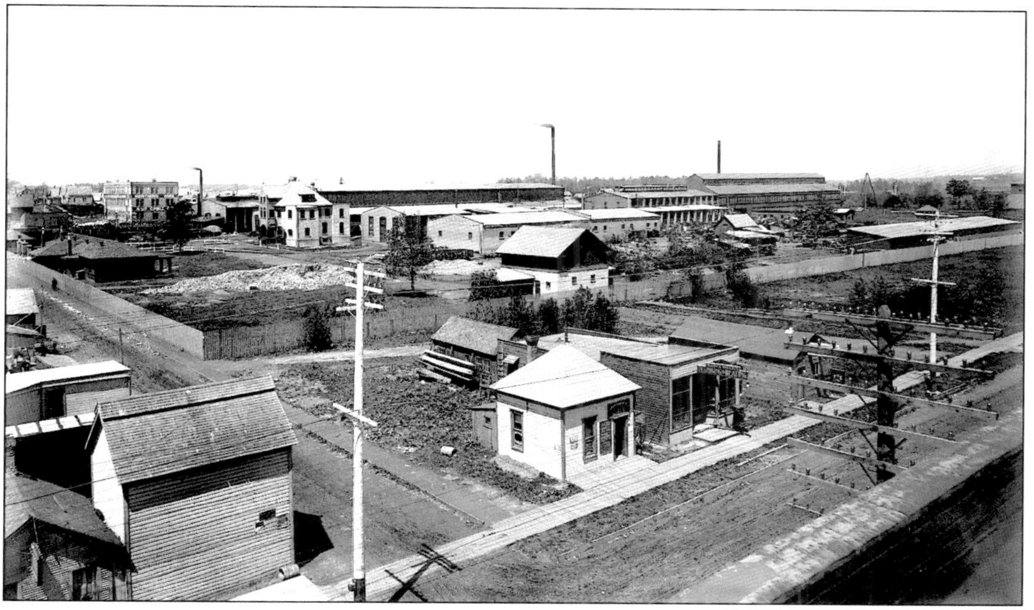

View of the Bucyrus plant as it looked in 1901 from atop the Hotel Blatz building, located on the northeast corner of Tenth and Milwaukee. The Racine Fire Engine & Motor Company building (formerly the Schutz Brothers Furniture Company) can be seen in the left background. Tenth Avenue runs diagonally across the bottom of the image.

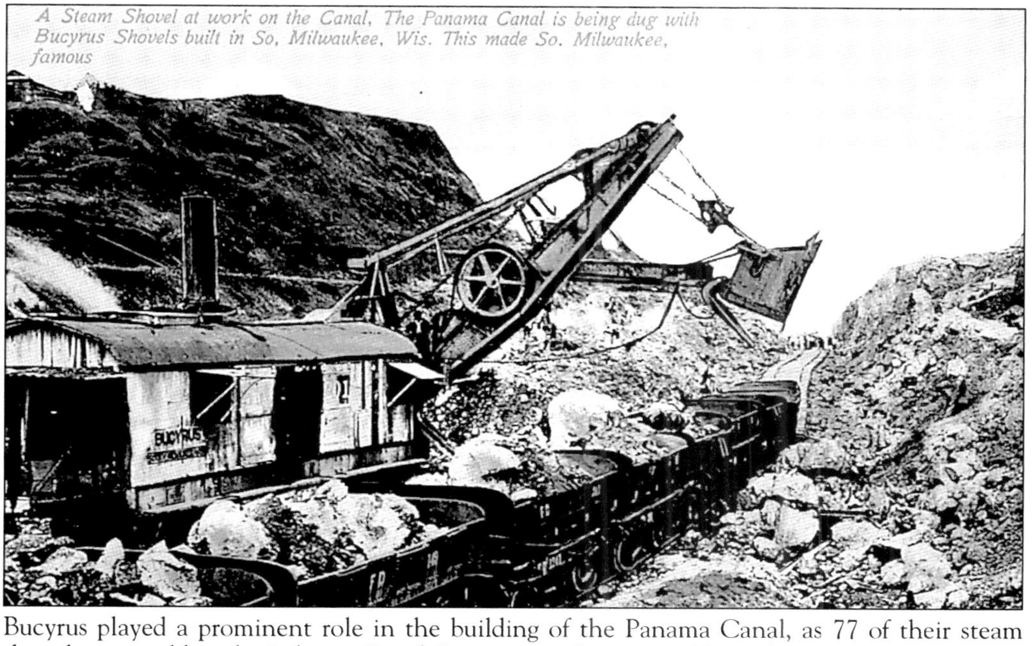

Bucyrus played a prominent role in the building of the Panama Canal, as 77 of their steam shovels were sold to the Isthmus Canal Commission between 1904 and 1907.

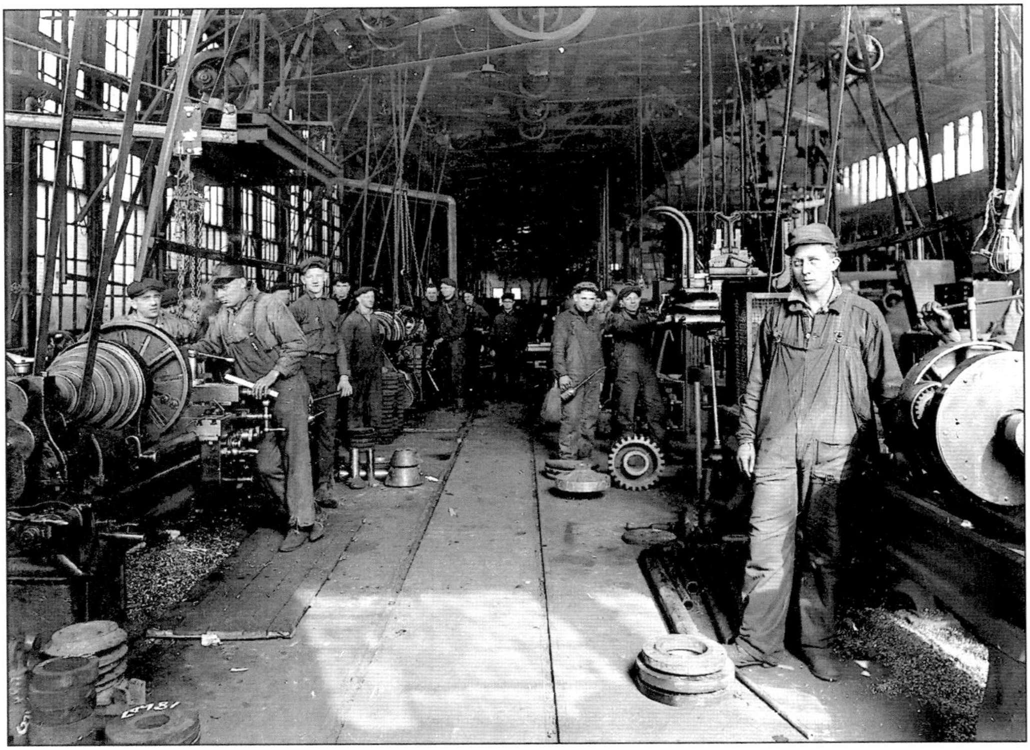

Bucyrus Machine Shop employees are seen hard at work, *c.* 1900.

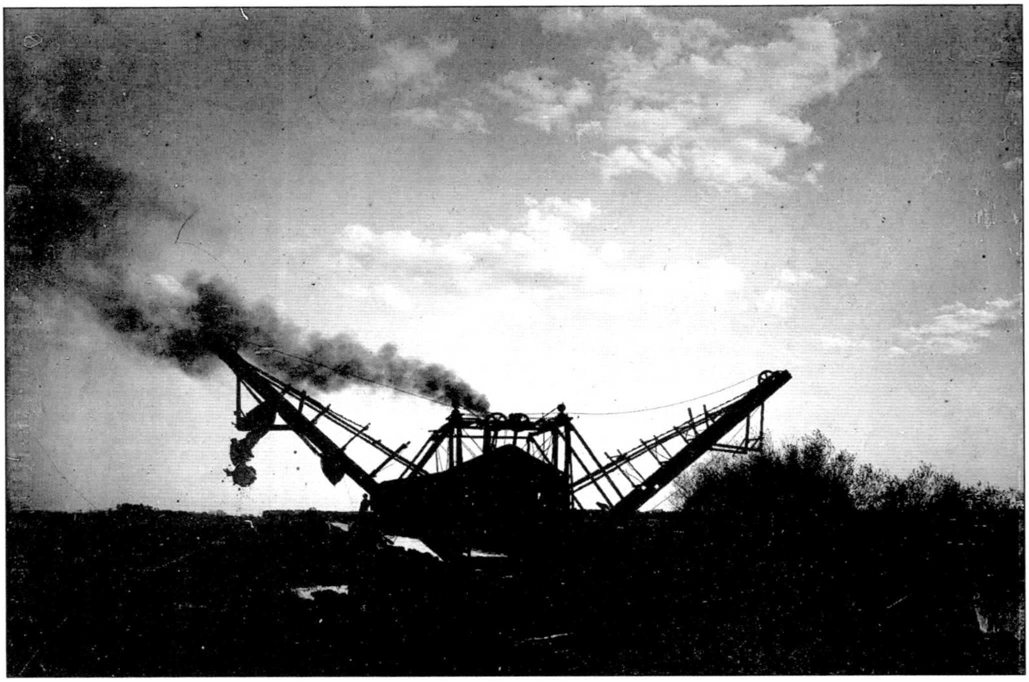

Silhouetted against the summer sky, a Bucyrus dragline toils away in Janesville, Wisconsin in 1912.

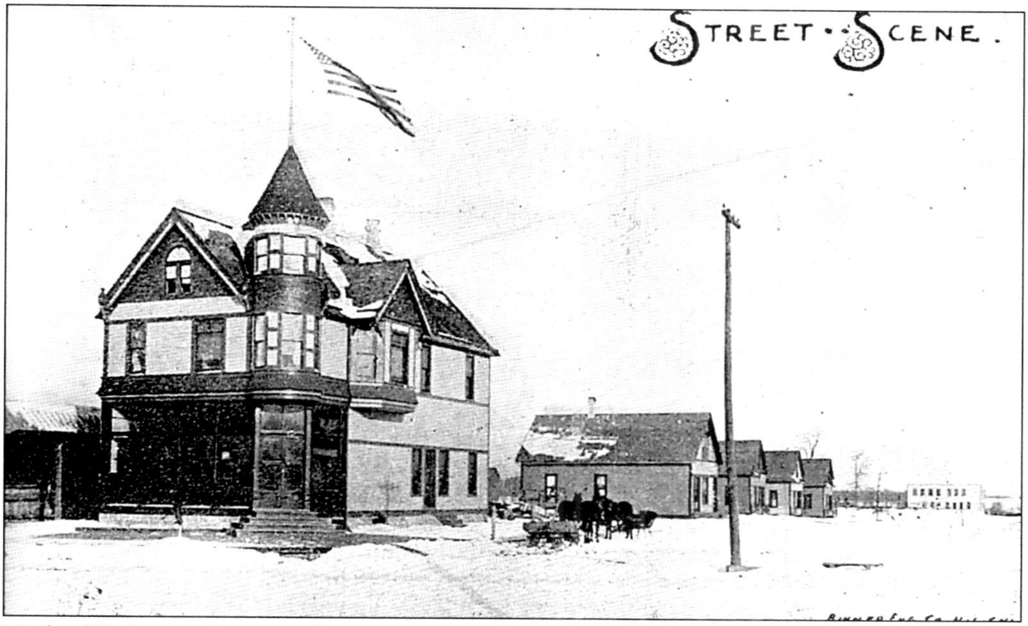

Michael Bedessem, former village treasurer and long time alderman, built the "South Milwaukee House" on the northeast corner of Tenth and Minnesota in 1892. It was described as being "one of the finest structures in the city." A popular watering hole for local politicians, the South Milwaukee House proudly served Cream City beer and John Graf's carbonated beverages. This historic building still stands today, though it is in need of restoration.

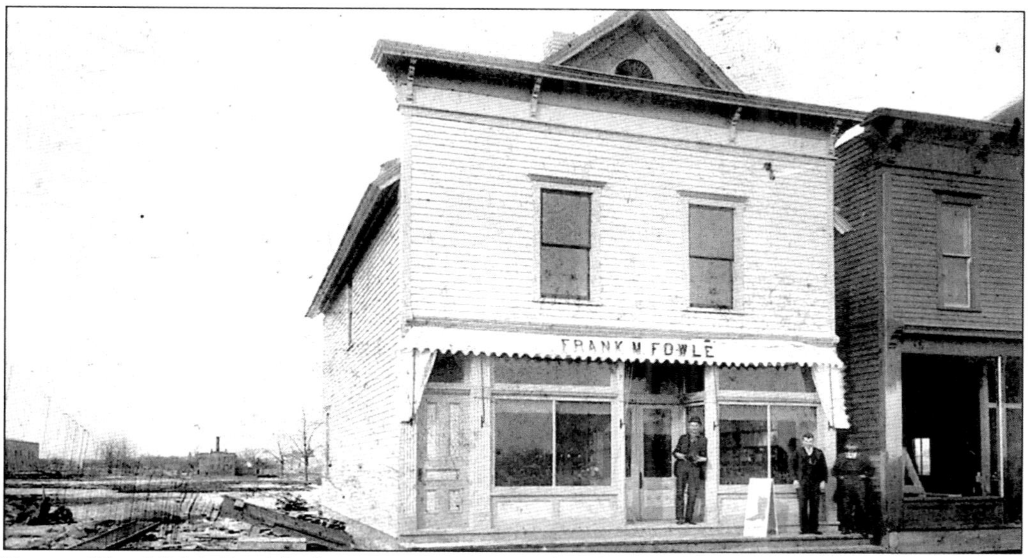

Francis "Frank" M. Fowle's shoe store at 1006 Milwaukee Avenue. Frank Fowle, grandson of pioneer John Fowle, is seen standing in the doorway. Visible in the background is the Adamant Paint & Color Company, which went up in flames in May 1893. (Courtesy of Judy Balestrieri.)

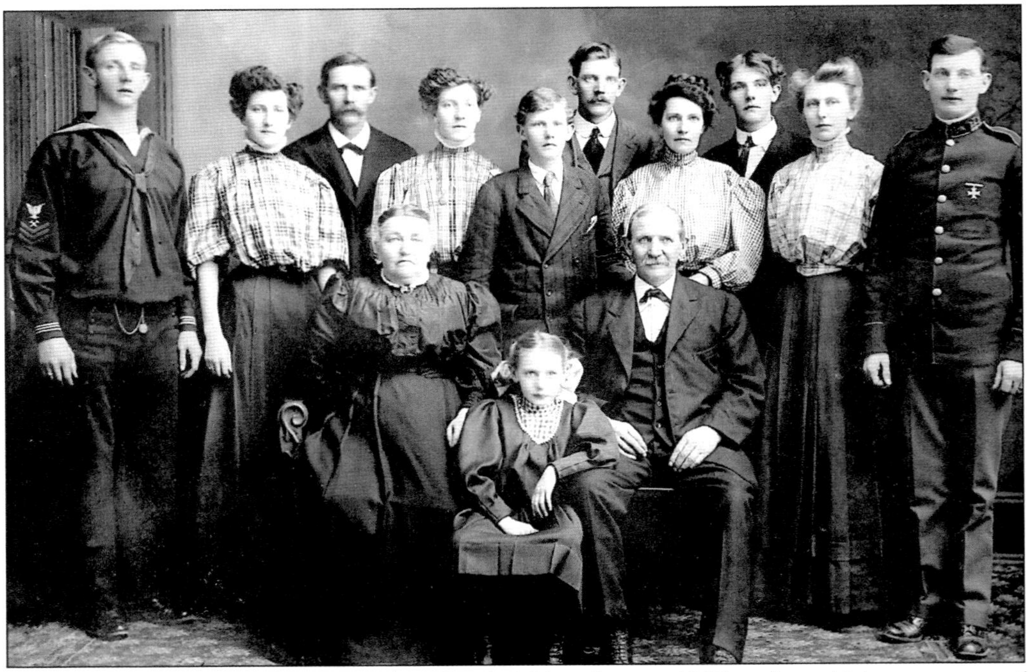

William (Willhelm) Ladwig moved to South Milwaukee in 1895 and would become one of the city's best known citizens. This family portrait was taken around 1910. Shown, from left to right, are: (standing) Frank Ladwig, Laurine (Ladwig) Walker, William Ladwig Jr., Sophie (Ladwig) Gumerman, Albert Ladwig, John Ladwig, Caroline (Ladwig) Fowle, Edward Ladwig, Elizabeth (Ladwig) Wrisley, and Frank Ladwig; (seated) Sophia (Jacho) Ladwig, Elfrieda (Ladwig) Pfeiffer, and William Ladwig Sr. (Courtesy of Judy Balestrieri.)

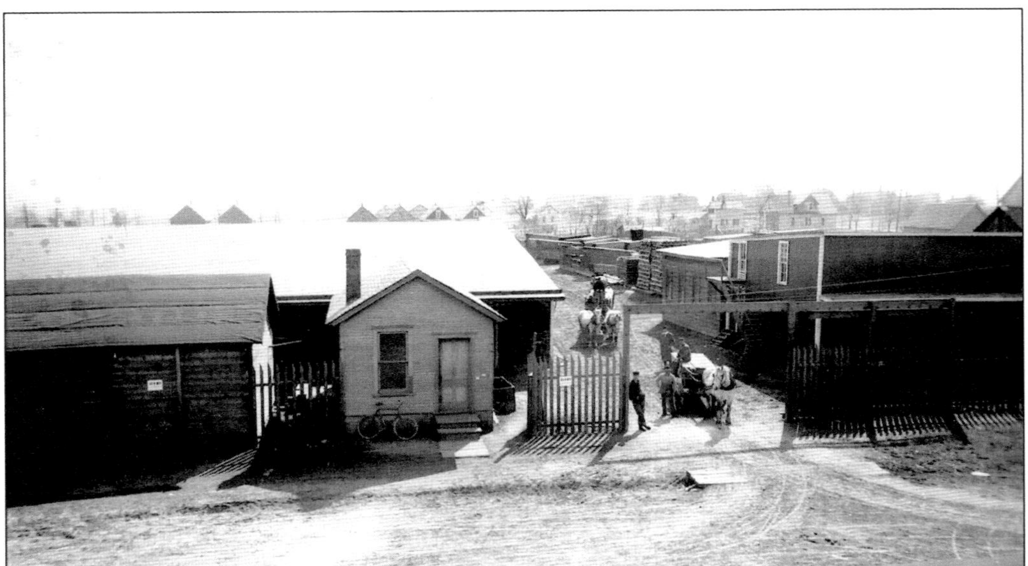

The South Milwaukee Lumber Company was located on Michigan Avenue between Eleventh and Twelfth. Established around 1895, the company served the community for well over 50 years.

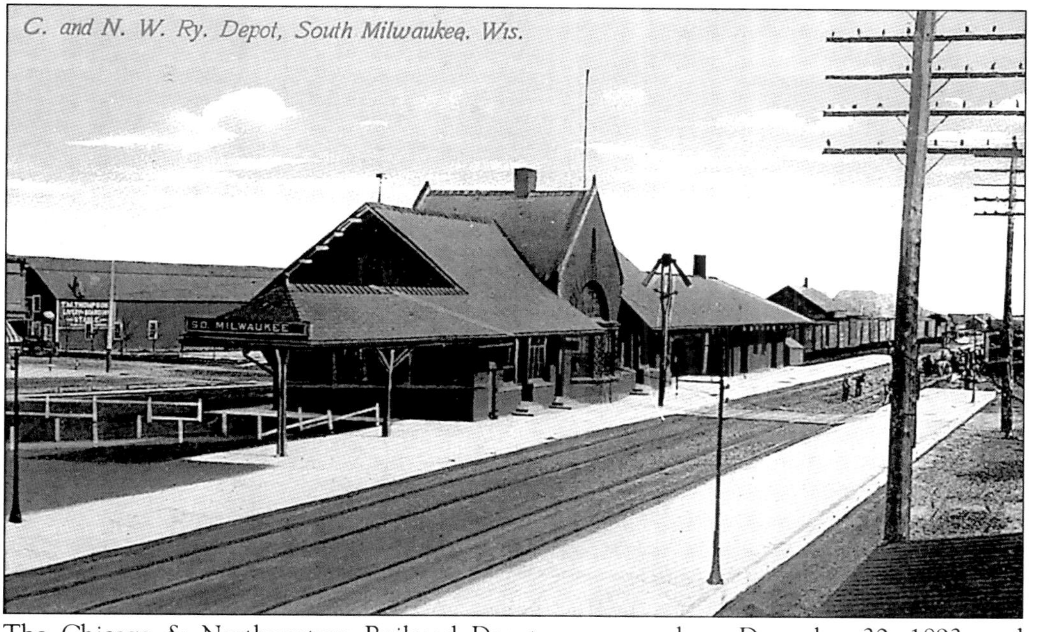

The Chicago & Northwestern Railroad Depot was opened on December 30, 1893, and continued regular passenger service until the late 1950s. Old-timers would recall that the Depot was a popular spot to gather on summer evenings and while away the time watching the trains rumble by. It was formally listed on the National Register of Historic Places in 1978.

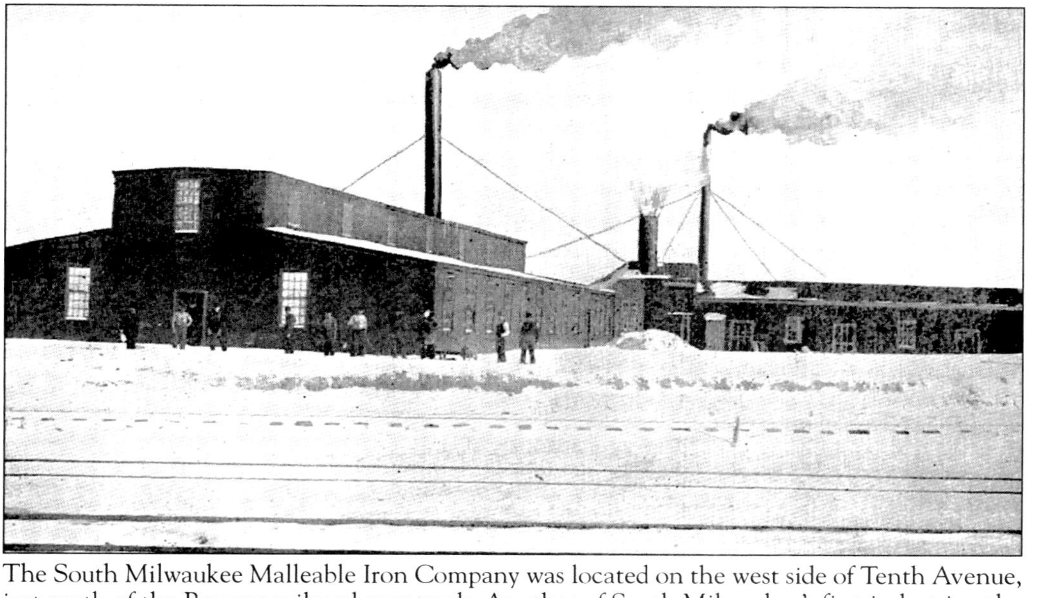

The South Milwaukee Malleable Iron Company was located on the west side of Tenth Avenue, just south of the Bucyrus railroad spur track. Another of South Milwaukee's first industries, the company folded when these buildings were burned to the ground on July 22, 1893.

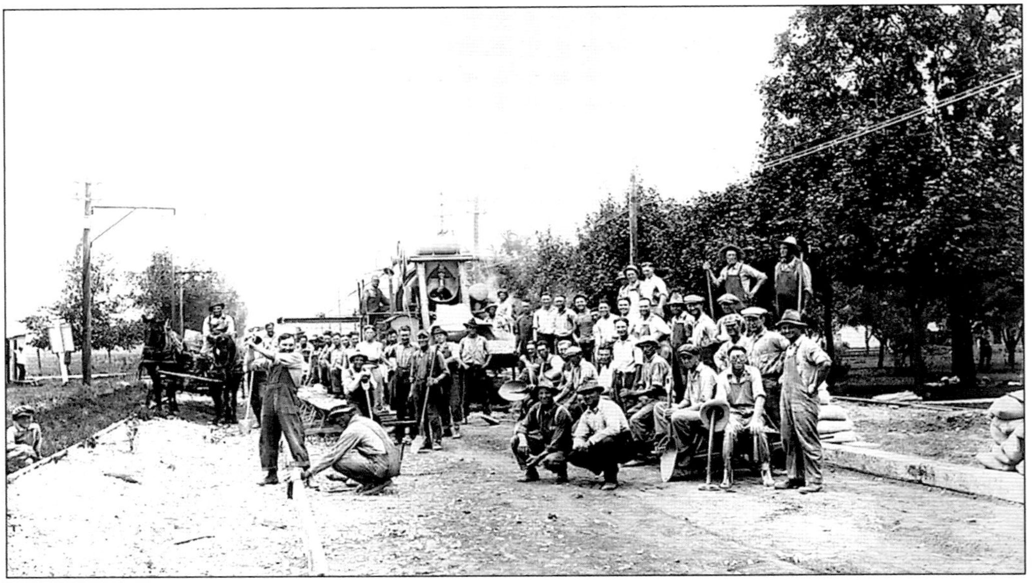

The Transit Milwaukee Electric Railway & Light (TMER&L) Company came to South Milwaukee in the summer of 1896. This suburban railway followed Chicago Avenue and provided much needed transportation for the hundreds of local factory workers, as well as for others going about their daily business. In 1902, a new line was added, running east down Milwaukee Avenue to Fifth and turning south towards Carrollville. This image is believed to show TMER&L construction crews at work.

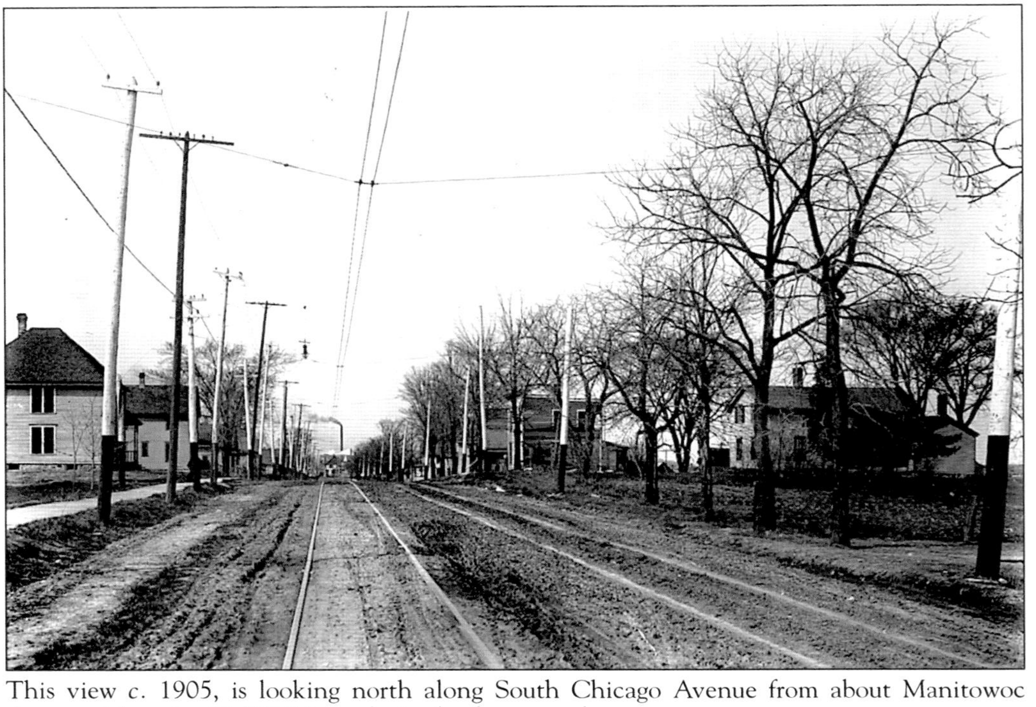

This view c. 1905, is looking north along South Chicago Avenue from about Manitowoc Avenue. Note the TMER&L tracks in the foreground

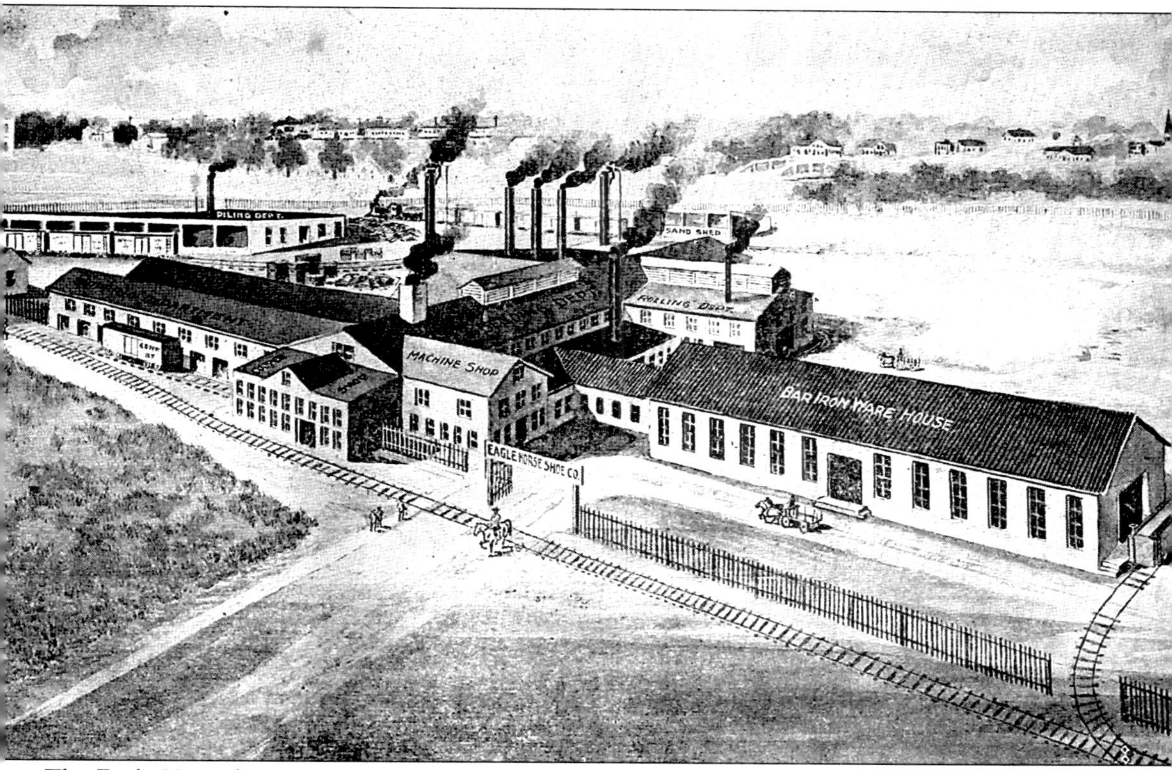

The Eagle Horseshoe Company. At one time considered the biggest horseshoe maker "west of Pittsburgh," the factory was located east of Tenth Avenue just north of the spur track. After suffering through a couple of costly fires, this once promising company slowly passed from the scene around 1910. In this image, several landmarks can be discerned in the background, including the high school on Tenth and Rawson, the Chicago Avenue bridge over Oak Creek, and the First Congregational Church.

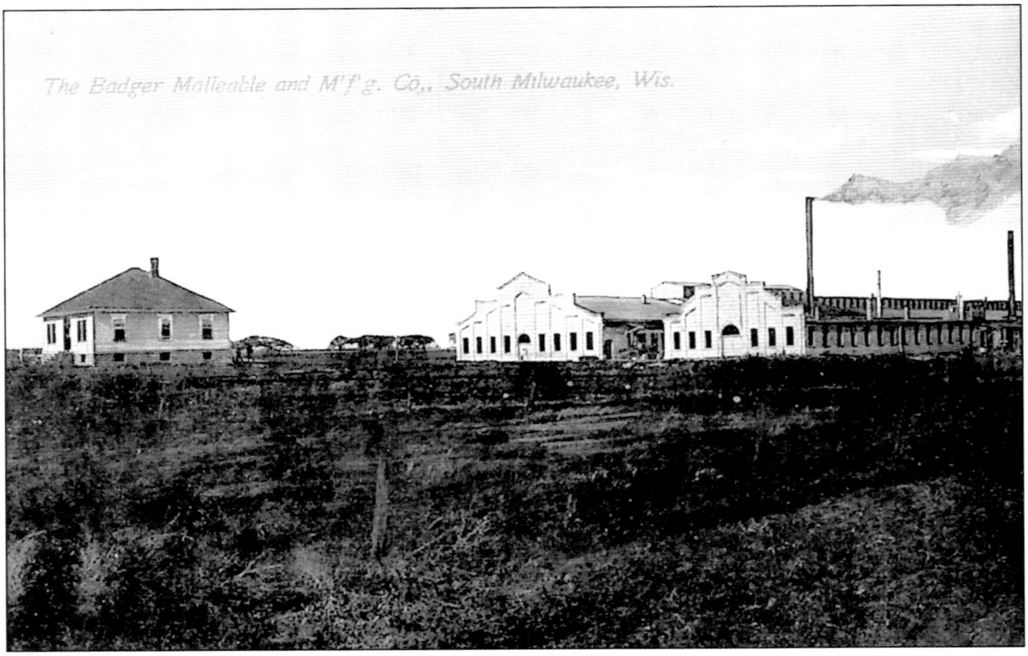

Badger Malleable & Manufacturing Company plant was built in 1908. By 1922, it had an annual capacity of 6,000 tons of various iron castings. The plant was located east of North Chicago Avenue, just south of Badger Avenue. Surviving through the Great Depression, Badger stayed in business until 1955.

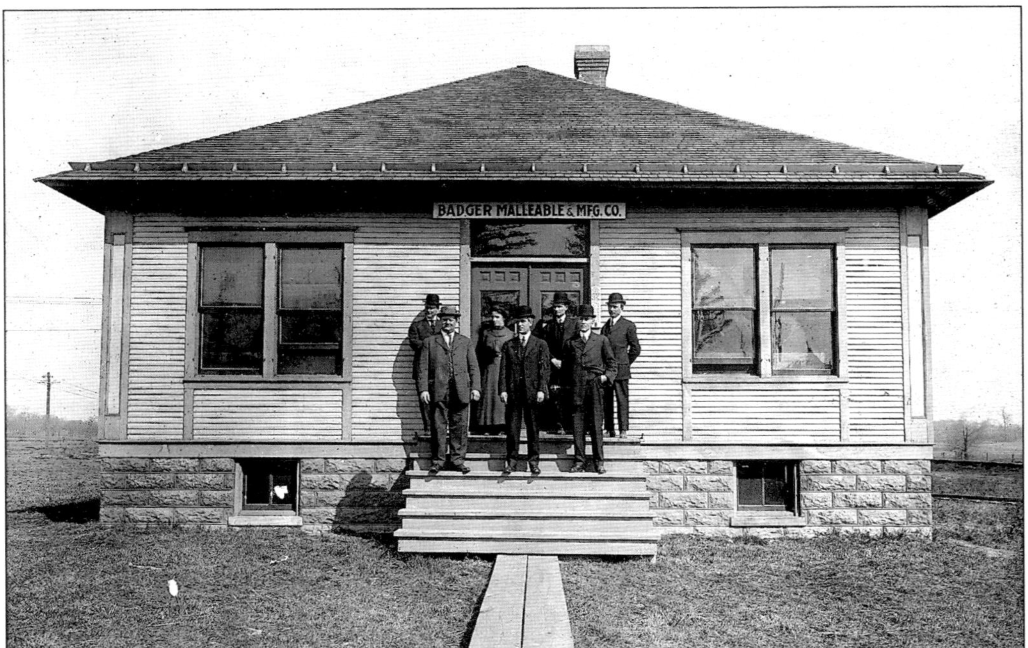

Officers of the Badger Malleable & Manufacturing Company pose before their new office building, c. 1908.

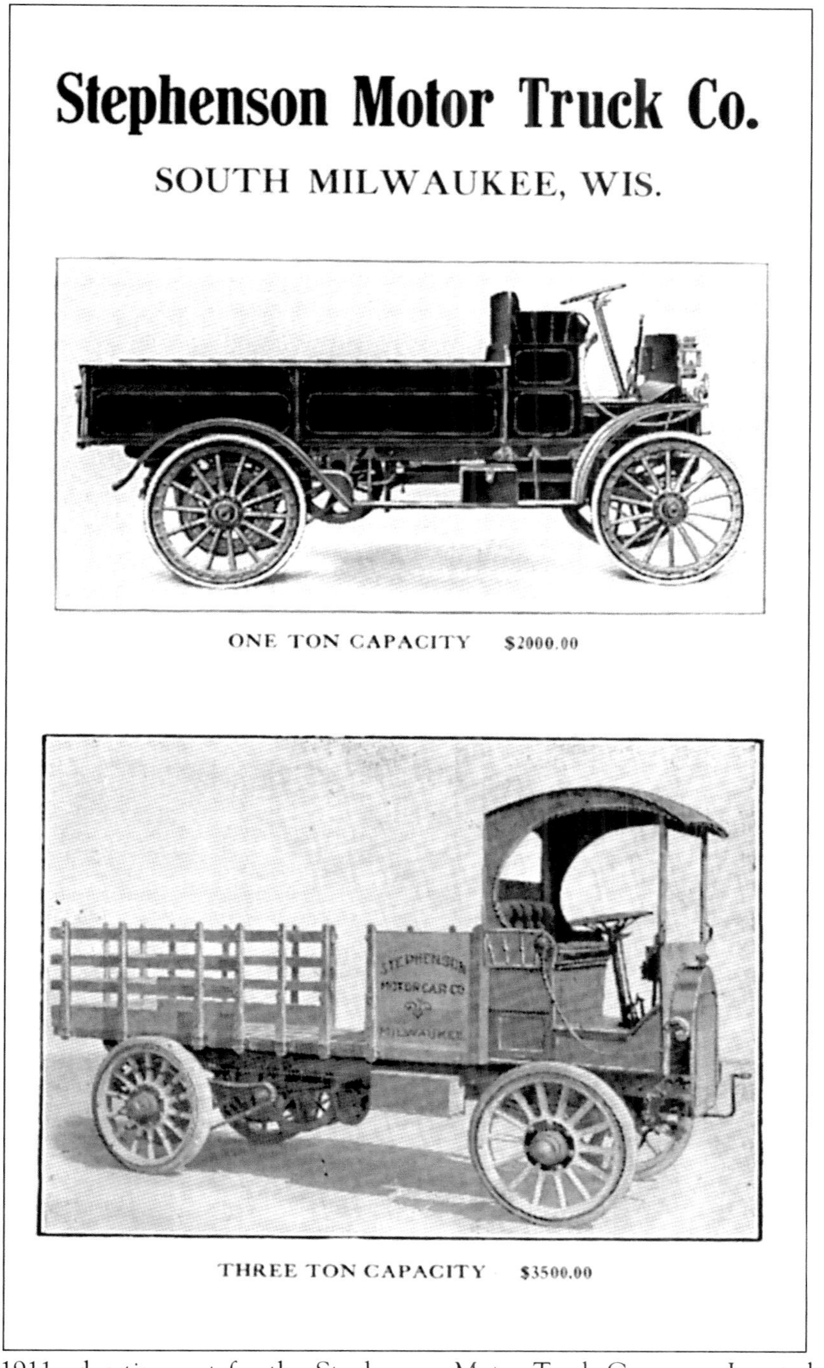

This is a 1911 advertisement for the Stephenson Motor Truck Company. Located at 1016 Davis Avenue on the city's north side, the company kept a boar in their yard as a mascot. On occasion, this creature would root its way under the fence and terrify the neighborhood children, sending some shinnying up trees to escape its fearsome snout. The company produced these vehicles in South Milwaukee until sometime around 1917.

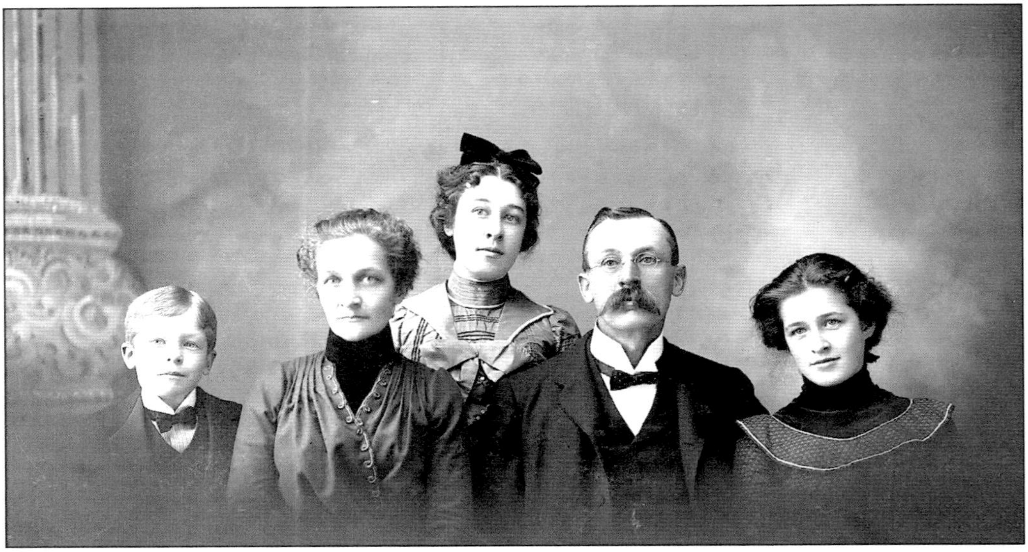

The Frederick Heidelberg family are pictured, *c.* 1900. The Heidelberg Blacksmith Shop was located just west of Chicago Avenue, north of the creek crossing. Dating from the 1890s, Heidelberg's Blacksmith Shop was always a popular meeting spot where local matters were freely discussed. Shown here are Amanda (Steller) and Frederick Heidelberg with their children, Harold, Elsie, and Winifred. Their home still stands at 716 Hawthorne Avenue

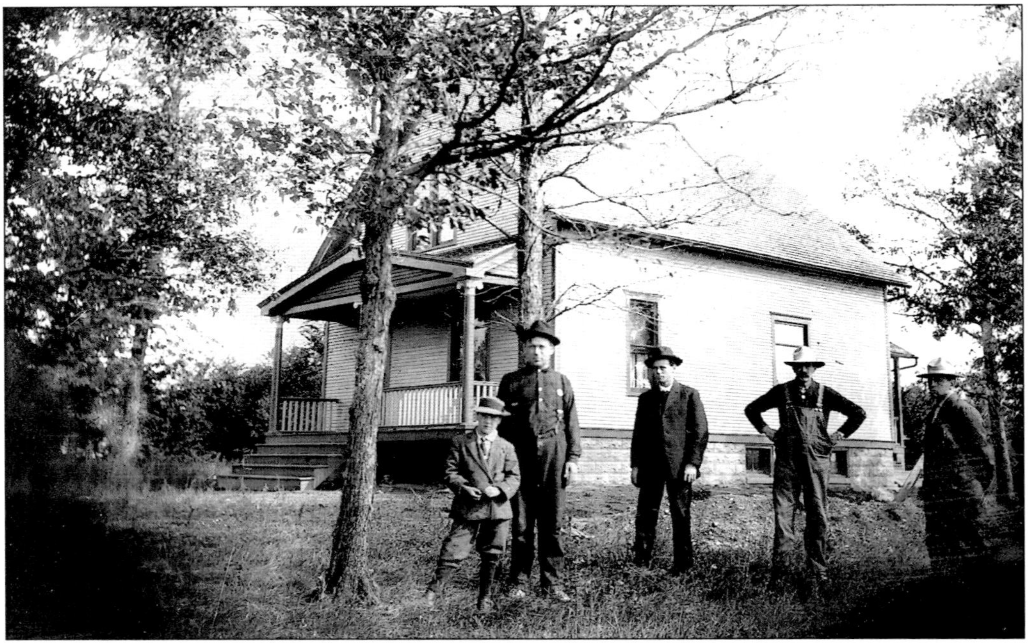

The Conrad Trieschmann family pose in front of their farmhouse *c.* 1895. For many years the Trieschmann farm was located on South Milwaukee's west side, north of Rawson Avenue and just east of Nicholson Road. The farmhouse stood until the 1970s, when it was torn down to make way for a new Baptist Church.

Three

Administration

When the Village of South Milwaukee (population 517) incorporated in late 1892, a provisional administration had to be established until regular elections could be held the following April. Meanwhile, when one of South Milwaukee's most prominent buildings, the three-story Lake View Club House on Milwaukee Avenue, burned to the ground during the early hours of March 2, 1893, it became obvious that the establishment of a fire department was to be a top priority. Under Village President Edward A. Bunn, the new village officers vigorously set about instituting a number of public improvements, including a new city hall, fire department, water utility, and sewage system.

The combination of commerce, industry, and civic support caused the population of the community to swell. On July 6, 1897, South Milwaukee became a city of the fourth class. When Mayor George C. Bush and his administration took over, the foundations of South Milwaukee had been firmly established, and the metamorphosis from rural settlement to industrial city was now complete.

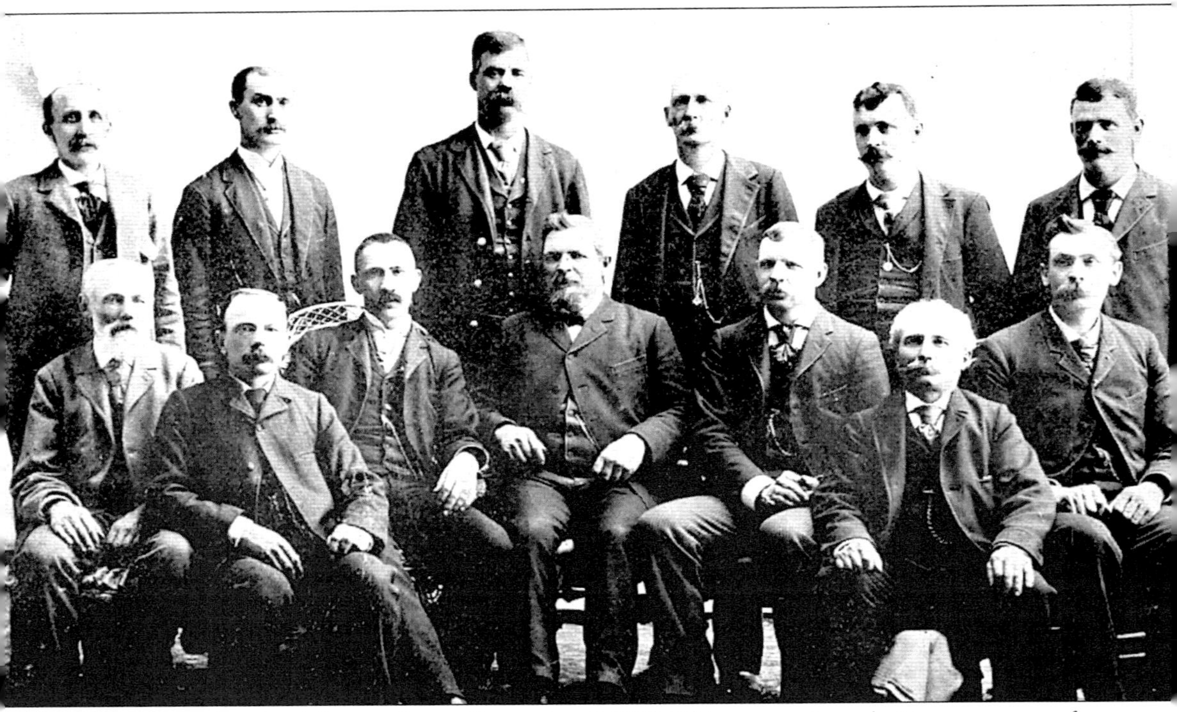

South Milwaukee's First village officers, April 1893. This energetic and visionary group of men set about bringing a great number of improvements to the fledgling community. Shown here, from left to right, are: (sitting) Charles Ahrens Sr., trustee; George Hook, trustee; George Morgan, trustee; Edward A. Bunn, president; William Fadel, trustee; Jacob Fink, trustee; and Frederick Heidelberg, trustee; (standing) Louis George, treasurer; P.J. Kelly, attorney; John Cullen, marshal; A.D. Bethel, assessor; Frank J. Boyle, clerk; and George Blake, constable.

George C. Bush was the first man to be elected mayor of South Milwaukee. Bush, a native of New York, moved to the Badger State in 1855. He served four years in the Civil War and was a member of Company B, 7th Wisconsin Volunteer Infantry Regiment. The 7th Wisconsin was part of the famed "Iron Brigade," which had earned renown in many of the bloodiest battles of the war.

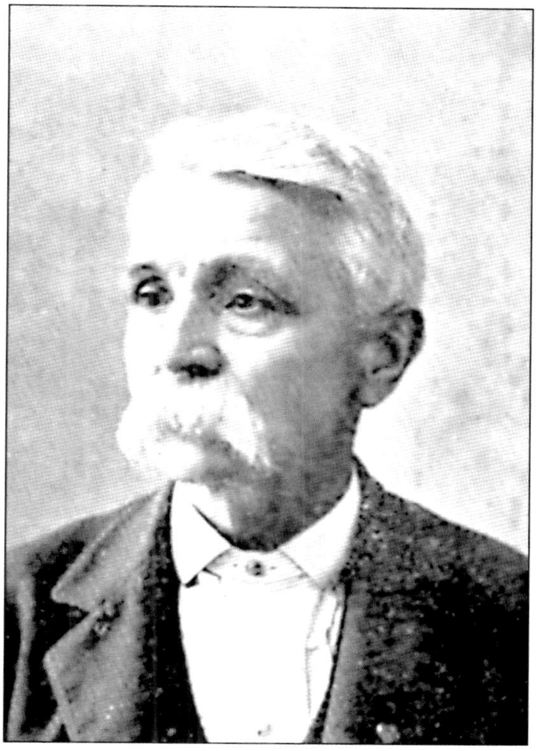

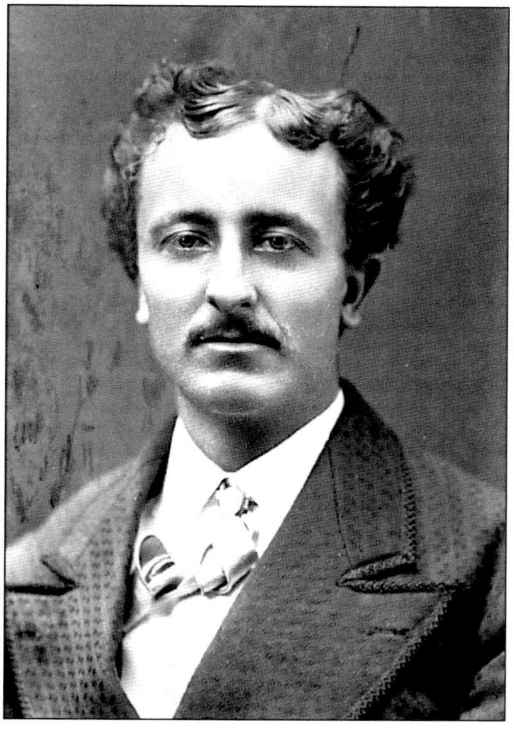

DeLos A. Fowle was mayor of South Milwaukee in 1899. His home still stands at 627 Hawthorne Avenue. (Courtesy of Judy Balestrieri.)

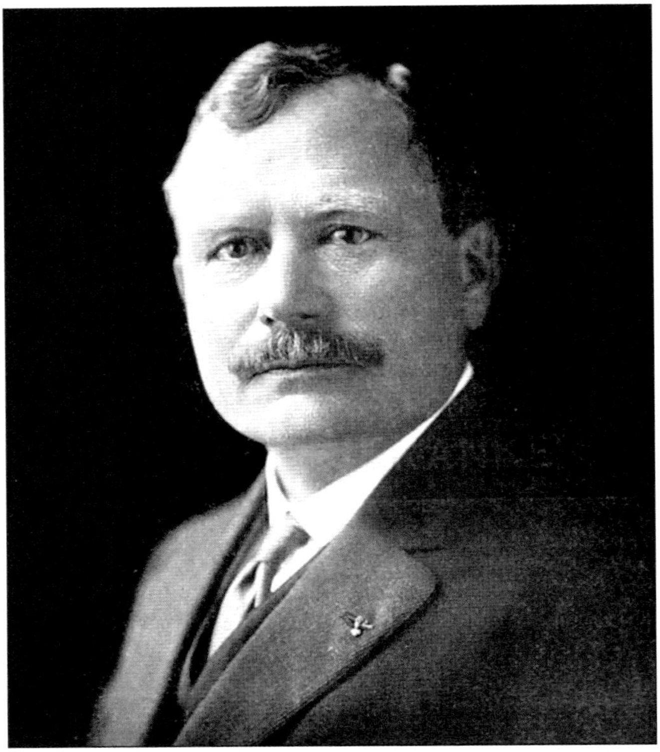

Charles Franke was elected to his first of eight nonconsecutive terms as mayor in 1902. He came to South Milwaukee around 1894 and purchased Frank Fowle's shoe business on Milwaukee Avenue. He later became the proprietor of the Hotel Blatz, located at 928 Milwaukee Avenue. Though sometimes controversial, Mayor Franke was known as a staunch defender of the rights of the ordinary citizen.

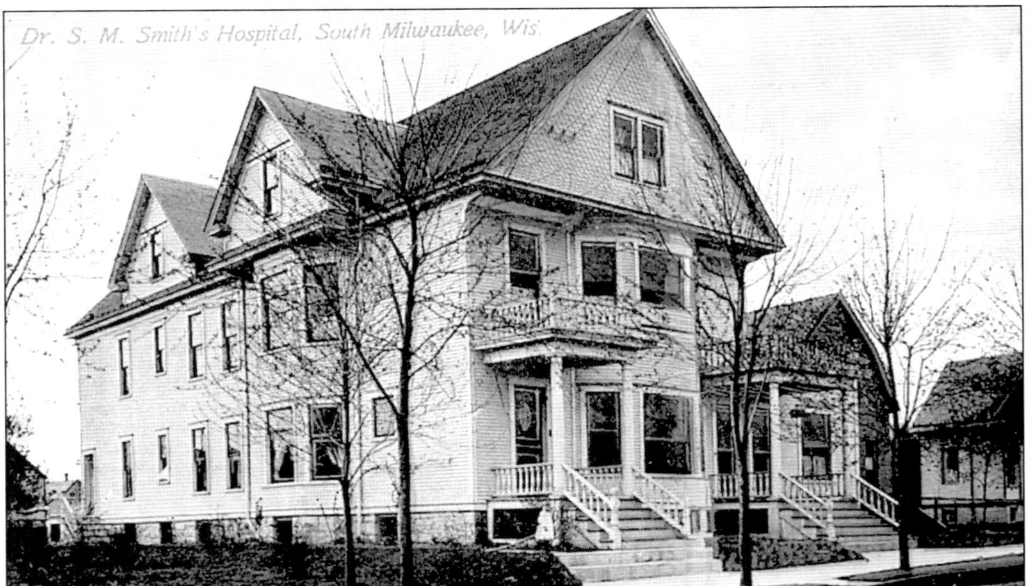

Dr. Sidney M. Smith, who received his medical degree in Canada, built this eight-bed hospital at 1215–17 Milwaukee Avenue in 1904. It was later enlarged to 20 beds and acted for a time as a training school for nurses. It served the community until Trinity Memorial Hospital was opened in Cudahy in 1958. Dr. Smith also served one term as the city's mayor from 1908 to 1910.

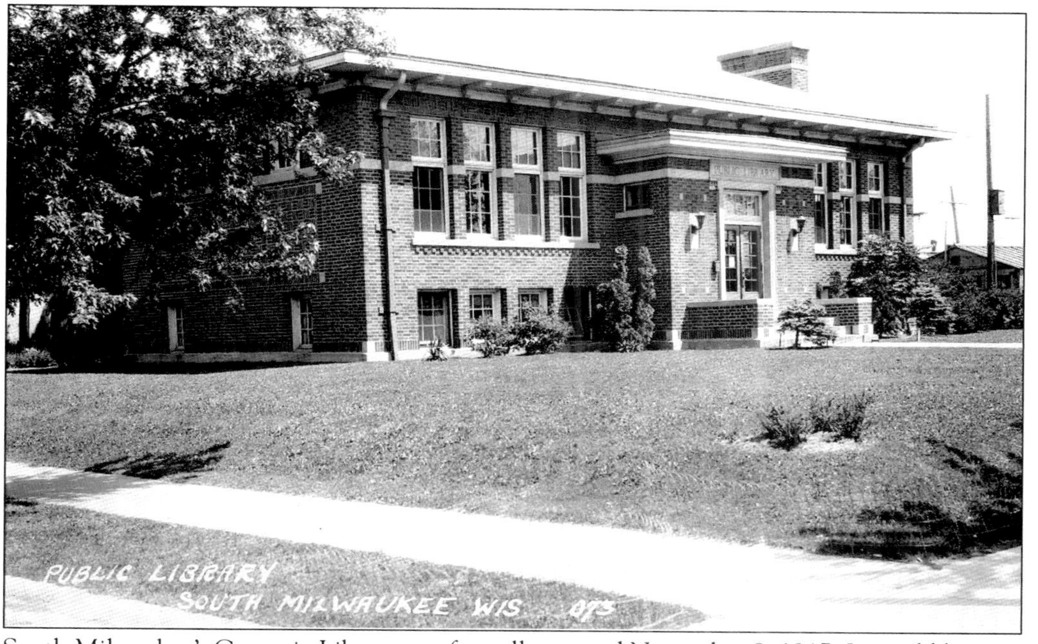

South Milwaukee's Carnegie Library was formally opened November 8, 1917. It would be torn down in 1966 and replaced by a new library built on the same spot.

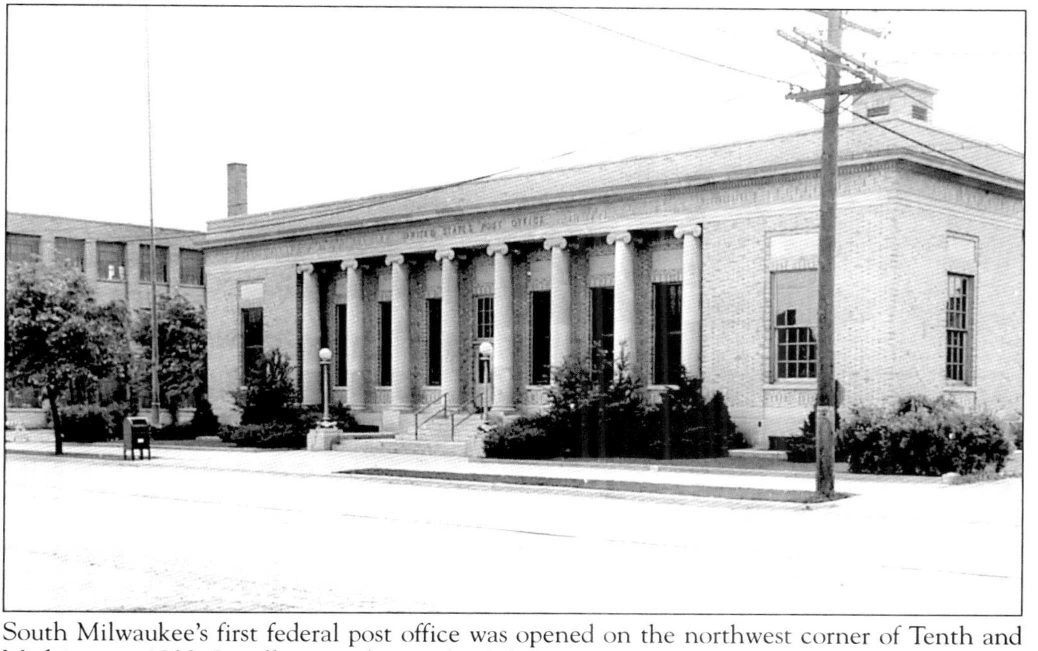

South Milwaukee's first federal post office was opened on the northwest corner of Tenth and Michigan in 1933. It still meets the needs of the community today. Visible at the left edge of this photograph is the Doerman Shoe Factory, built in 1923 and one of South Milwaukee's steadiest employers during the Great Depression.

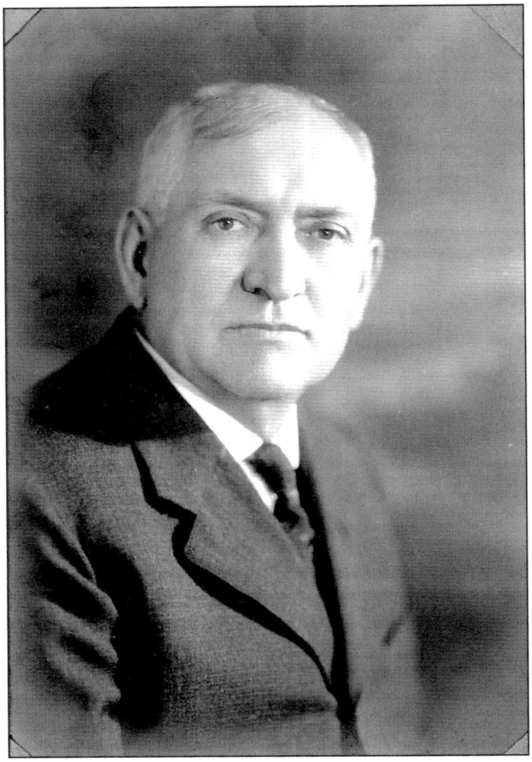

One of the signers of South Milwaukee's original application for incorporation in 1892, businessman Henry W. Donsing was one of the city's most prominent citizens. In 1897, Donsing built the Palace Meat Market at 1009 Milwaukee Avenue. On the second floor of this building was one of the city's most popular halls. In 1924, Donsing built South Milwaukee's first apartment building, located at 915 Minnesota Avenue. He died in 1935.

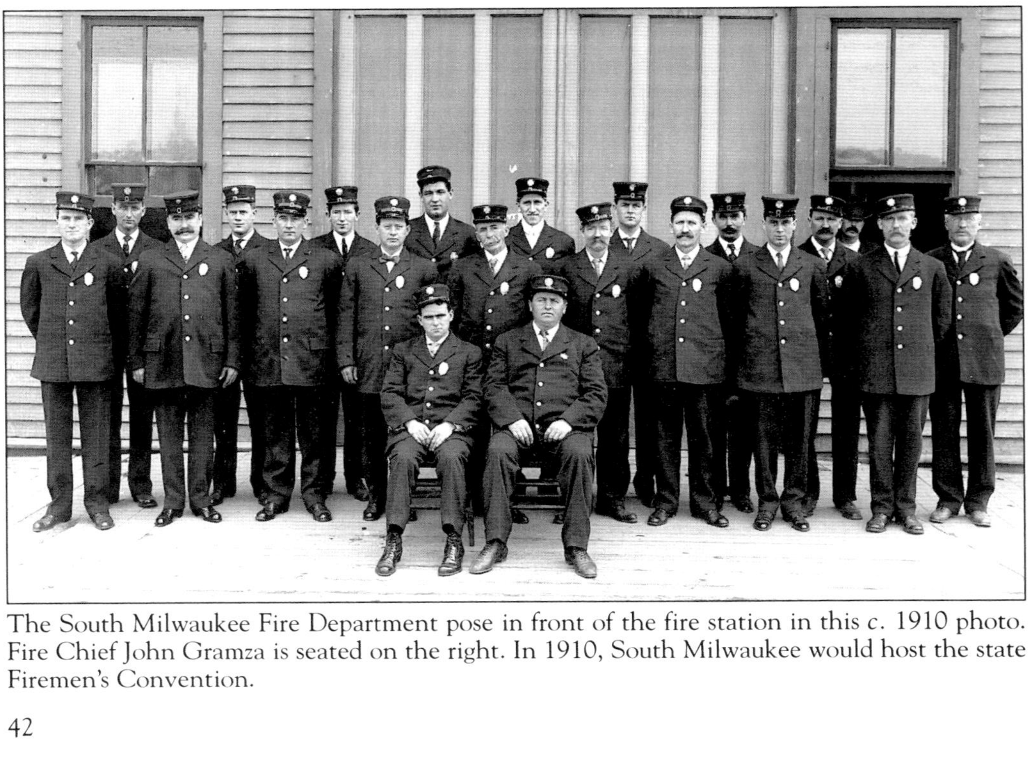

The South Milwaukee Fire Department pose in front of the fire station in this *c.* 1910 photo. Fire Chief John Gramza is seated on the right. In 1910, South Milwaukee would host the state Firemen's Convention.

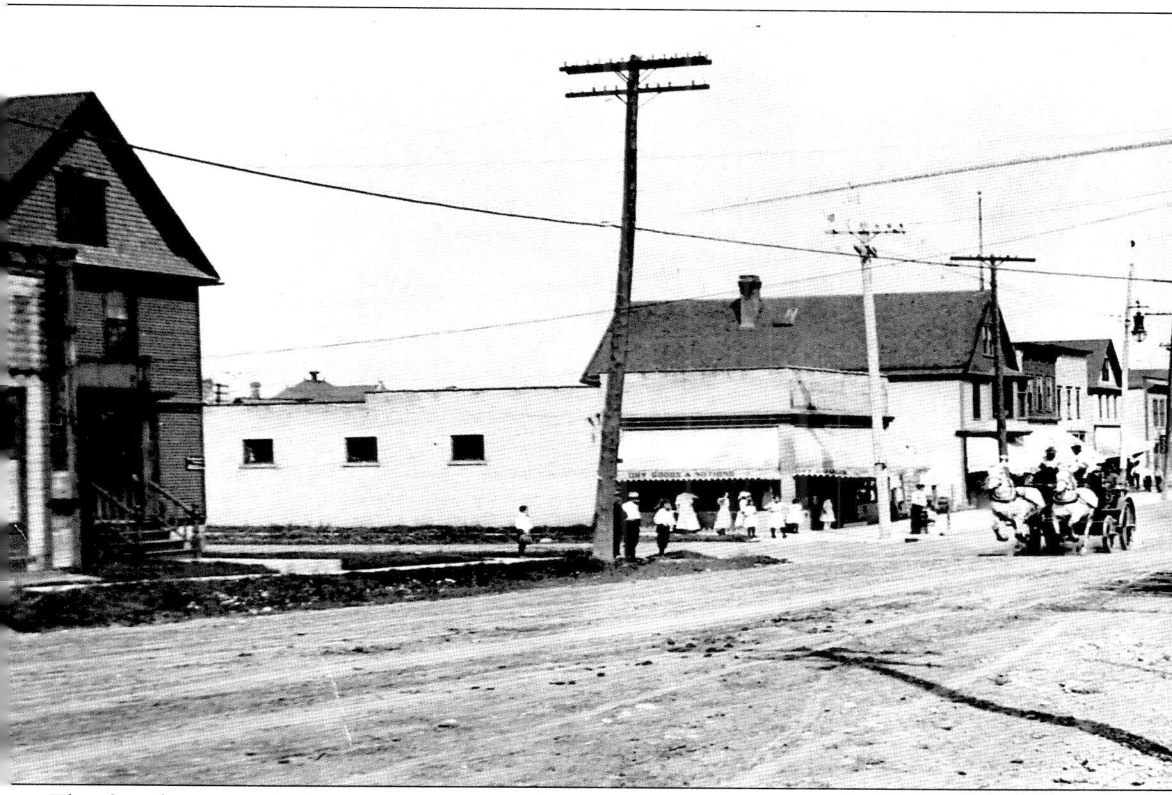

The fire department's horse-drawn chemical engine unit races to action near Twelfth and Milwaukee Avenues in this *c.* 1915 image. The city's fire department would rely on horses until the first gasoline powered vehicle was purchased in 1921. Zucker's Department Store, a Milwaukee Avenue landmark, is seen on the corner. Looming in the background is the South Milwaukee Hotel. (Courtesy of Joe Szatmary.)

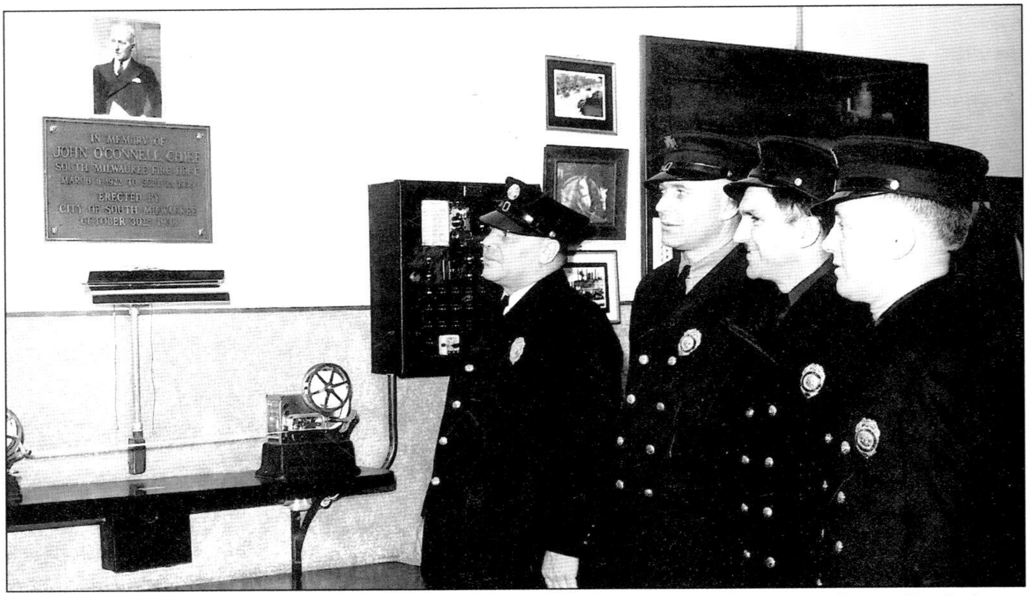

Firefighters pictured are John Brodhagen Sr., Peter Brink, Arthur Monroe, and Max Dinkelman c. 1938. Dinkelman was promoted to fire chief in 1960, a position he held for the next 14 years. In 1967, Chief Dinkelman received numerous commendations for heroism when he was credited with saving dozens of lives seconds before a tremendous gas explosion ripped through St. Adalbert's Church. Suffering severe leg injuries during this action, Dinkelman's wounds would never fully heal.

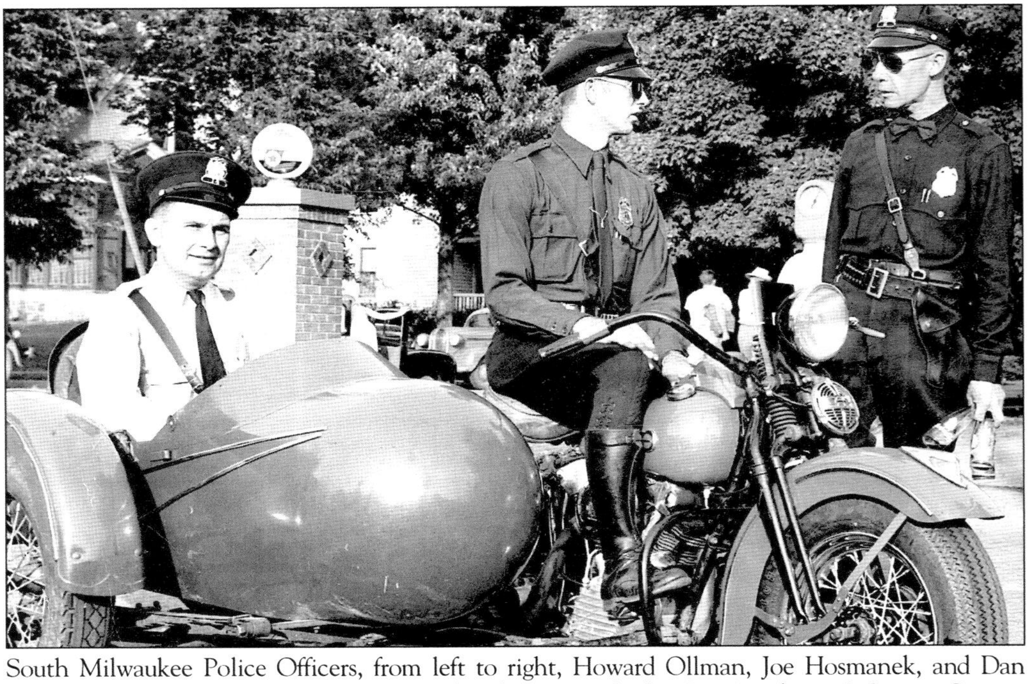

South Milwaukee Police Officers, from left to right, Howard Ollman, Joe Hosmanek, and Dan Grady, take a break in this 1947 photograph. They are parked at Ray Landergott's Service Station on the southeast corner of North Chicago and Hawthorne Avenues. (Courtesy of Joe Hosmanek.)

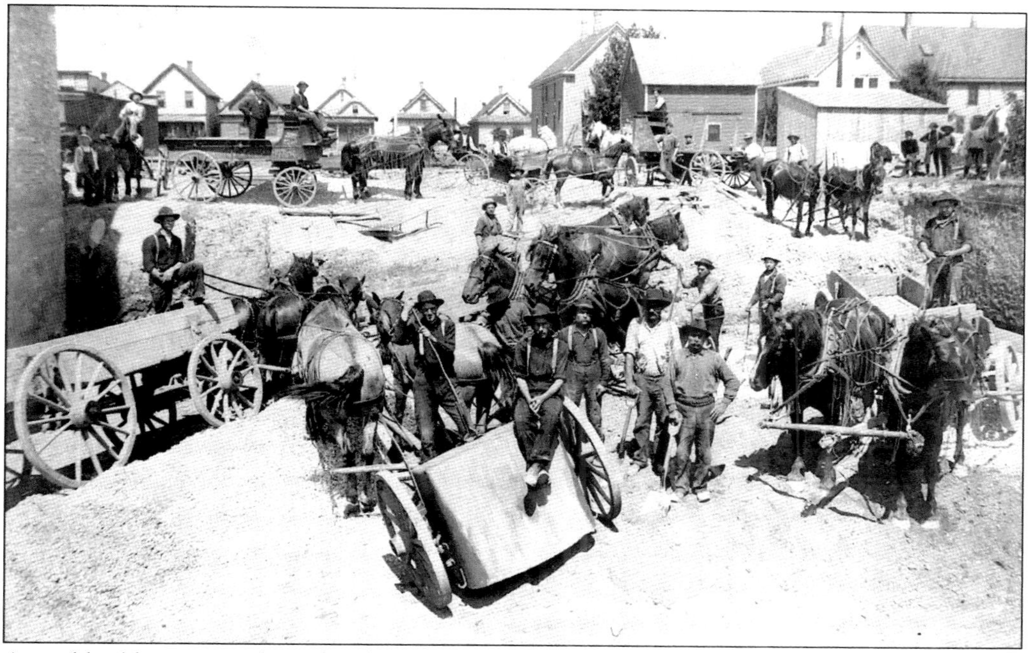

A road building crew takes a break to pose for this picture c. 1895.

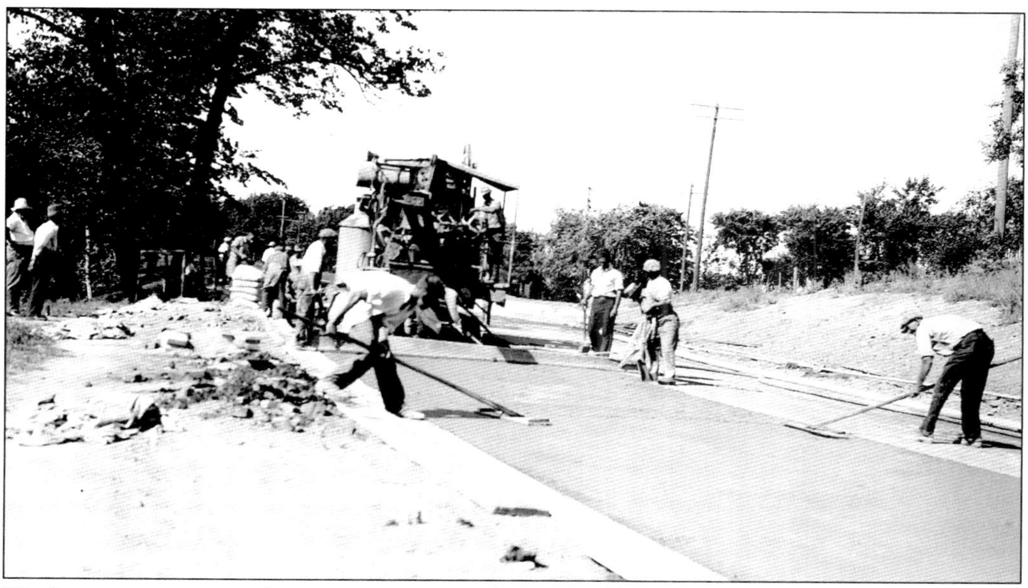

Workers pour concrete during construction of a new Mill Road in August 1932.

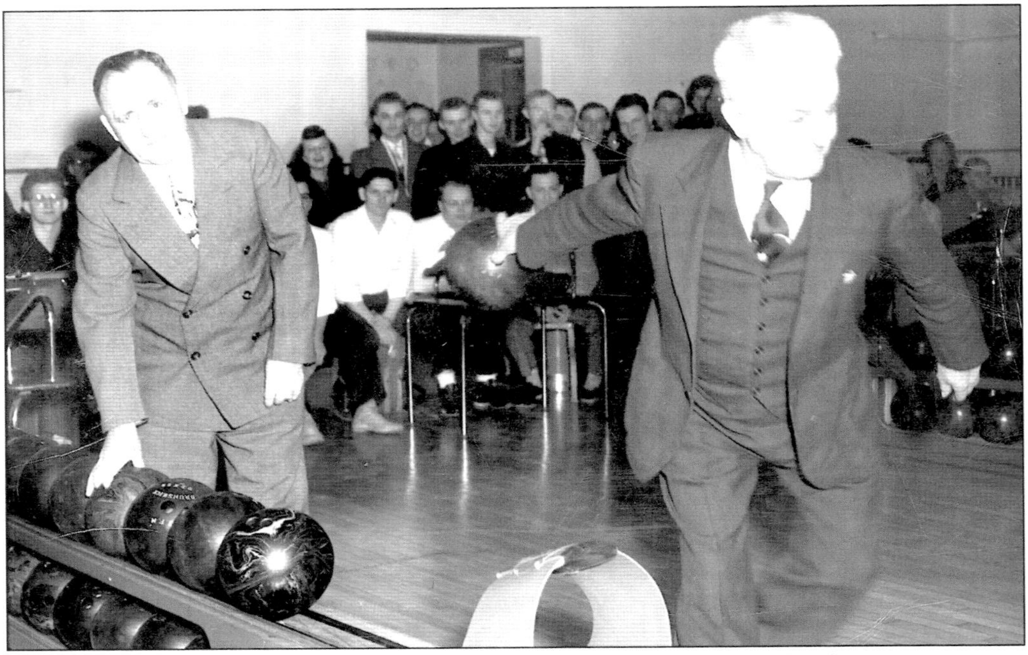

An overdressed Mayor Charles J. Plotz (right) shows off his bowling skills. Plotz spent 18 years as the very popular mayor of South Milwaukee and was instrumental in organizing civic support for the first Spectacle of Music parade in 1946.

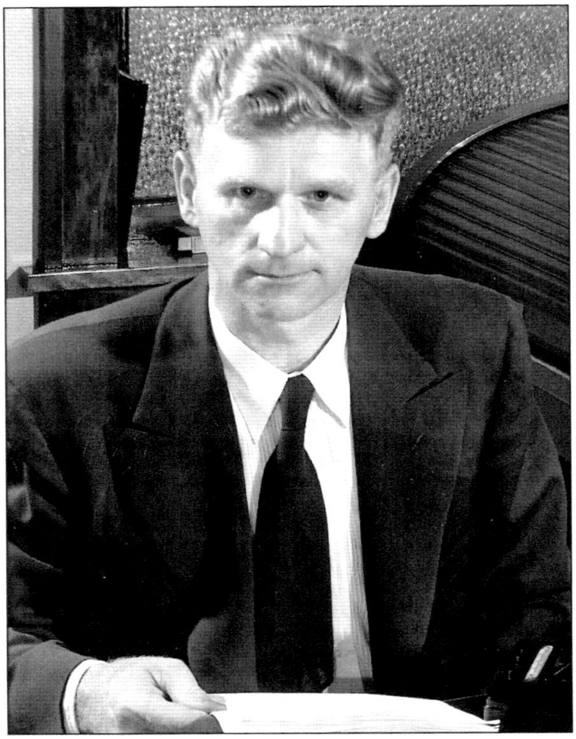

Henry Tylicki was South Milwaukee's police chief from 1949 to 1982.

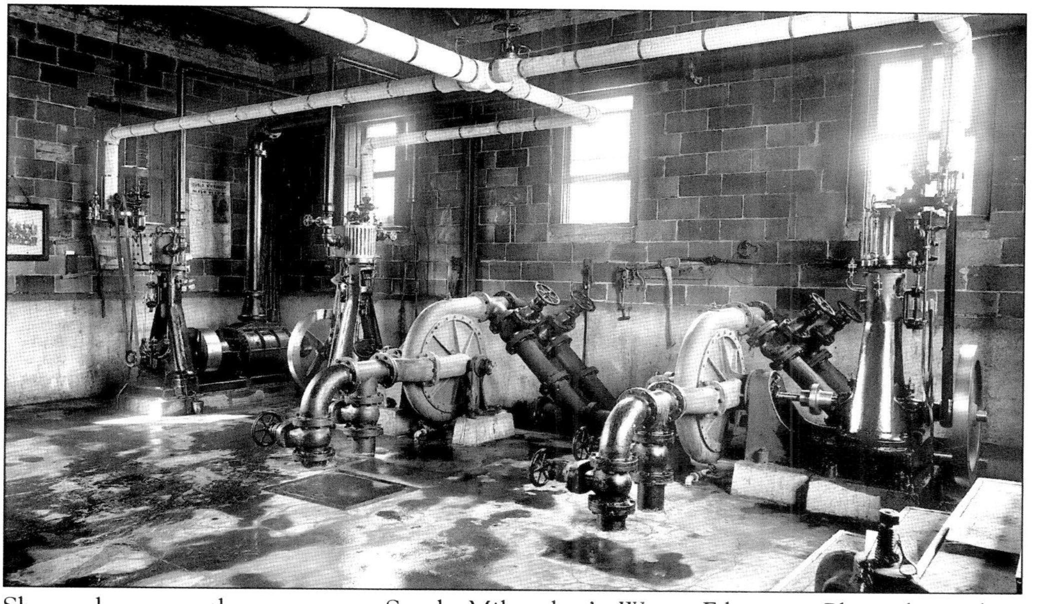

Shown here are the pumps at South Milwaukee's Water Filtration Plant, located at the east end of Montana Avenue, in 1911. Though he only served one term as mayor, Dr. Sidney M. Smith successfully lobbied for the construction of this, the first water filter process plant on the Great Lakes.

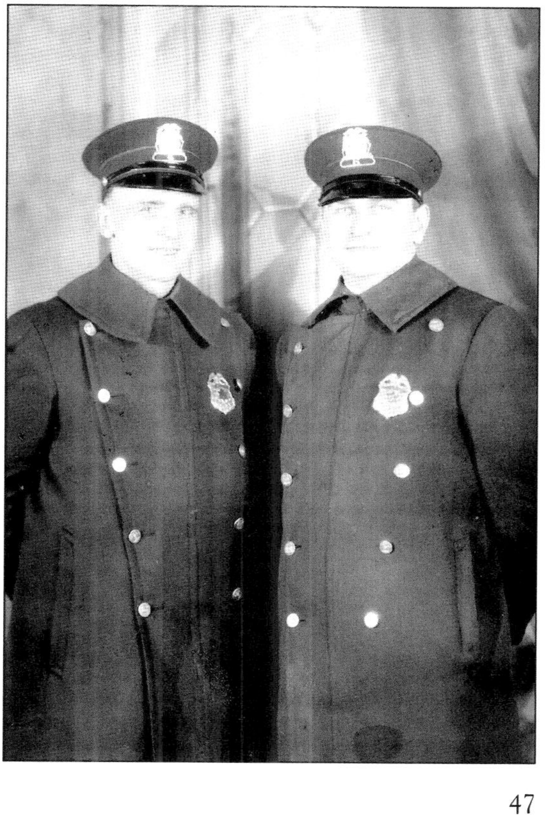

Two South Milwaukee police officers pose in this 1920s photograph. (Courtesy of Edie Ottman.)

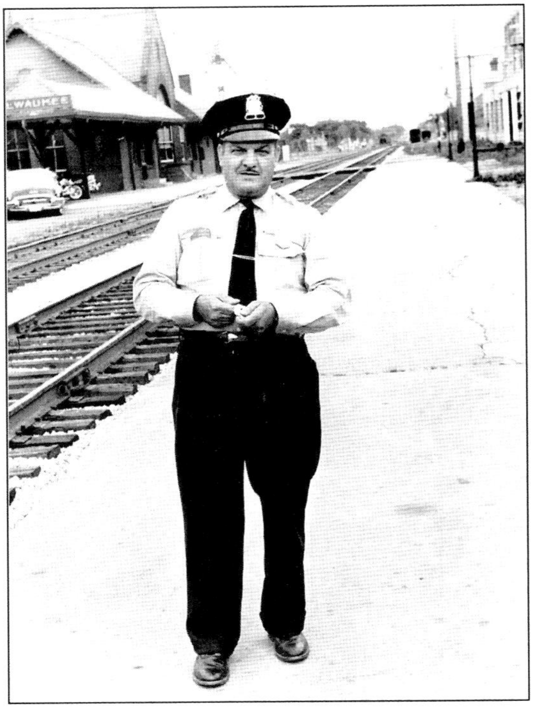

Edward Broskowski was South Milwaukee constable from 1942 to 1986. Edward's parents, Herman and Anna Broskowski, were Polish immigrants who arrived in South Milwaukee around 1902. Together, with their eight children, they would become one of the most well-known and industrious families in town.

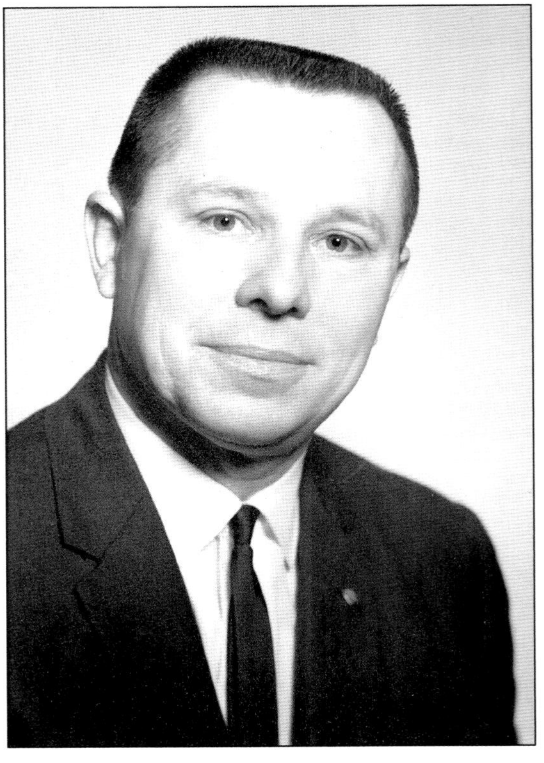

Chester W. Grobschmidt would serve as South Milwaukee's mayor from 1966 to 1994. One of Grobschmidt's most noted achievements as mayor was his successful effort to maintain local control of South Milwaukee's Sewage Treatment Plant by keeping out of the Milwaukee Metropolitan Sewage District.

Four

Churches and Schools

Since churches and schools are the foundations of any community, one of the first priorities of the early settlers to the area was to make sure that the spiritual and educational needs of the pioneer families be met. In 1837, the first religious meetings were held in the home of Oliver Rawson. By 1842, a single crudely built structure, located on the west side of the Chicago Road north of Hawthorne Avenue, served as both church and school. The first permanent public school building, completed around 1852, was built near the same site. In 1871, a new four-room brick schoolhouse was constructed, located at the southwest corner of Tenth and Rawson Avenues. This building was expanded in 1893 with the addition of a new high school. After South Milwaukee became a city in 1897, new elementary schools were added to meet the demands of the growing populace.

Dedicated on July 26, 1855, the First Congregational Church, which is still located on North Chicago Avenue, became the first regular house of worship in what is now South Milwaukee. In 1869, St. Mark's Episcopal Church was built on Rawson Avenue. After South Milwaukee became incorporated in 1892, many religious denominations were established to meet the village's growing demands. Zion Evangelical Lutheran Church was first, quickly followed by St. John's and St. Mary's Catholic Churches. St. Mary's predominantly served the city's German-speaking populace. St. Adalbert's Catholic Church was organized in 1896 and used largely by the Polish citizens. In March 1893, the Methodist Episcopal Church was organized. In 1924, the Holy Resurrection Armenian Apostolic Church at 909 Michigan Avenue became what is believed to be Wisconsin's first Armenian church.

By 1930, South Milwaukee's churches had been firmly established, laying the framework for the spiritual well-being of the community.

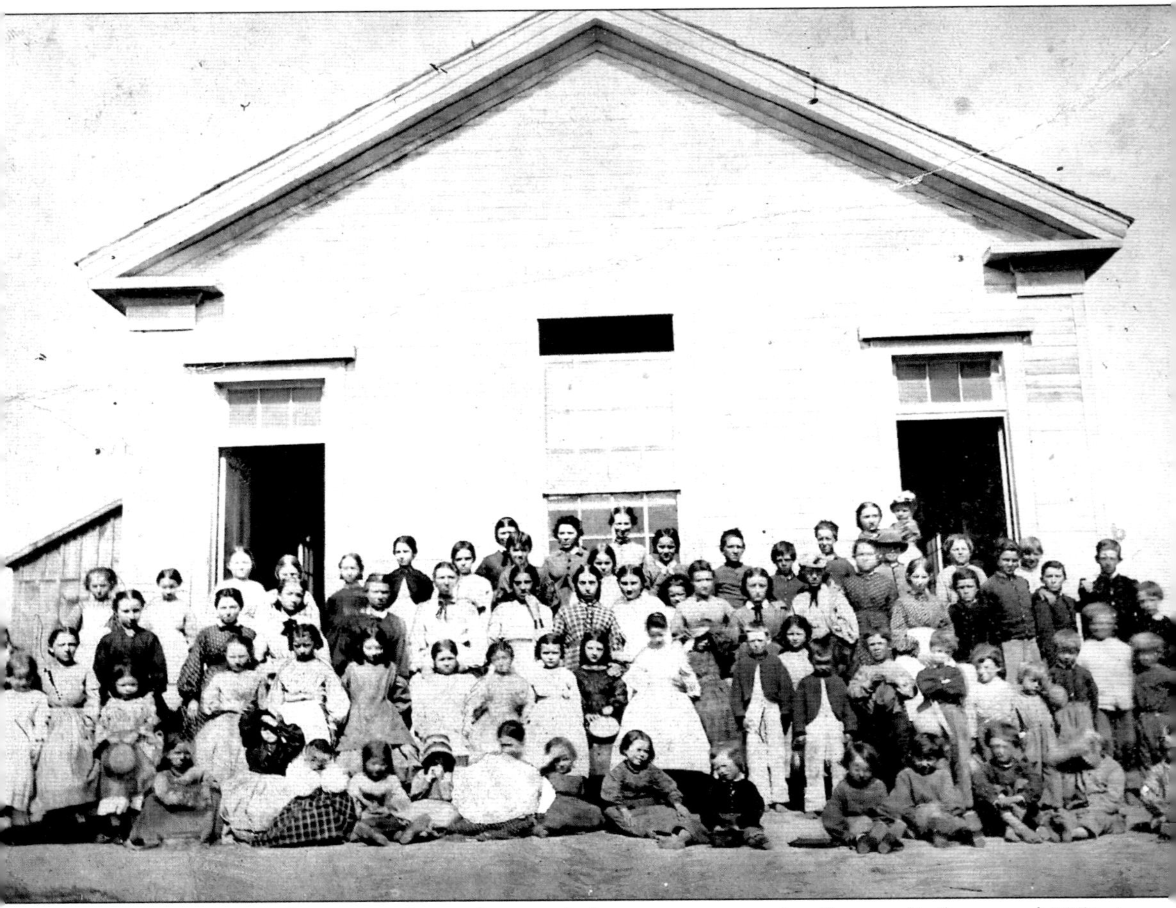

Taken c. 1857, this image shows the town's first permanent schoolhouse. Built around 1852, it was located just south of the First Congregational Church. In 1880, the building was moved to the west side of Tenth Avenue, just south of the railroad spur. Accounts of the time mention that the moving contractor had quite a difficult time moving the building across the North Chicago Avenue bridge over the creek.

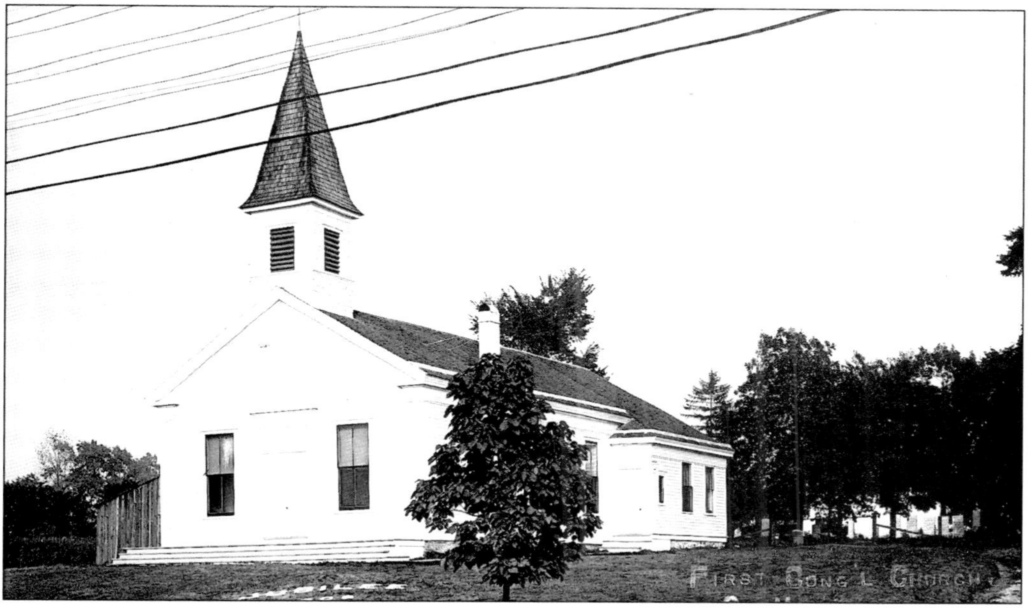

The First Congregational Church is located on North Chicago and Pine. South Milwaukee's oldest church, the building has undergone considerable remodeling over the years, though a portion of the original building remains in use today.

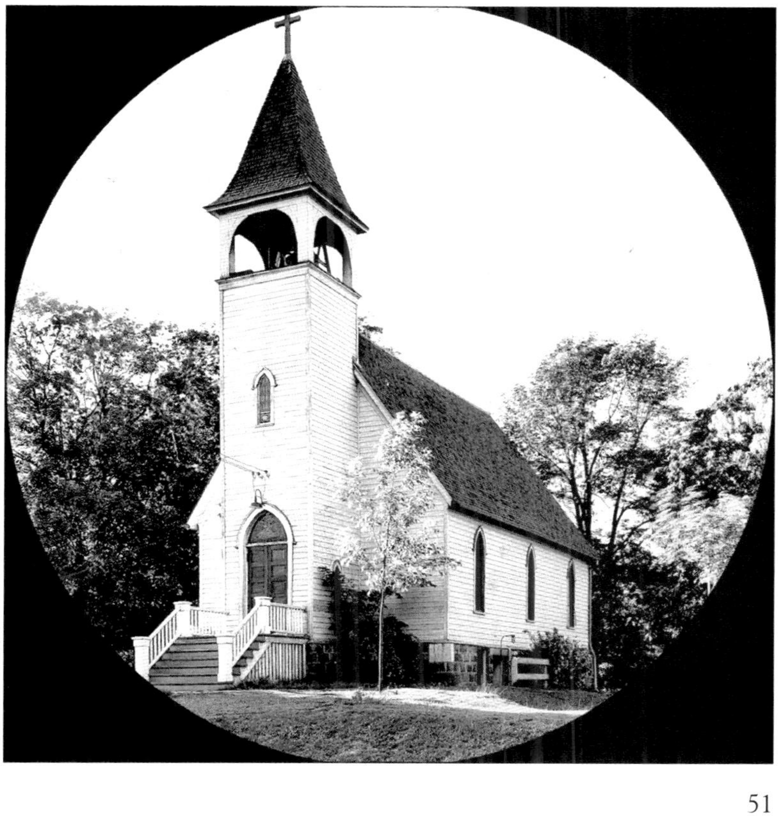

St. Mark's Episcopal Church was built on Rawson Avenue in 1869. The bell tower was added in 1893. In 1959, a new church building was erected on the site.

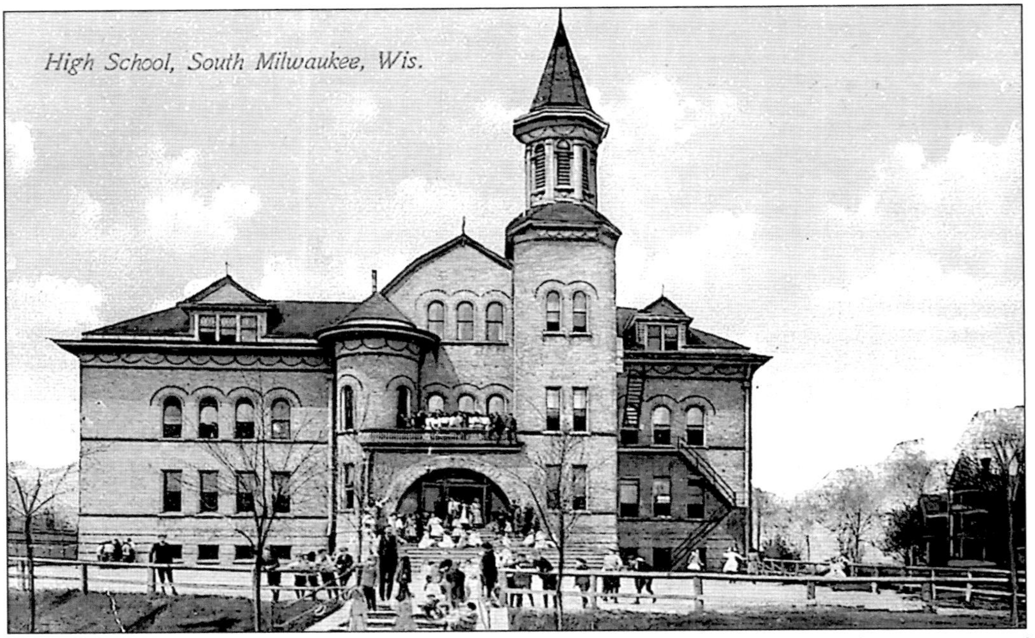

The South Milwaukee High School and First Ward School stood on the southwest corner of Tenth and Rawson Avenues. Grades one through six occupied the first floor, while grades seven through twelve used the second and third floors. The Edward Rawson house can be seen at the right edge of this *c.* 1907 image.

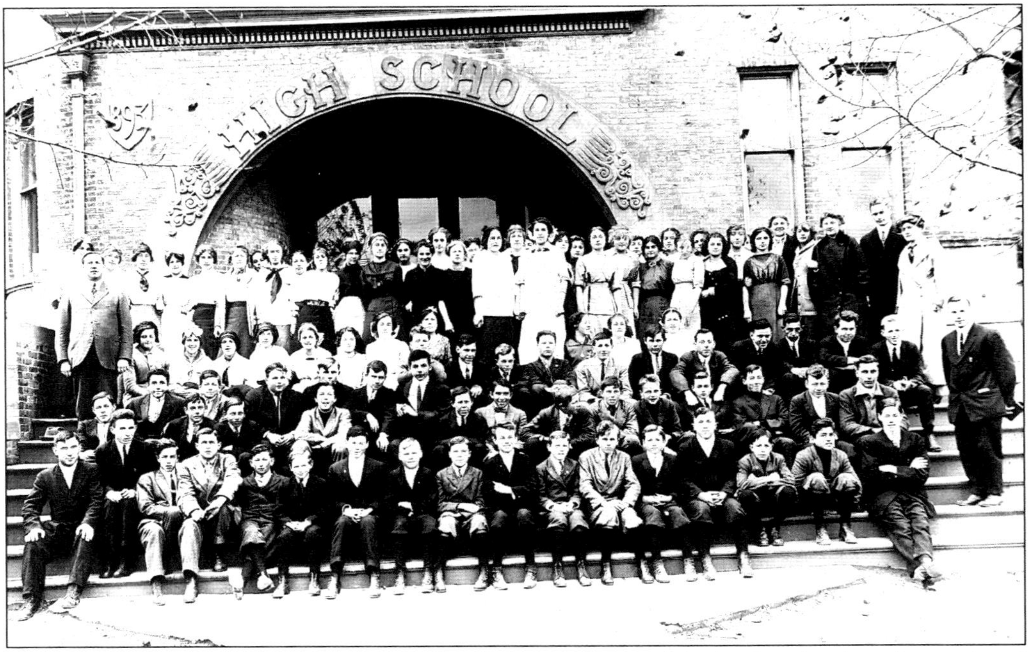

Students and staff of the First Ward School pose in front of the high school in this undated photograph.

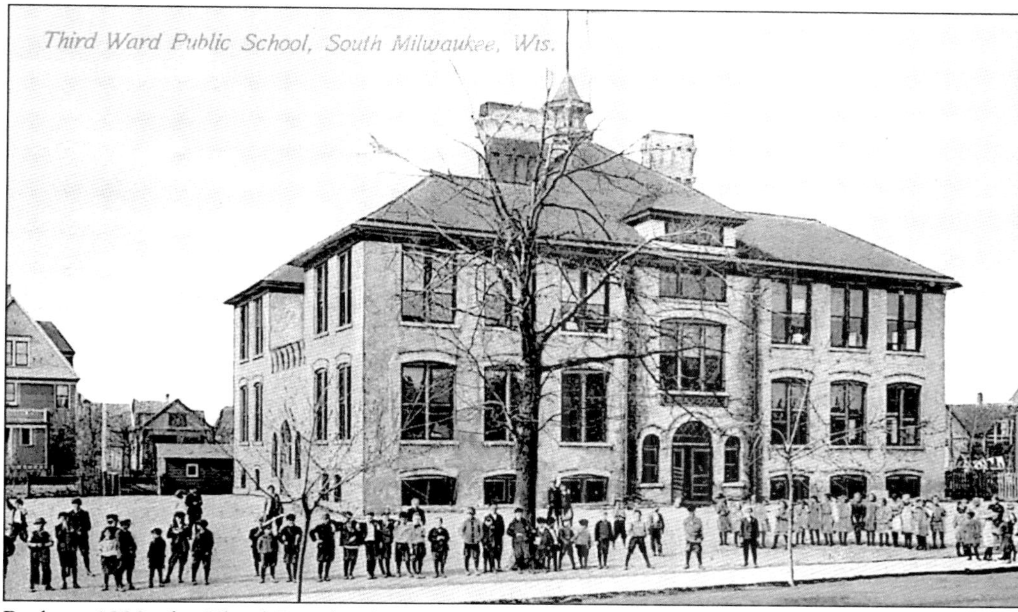

Built in 1899, the Third Ward School was located on the northeast corner of Thirteenth and Michigan. Designed to relieve congestion at the school on Tenth and Rawson, the Third Ward School was used until the new Parkway Elementary School was completed in 1954. The old Third Ward School was torn down around 1977 to make room for an apartment complex. Today, only the old flagpole remains.

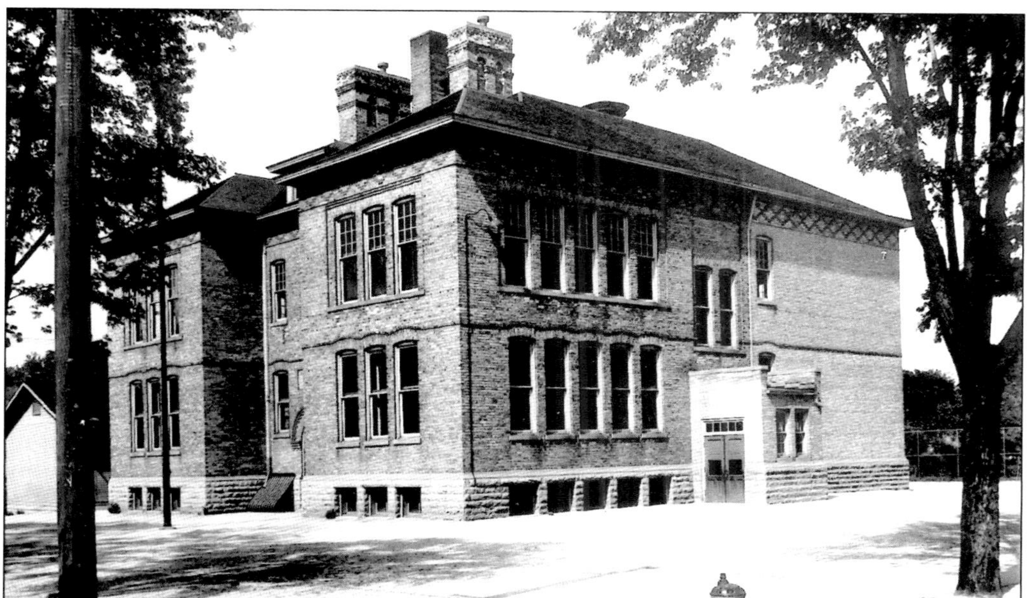

Located on the northeast corner of Eighth and Marquette, the Second Ward School was built in 1905. In use until 1957, when the new Lakeview Elementary was opened, the Second Ward School was sold to St. John's parish. Renamed as the Marquette School, it was used by St. John's as a parochial school until 1968. Afterwards, the building was sold to a developer and razed.

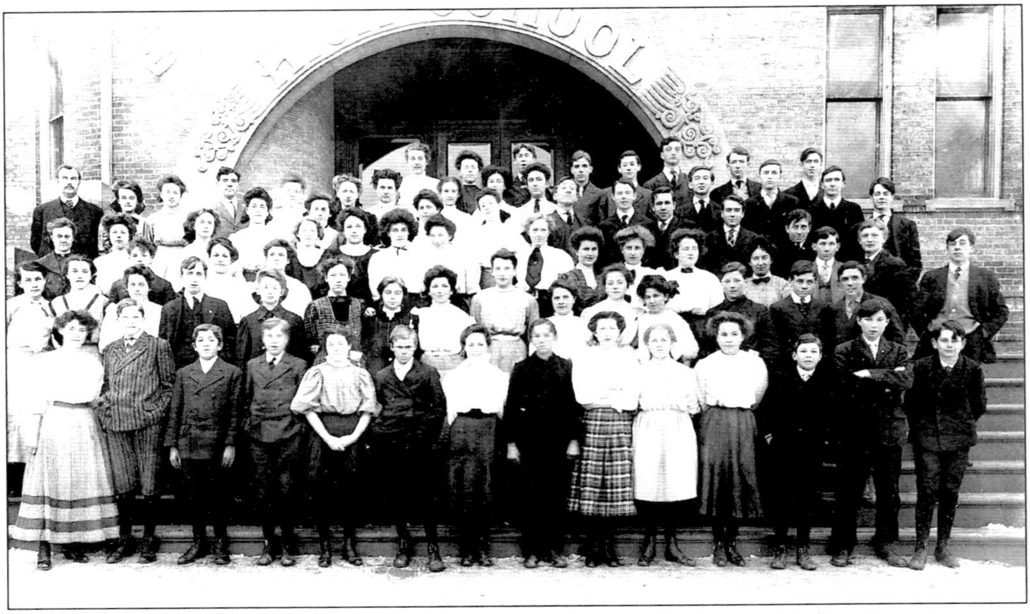

Students from grades seven through twelve pose in front of the high school.

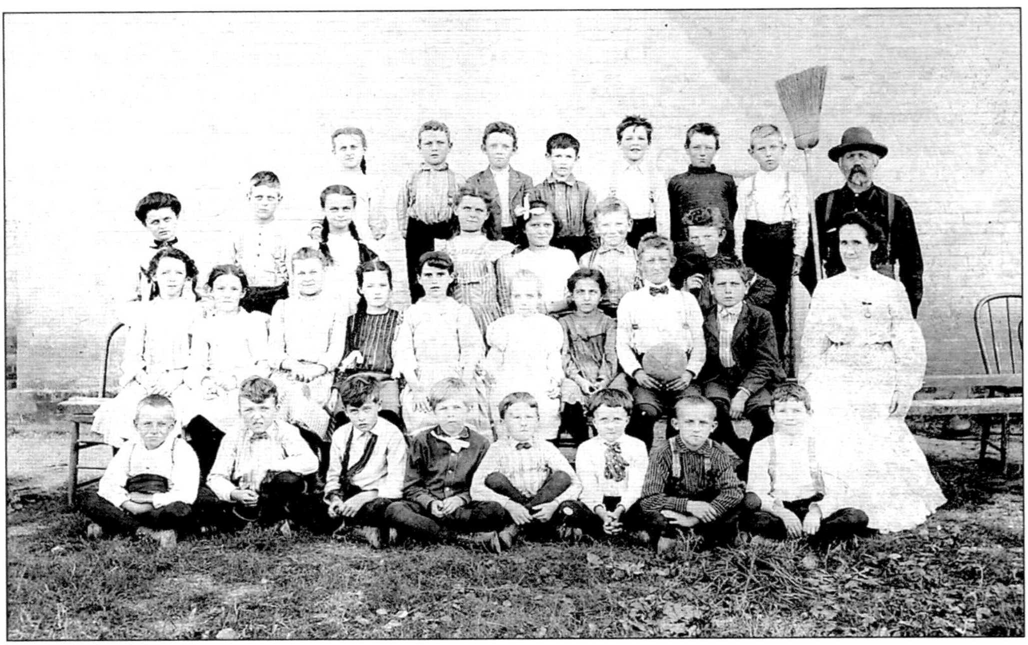

The fourth grade class of the Third Ward School sit for this portrait taken on September 26, 1903. The man on the right holding the broom is Mr. Stosick, the school's janitor.

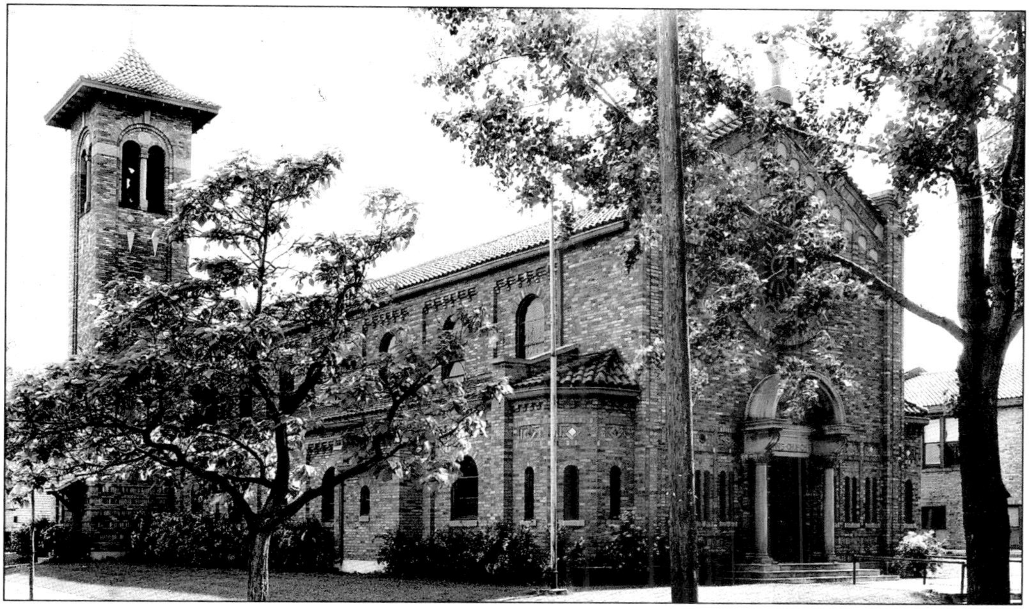

St. John's Catholic Church, on the southwest corner of Eighth and Marquette. The cornerstone for this building was laid on November 2, 1924. The first Catholic Church to be organized in South Milwaukee, St. John's was intended for the English-speaking Catholics of the community. In 1965, a new St. John's church was built across the street.

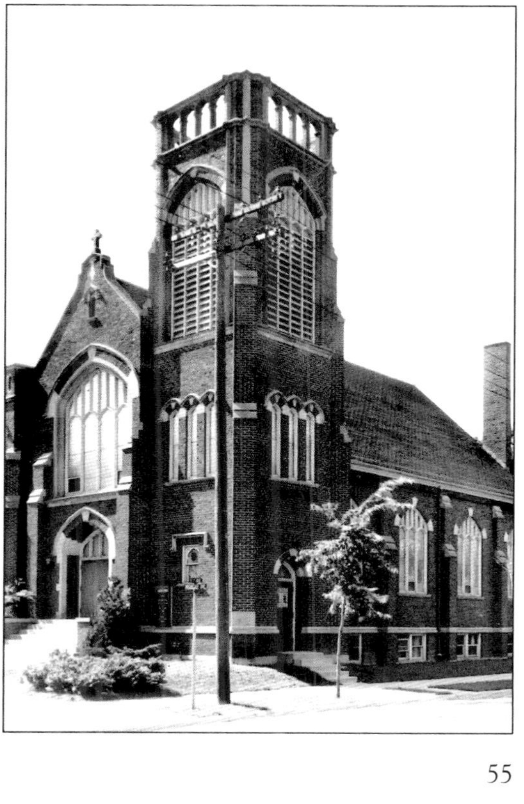

Zion Evangelical Lutheran Church was first organized on July 3, 1892 at the home of John Ahrens. By September, a frame church had been built on the corner of Sixth and Milwaukee Avenues. At Zion, all church services were conducted in German until 1912. In August 1924, the cornerstone for a new church was laid out on the northwest corner of Ninth and Michigan, where the church remains today.

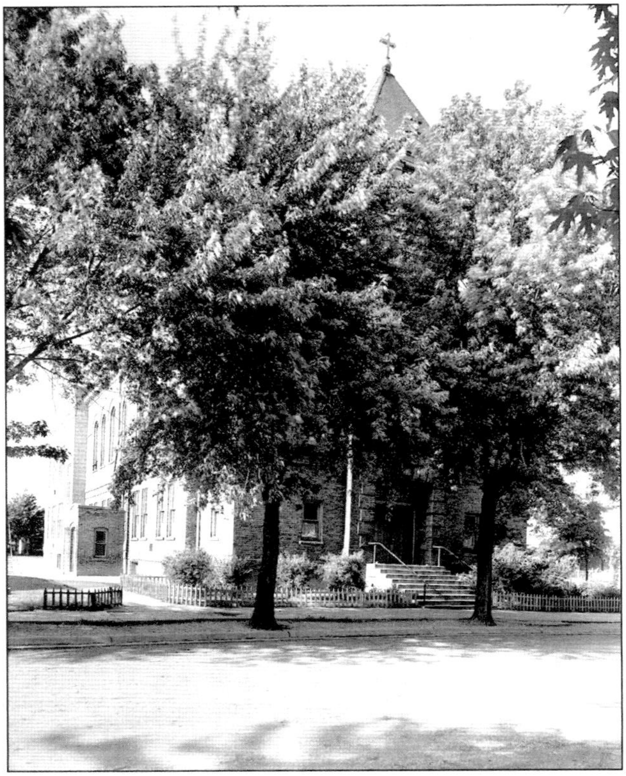

Located near Thirteenth and Manitoba, St. Mary's Catholic Church was built in 1894. It served the community's German-speaking Catholics. By 1911, the congregation listed some 455 members.

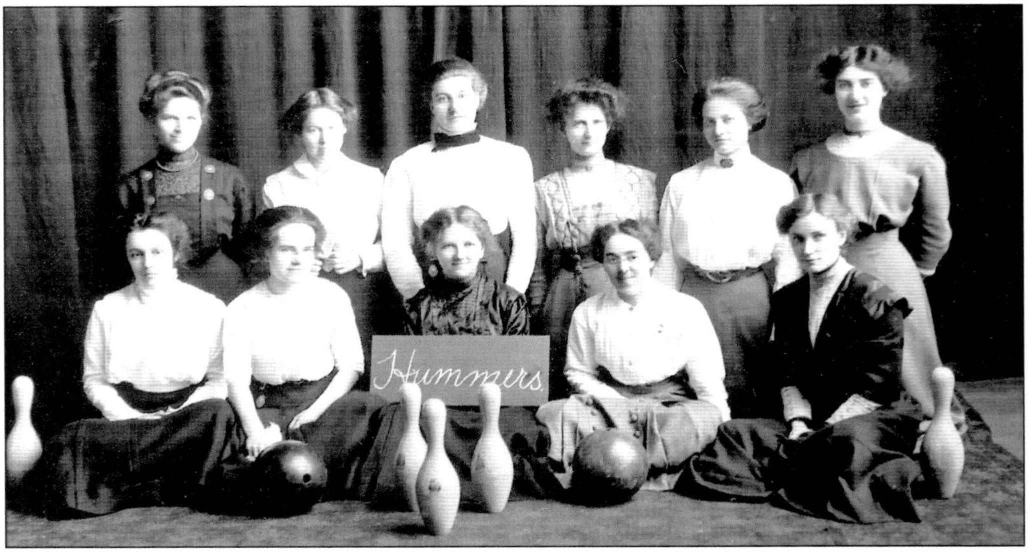

In 1911, St. Mary's had opened a fine new hall, which contained a bowling alley. The "Hummers"were one of the teams in the St. Mary's Ladies' Bowling League, and consisted mainly of local schoolteachers.

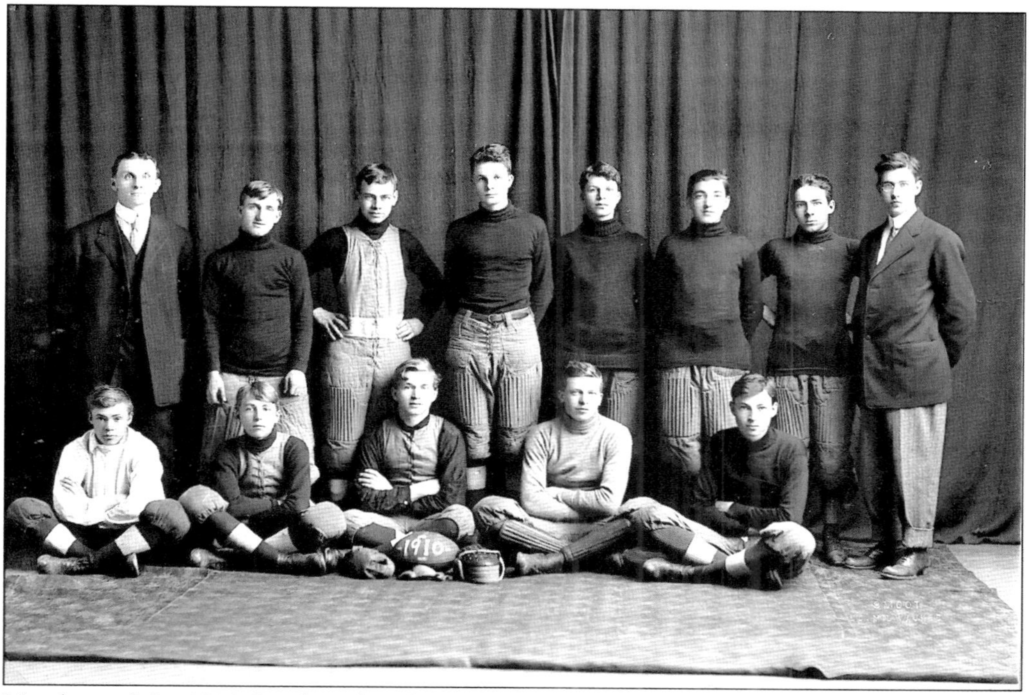

Members of the 1910 South Milwaukee High School Football Team pose in the uniform of the day.

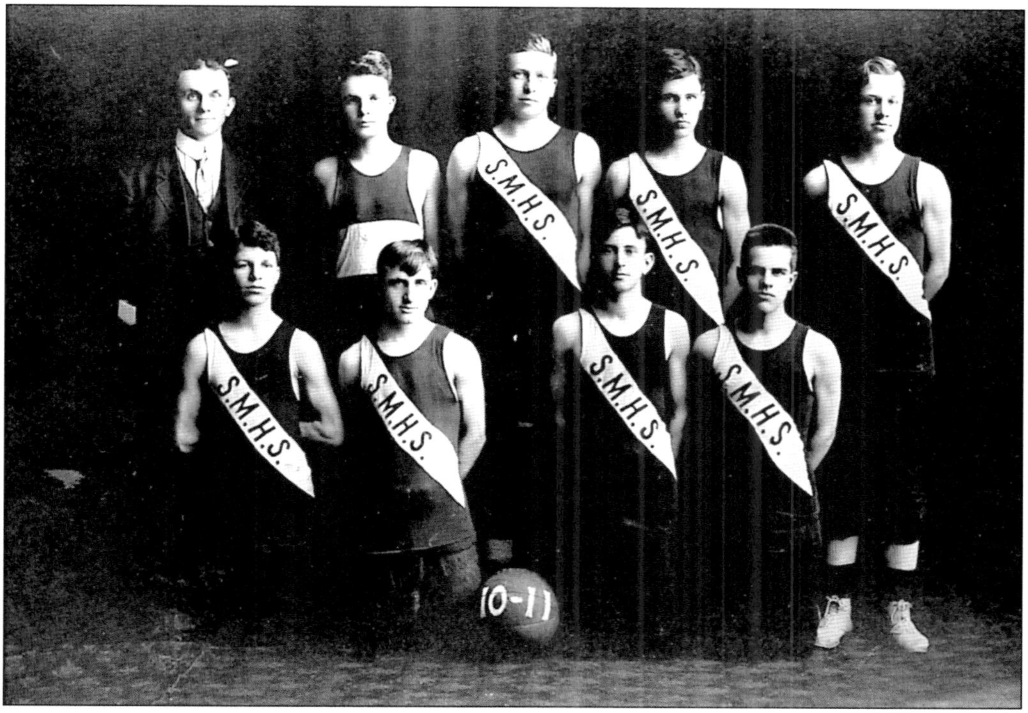

The 1911 South Milwaukee High School Basketball Team poses proudly.

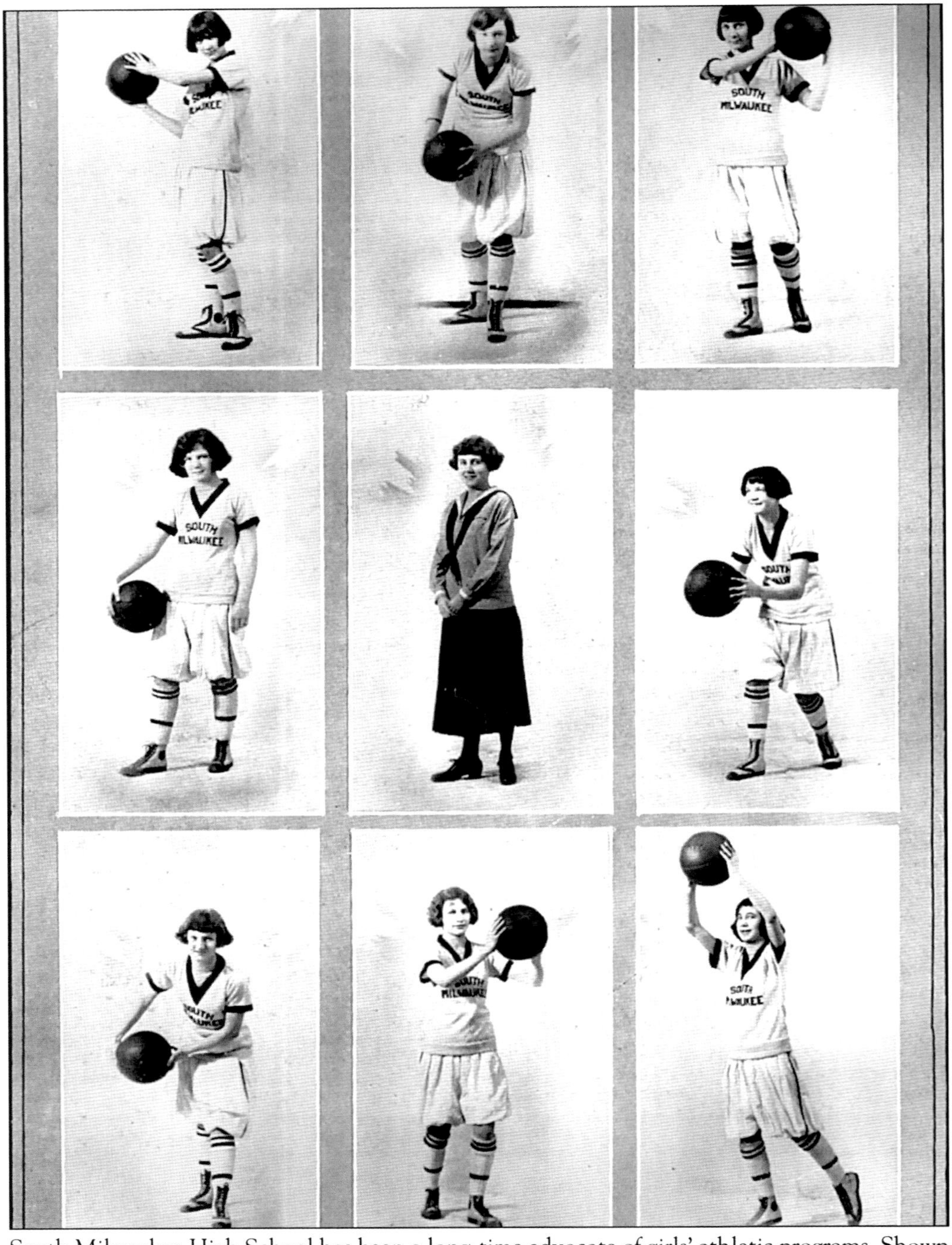

South Milwaukee High School has been a long-time advocate of girls' athletic programs. Shown here is the 1924 girls' basketball team. Under the tutelage of Miss Adelaide Hartopp, the Lady Cagers garnered a respectable season record of 7–2. Pictured here, from left to right, are: (top row) Alice Novak, Vera Nichols, and Martha Schmidt; (middle row) Eileen O'Leary, Coach Hartopp, and Mabel Gates; (bottom row) Mary Cook, Eva Schottlaender, and Ora Welbes.

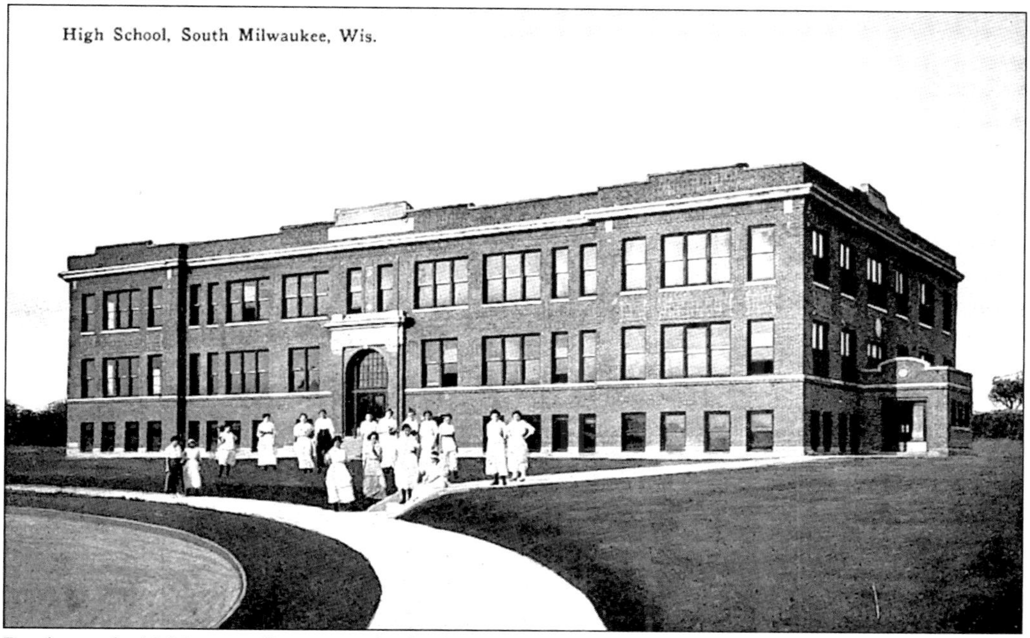

By the early 1900s, enrollment at the high school at Tenth and Rawson had grown to the point where a new facility was necessary. Opened in 1914, the new high school was built on Pine Street and Memorial Drive at a cost of $100,000.

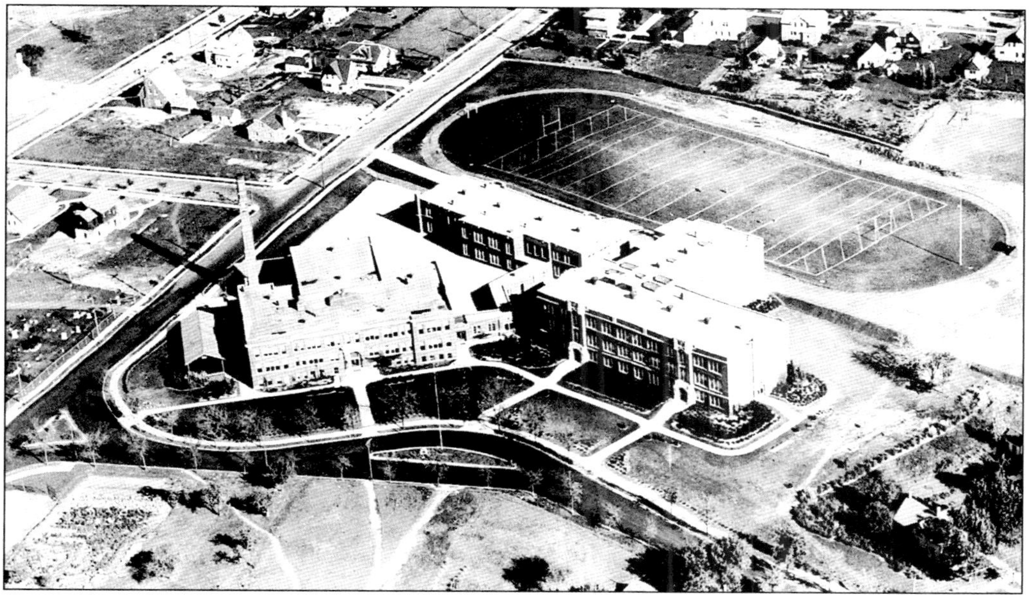

In 1929, a new junior high school was built next to the high school on Memorial Drive. By 1932, a fine new athletic field and vocational school were added. This 1935 aerial view shows what was then called "one of the most beautiful school plants in the state."

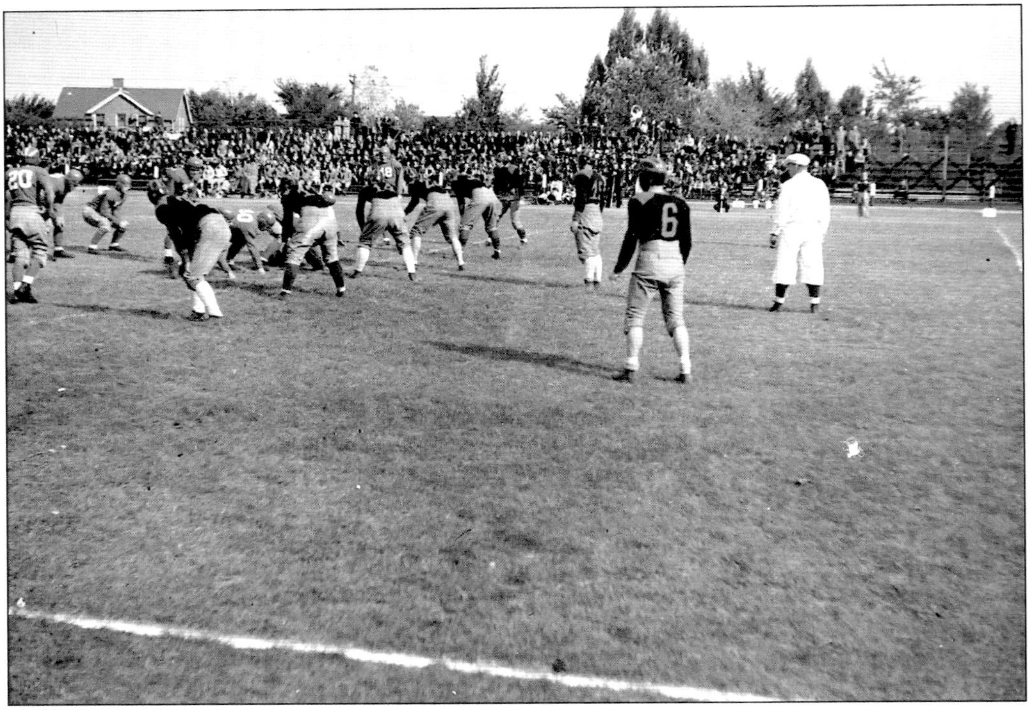

This photograph captures South Milwaukee High School football action, 1938 style. That year, South Milwaukee High School students voted to change the school's nickname from the "Cardinals" to the "Red Rockets."

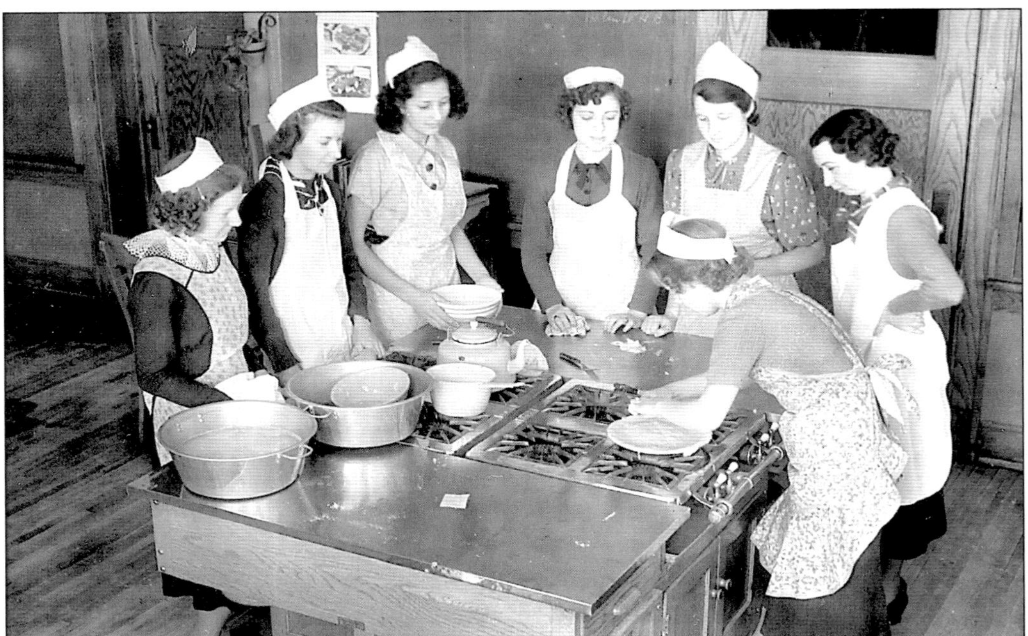

Students in a home economics class works to perfect their stovetop technique, 1938.

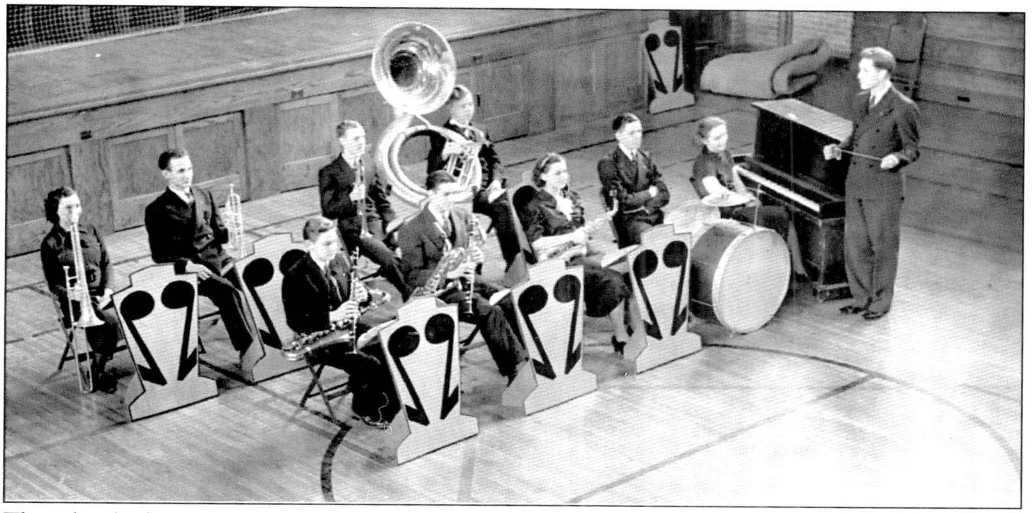
The school's dance orchestra gets ready to swing at a 1938 performance at the school's gymnasium.

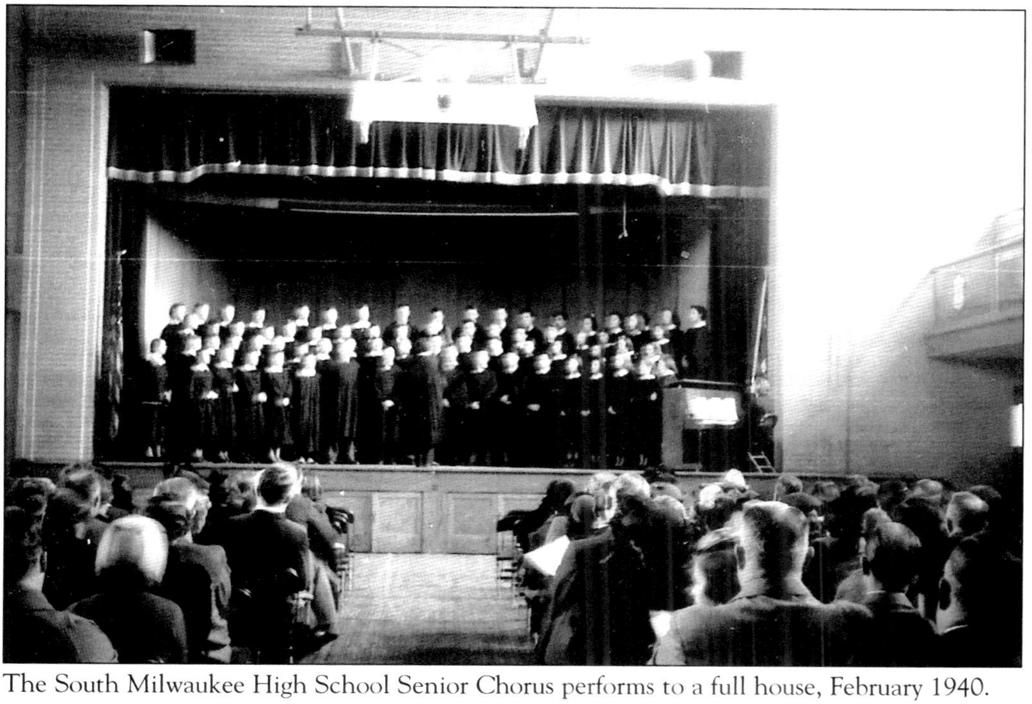
The South Milwaukee High School Senior Chorus performs to a full house, February 1940.

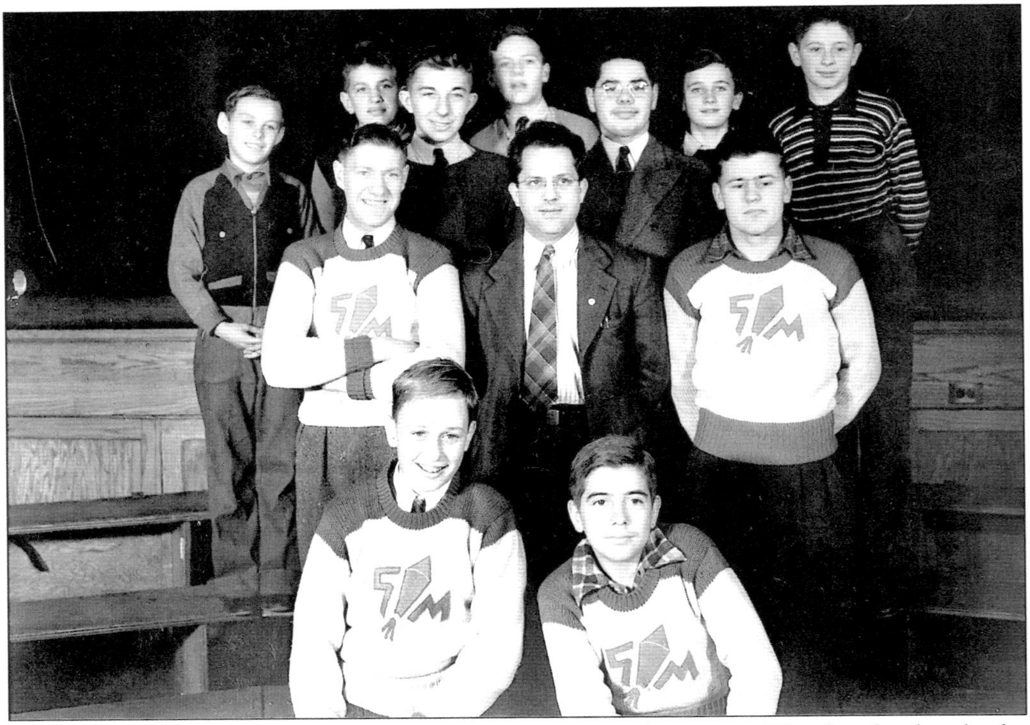

The 1942 "Red Rocket" cheerleader squad sports spirited sweaters. The female cheerleader squad was known at the time as the "Rocketeers."

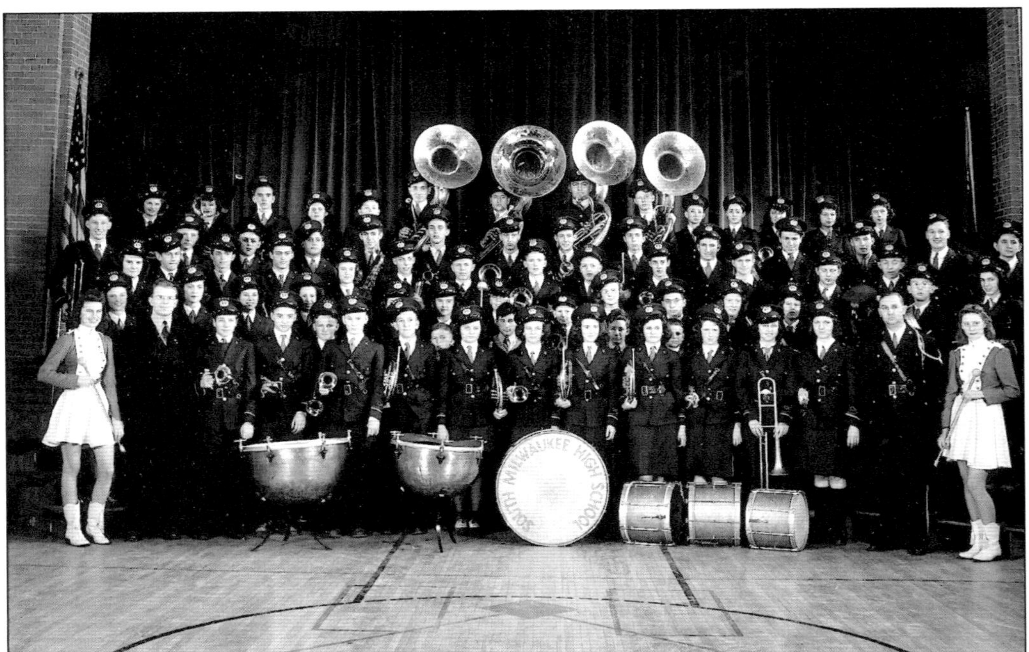

The South Milwaukee High School Marching Band assembled for this 1942 photograph.

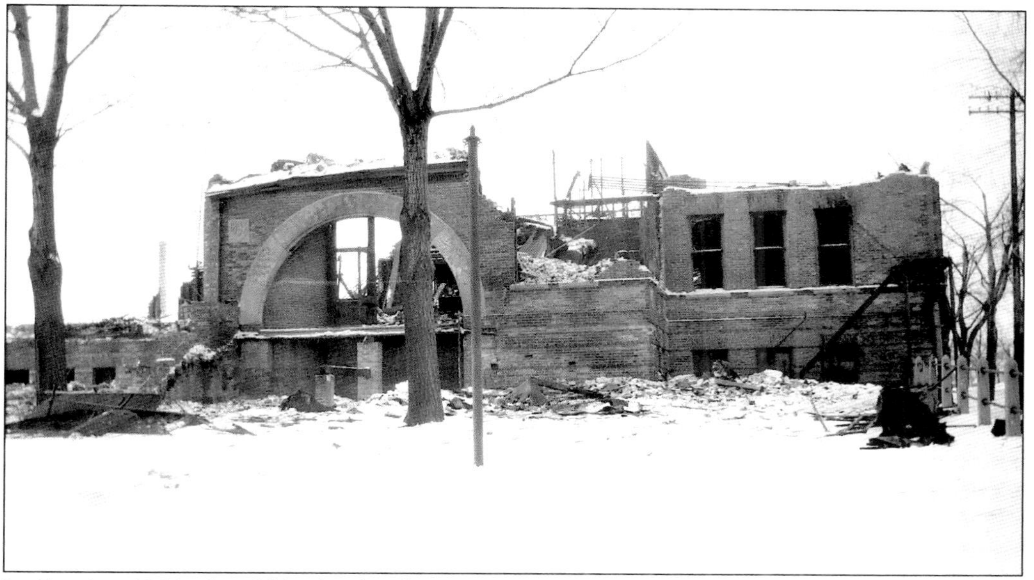

In October 1929, the old high school on Tenth and Rawson was completely destroyed by fire. This photo taken in January 1930 shows the aftermath. Afterwards, Bucyrus would purchase the property and erect a new plate shop on the old school site.

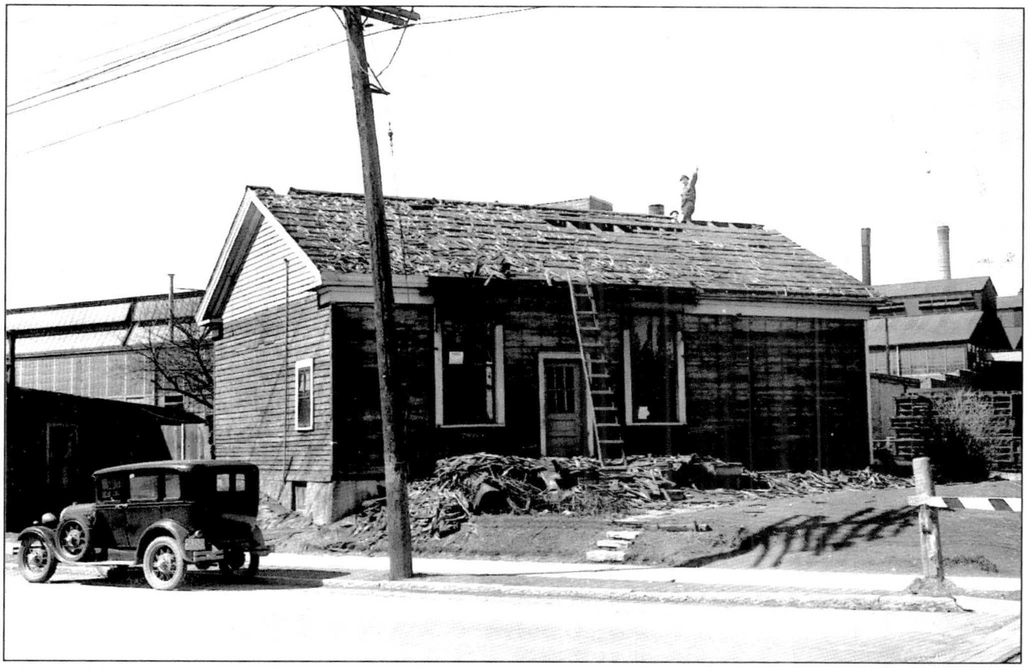

The old "pioneer school" located at 1702 Tenth Avenue is pictured shortly before it was torn down and the site taken over by Bucyrus.

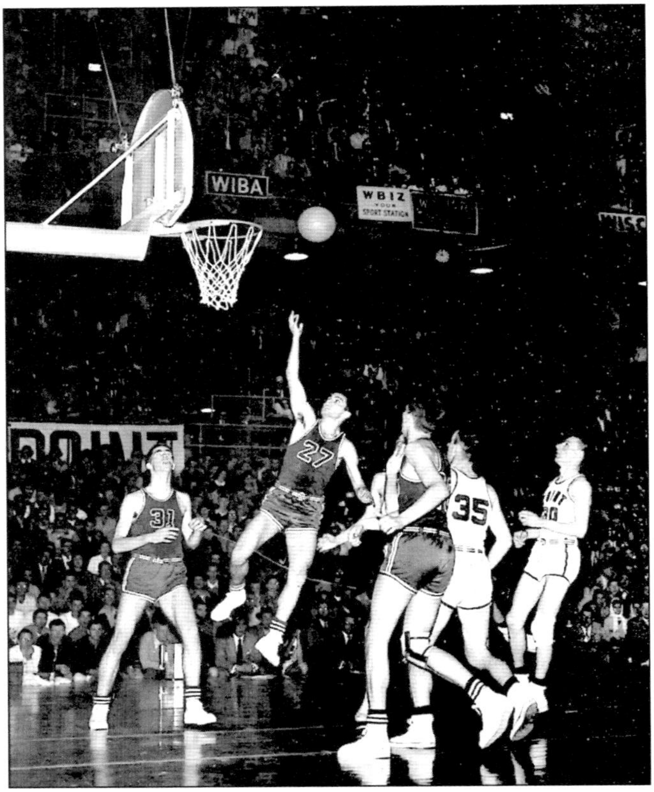

In 1952, under the leadership of Coach Larry Jansky, the South Milwaukee Boys' Basketball Team won the WIAA State Championship in Madison. Here, we see Rocket guard Jack Vahradian (No. 27) take the ball to the hoop while teammates Rollie Blanchett (No. 31) and Jay Schauer (back to camera) crash the boards. The next time the South Milwaukee Boys' Basketball Team would win the state title would be in 1976.

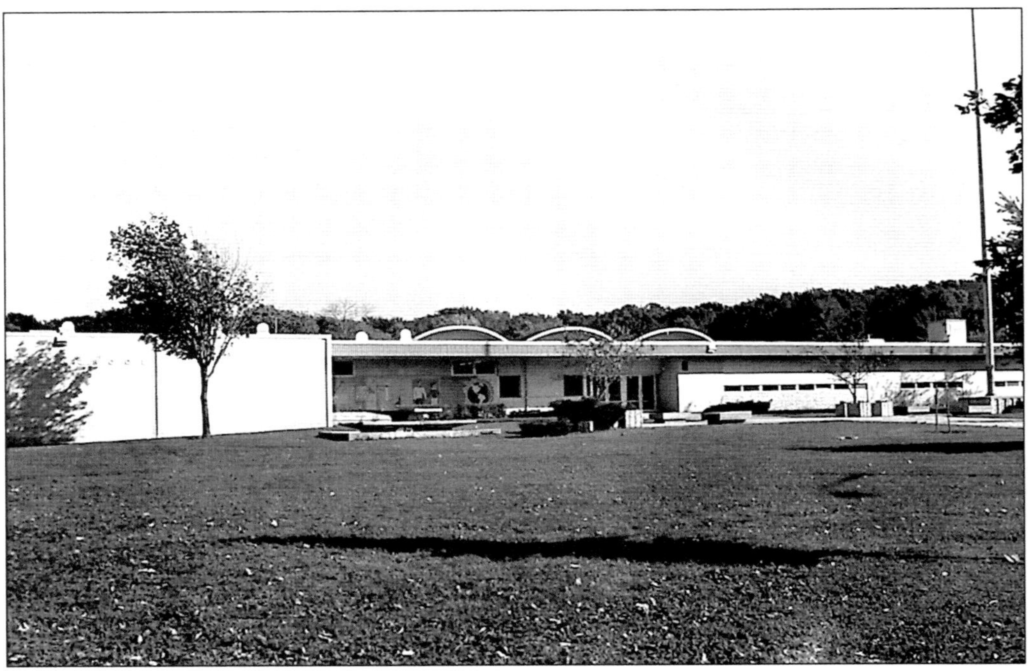

A new high school was built on Fifteenth Avenue and Beech Street in 1961.

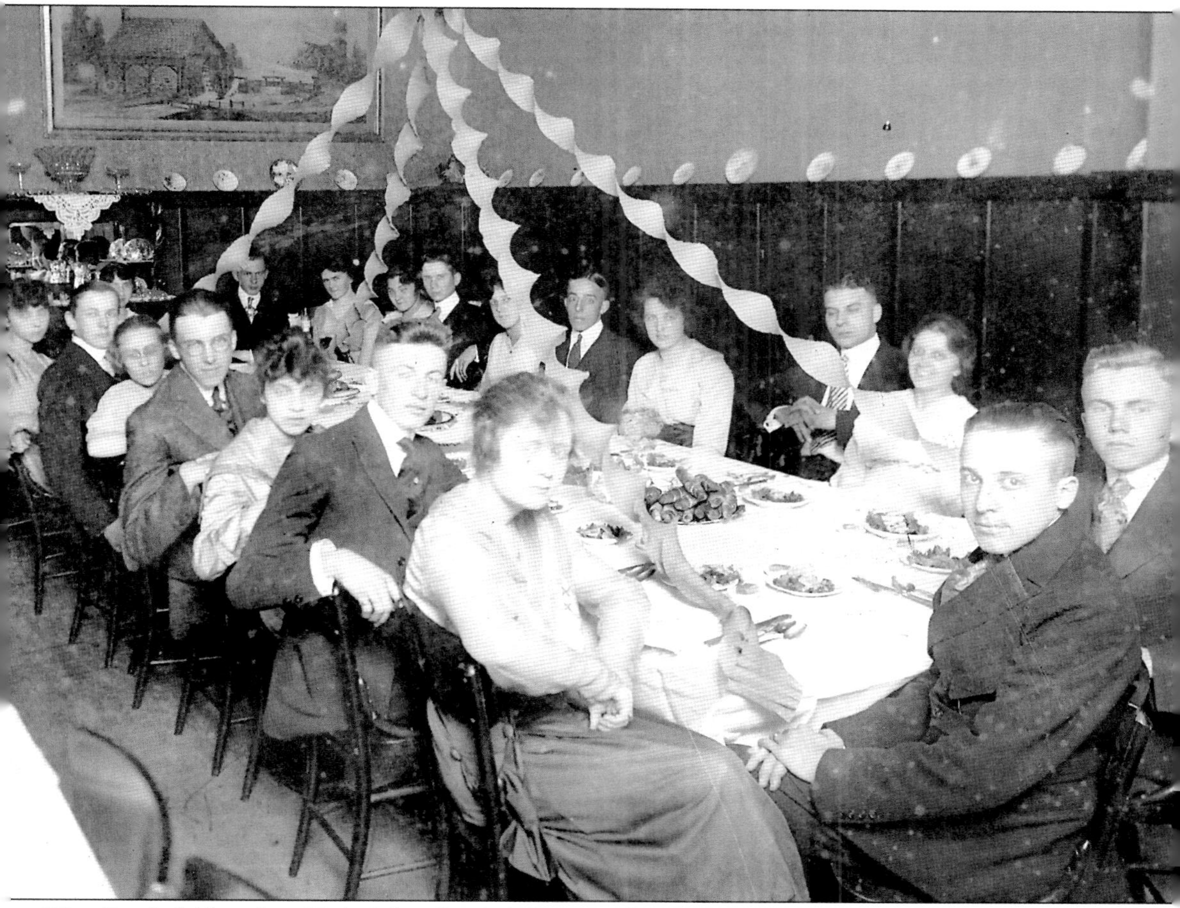

This South Milwaukee High School's 1917 Senior Class Banquet was held at Vollmer's Hall, located at North Chicago and Hawthorne Avenues. Vollmer's Hall was commonly used for many school functions.

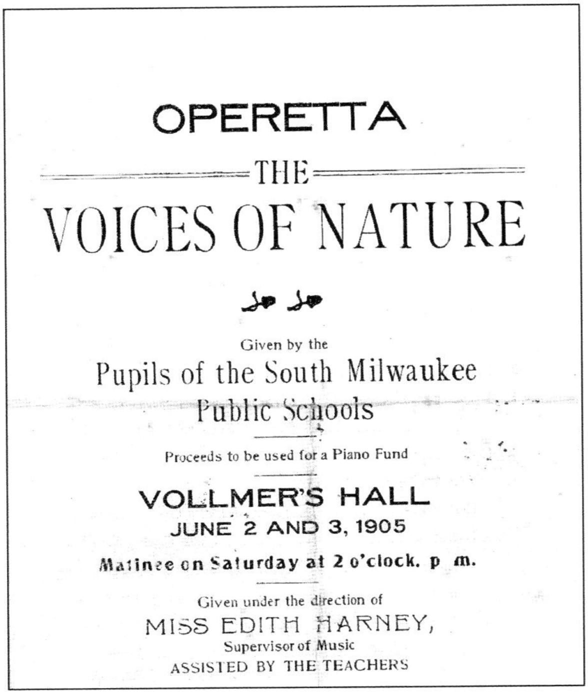

OPERETTA

THE

VOICES OF NATURE

Given by the

Pupils of the South Milwaukee

Public Schools

Proceeds to be used for a Piano Fund

VOLLMER'S HALL

JUNE 2 AND 3, 1905

Matinee on Saturday at 2 o'clock. p m.

Given under the direction of

MISS EDITH HARNEY,

Supervisor of Music

ASSISTED BY THE TEACHERS

This spectator program is for a South Milwaukee Public Schools operetta, 1905. Held at Vollmer's Hall, proceeds from this musical would go to a piano fund.

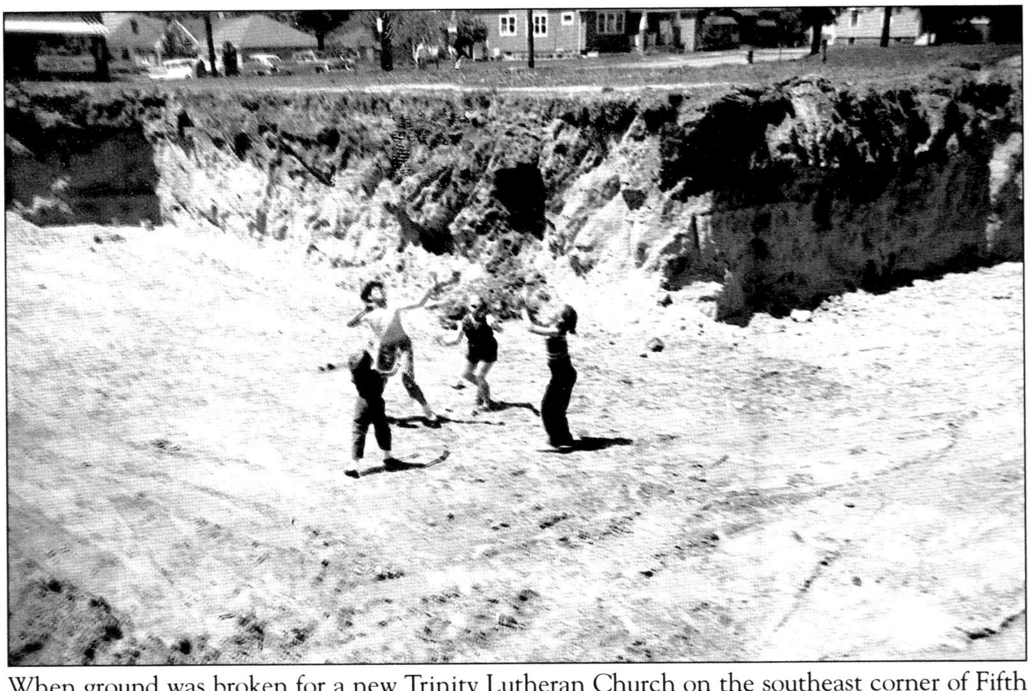

When ground was broken for a new Trinity Lutheran Church on the southeast corner of Fifth and Marshall in 1959, the basement excavation served as an ad hoc playground for some of the neighborhood children.

Five

Scenes from the Street

The independent nature of South Milwaukee has always fuelled its desire for self-sufficiency. To be sure, local businesses have continuously attempted to meet the material needs of the community. Additionally, the city's location on the old Chicago Road has always insured a steady flow of travelers through the area, further expanding the market for providers of various goods and services.

When the Yellowstone Trail, one of this country's first transcontinental highways, came through South Milwaukee in 1915, it incorporated part of the old Chicago Road and heralded the age of cross-country automobile travel in America. Like many other cities that the trail passed through, South Milwaukee soon benefited from this development. On July 2, 1921, the local newspaper, *The Journal*, reported, "South Milwaukee is especially favored above many cities with an unusual number of tourists." By the late 1920s, the city could offer nearly a half dozen hotels, a fine campground, and many other amenities to meet the demands of the traveling public.

This heady combination of commerce, recreation, and travel helped create a thriving downtown environment, which would make South Milwaukee a lively place indeed. . . .

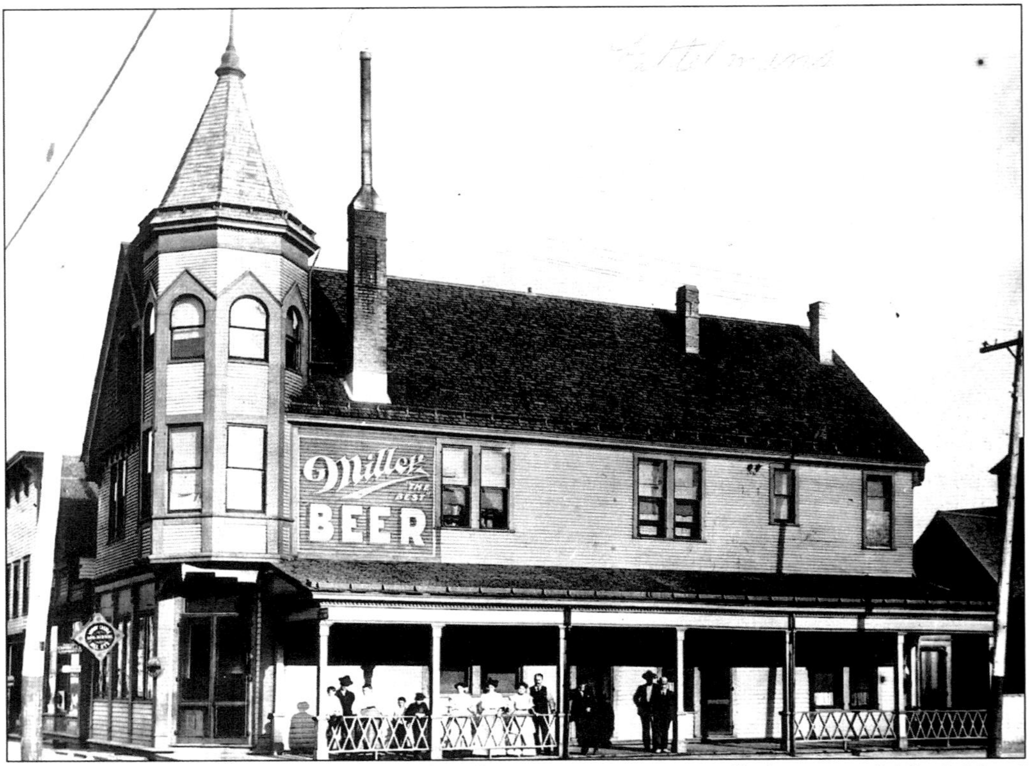

Built in 1894, this building at 1029 Milwaukee Avenue was originally known as Miller's Hotel and Tavern. Later, this building would become Pittelman's grocery store, a downtown South Milwaukee landmark until it was torn down in the late 1940s.

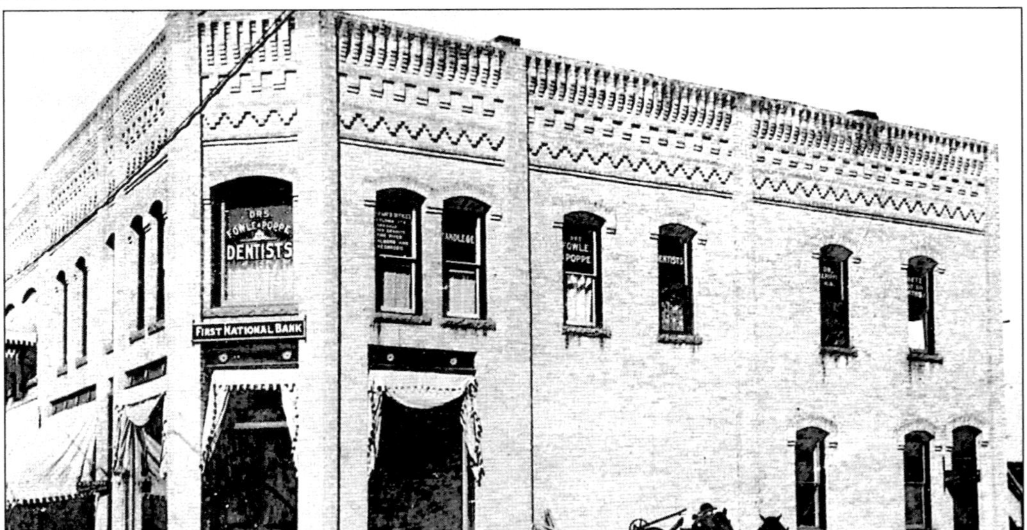

Established in 1893, South Milwaukee's First National Bank was located on the southeast corner of Tenth and Milwaukee Avenues. The bank's first president was Fred W. Rogers. It would become a state bank in 1897. The building was razed in 1960 when a new bank was built nearby.

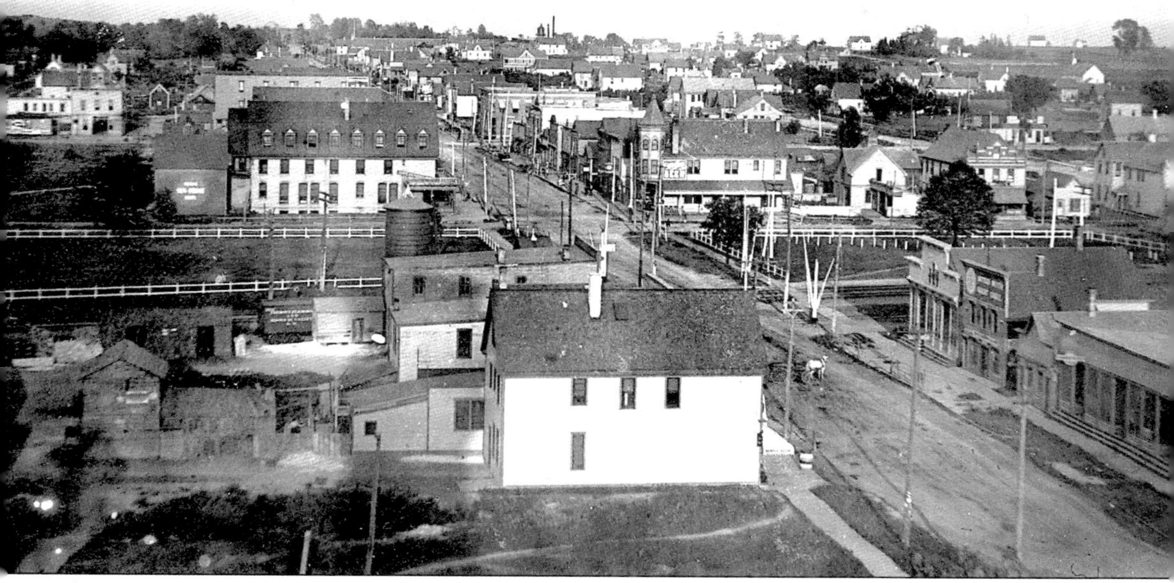

Taken from atop the city's water tower, which was built in 1894 on the site of the Lake View Club House, this 1902 view faces east and shows all the city's downtown landmarks of the time. As the name once implied, Lake Michigan can clearly be seen in the distance.

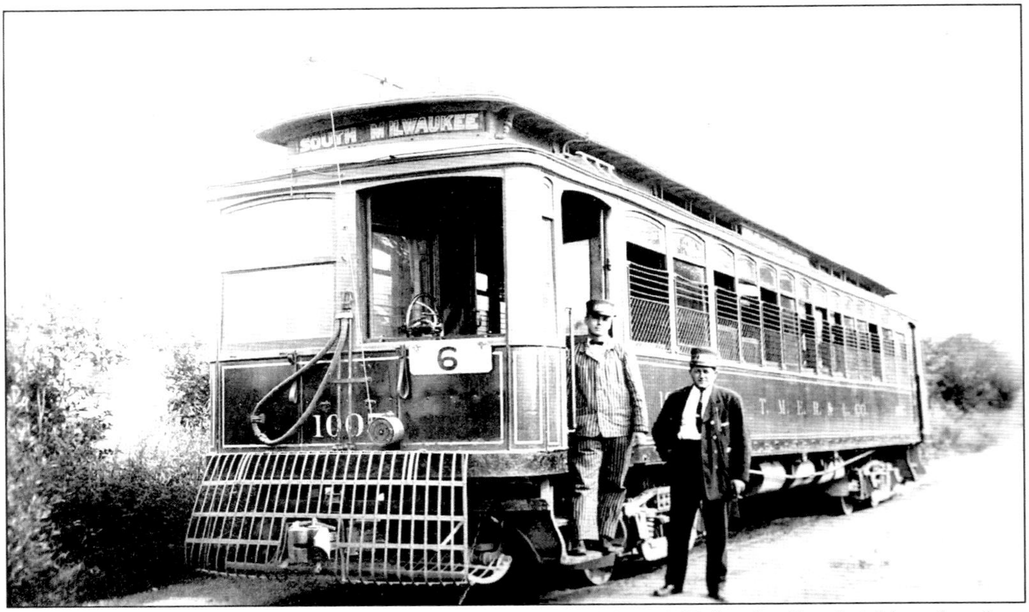

The motorman and conductor for TMER&L Streetcar No. 1007 for the South Milwaukee line pose in this undated photograph. The TMER&L served South Milwaukee until service was discontinued in 1938.

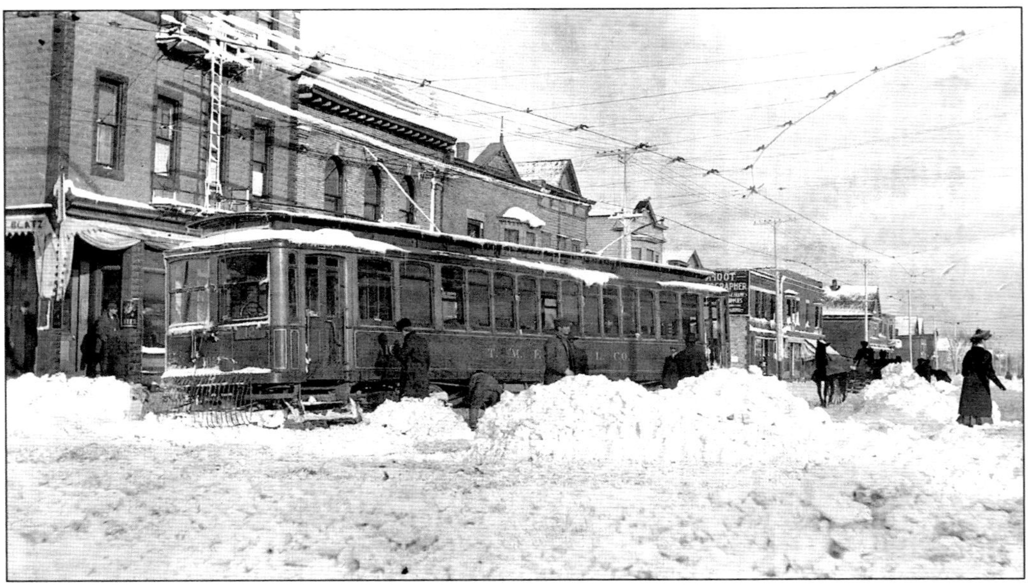

A TMER&L streetcar battles a rugged Wisconsin winter near Tenth and Milwaukee Avenues.

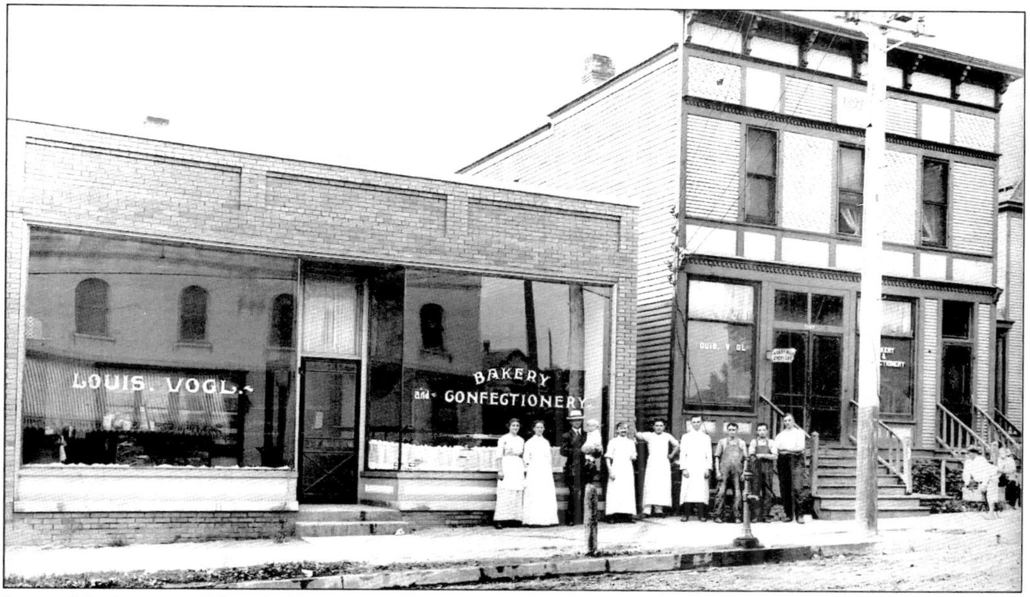

Louis Vogl opened his bakery at 1205–1207 Milwaukee Avenue around 1904. His business prospered, and Vogl was able to employ quite a number of workers, including bakers, helpers, drivers, and stable hands. This photo, taken around 1907, shows Vogl holding his son Henry. Vogl's wife Sophia stands on his right. The others are believed to be workers and helpers.

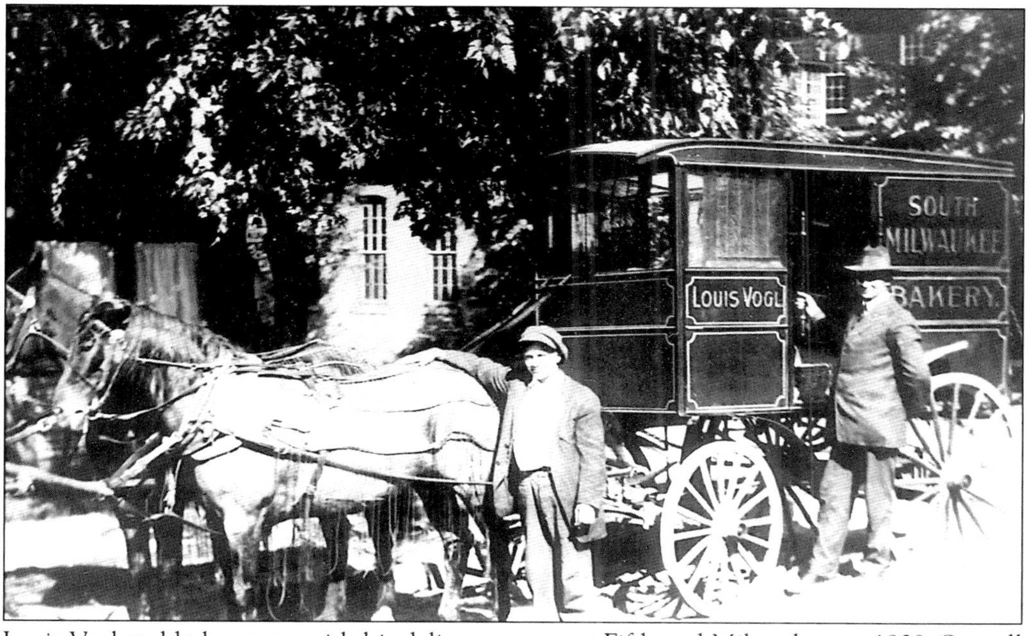

Louis Vogl and helper pose with his delivery wagon at Fifth and Milwaukee, c. 1909. Stowell Manufacturing is seen in the background. Each morning, Vogl would make the rounds to delivery his freshly baked goods. Neighborhood housewives would listen for the bugle call that announced his arrival to their area. They would then scurry out to the roadside and use their aprons to carry the still warm bakery back inside.

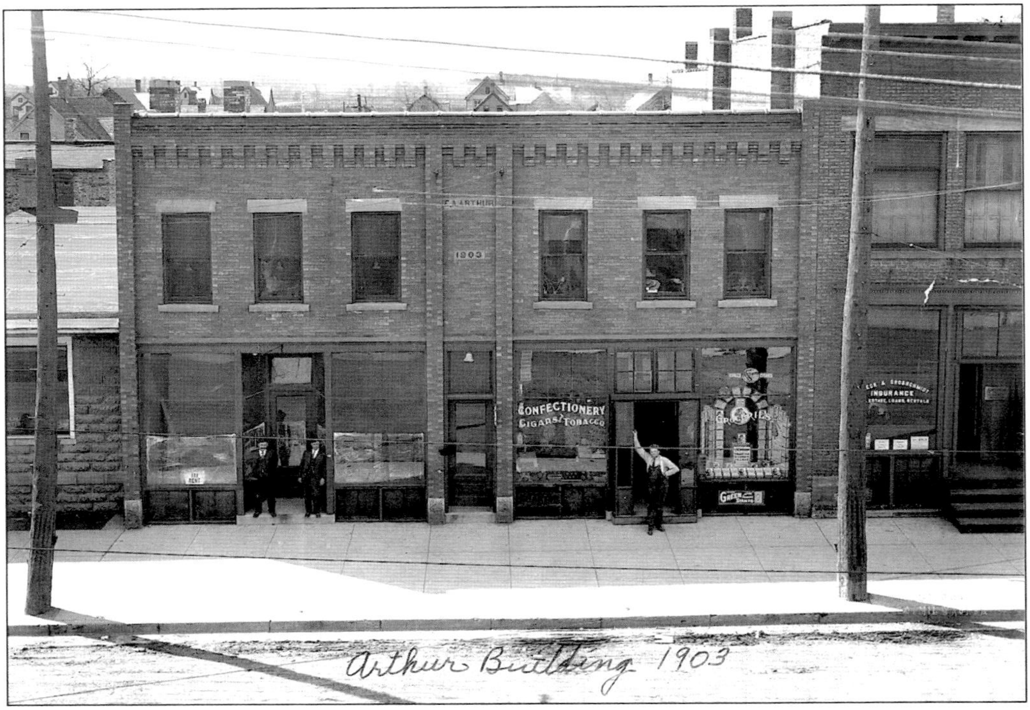

Built in 1903, the E. Arthur building still stands at 925–927 Milwaukee Avenue.

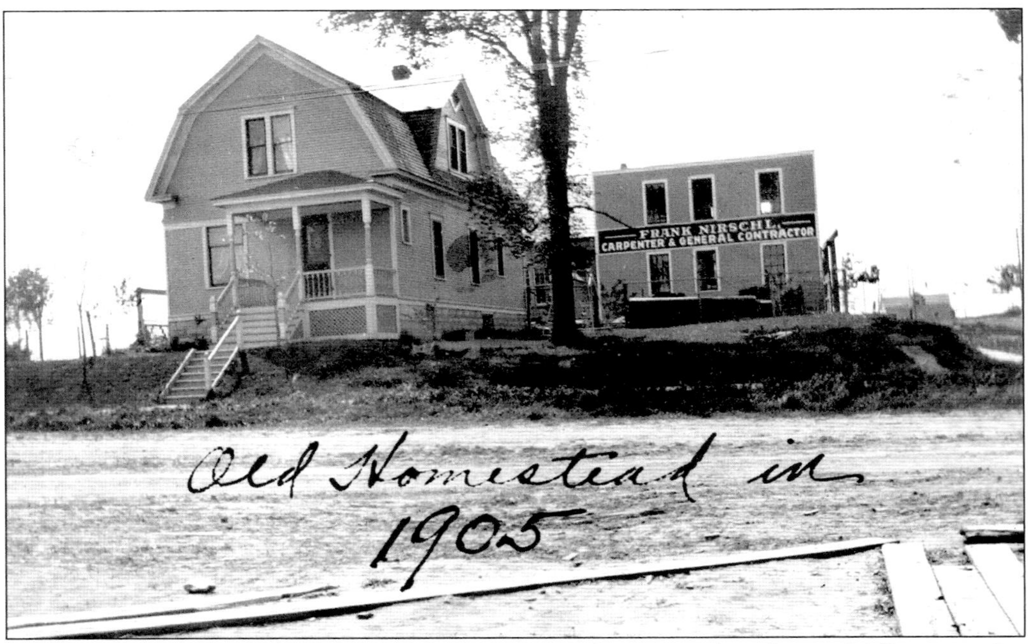

Frank Nirschl was a successful building contractor who operated a Planing Mill next to his home at 2502 South Chicago Avenue.

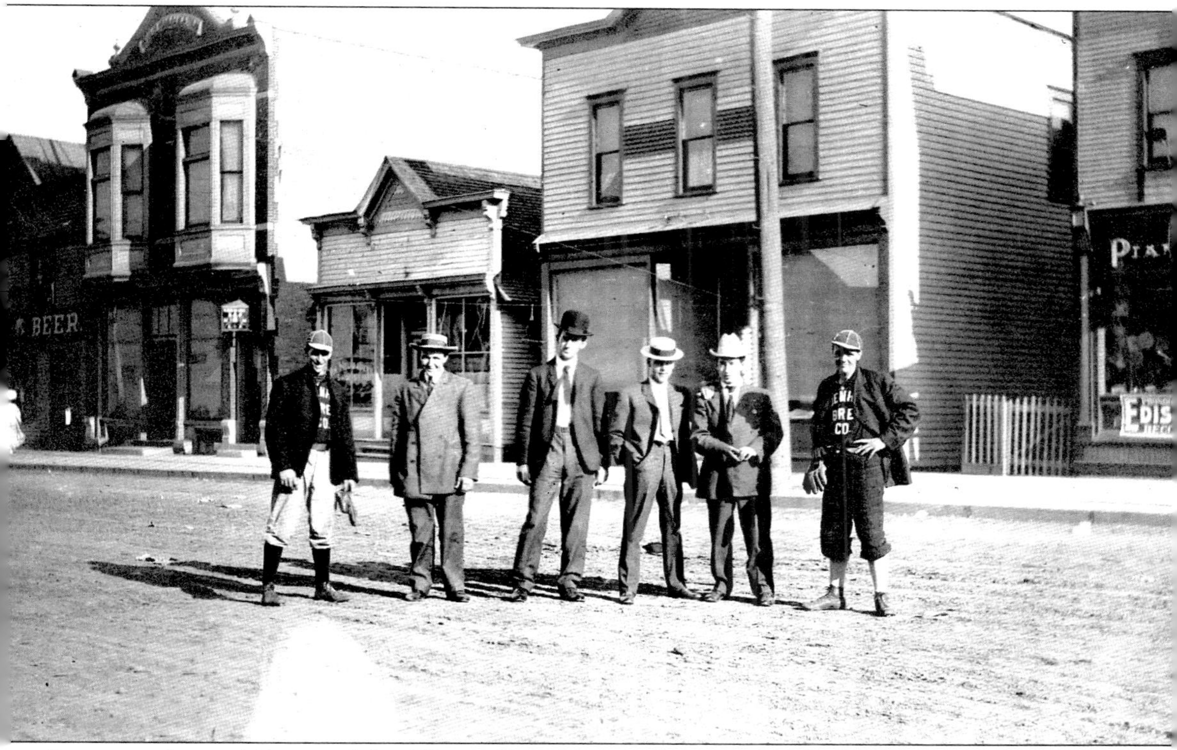

Posing in front of Captain John Wexstaff's tavern on the 1000 block of Milwaukee Avenue are members of his baseball team, co-sponsored by the Schoenhofen Brewing Company of Chicago, Illinois. Pictured here in this c. 1900 photo, from left to right, are Sam McCreedy, Will Morehead, John Sweeney, A.W. Walter, Frank Metzger, and Ridgely Fletcher. The Palace Meat Market building can be seen in the background, second building from the left.

Captain Wexstaff, retired Great Lakes ship captain, opened a tavern on Milwaukee Avenue around 1895. In 1902, he would open a new tavern on the southeast corner of Tenth and Madison Avenues. Captain Wexstaff would act as the city's informal weatherman by calling the weather service station in Milwaukee each morning. He would then run the appropriate flags up his flagpole to inform passersby what kind of weather to expect.

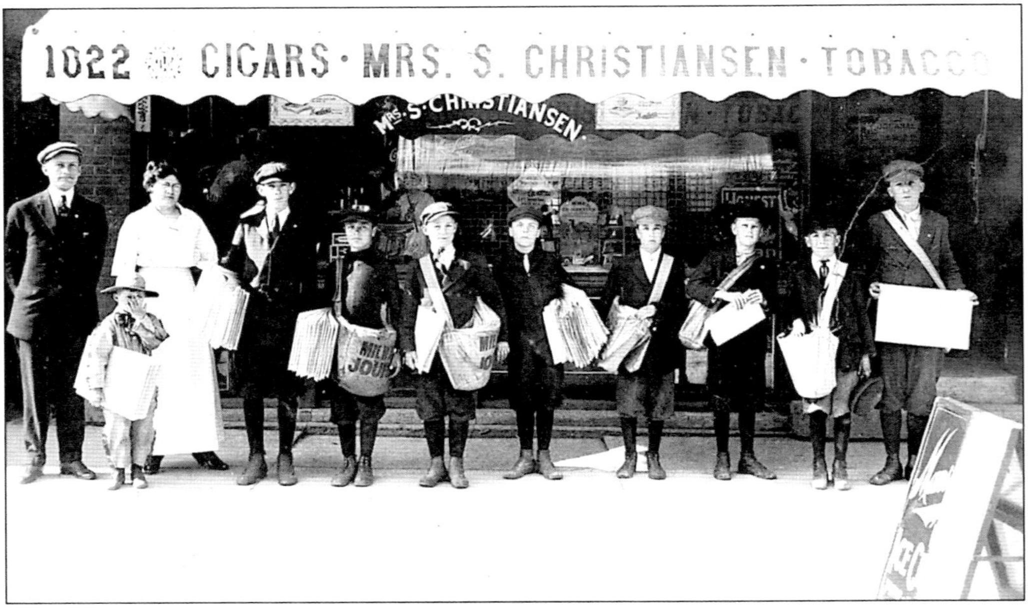

For many years, Mrs. Selma Christiansen's candy, tobacco, and newsstand was a Milwaukee Avenue institution.

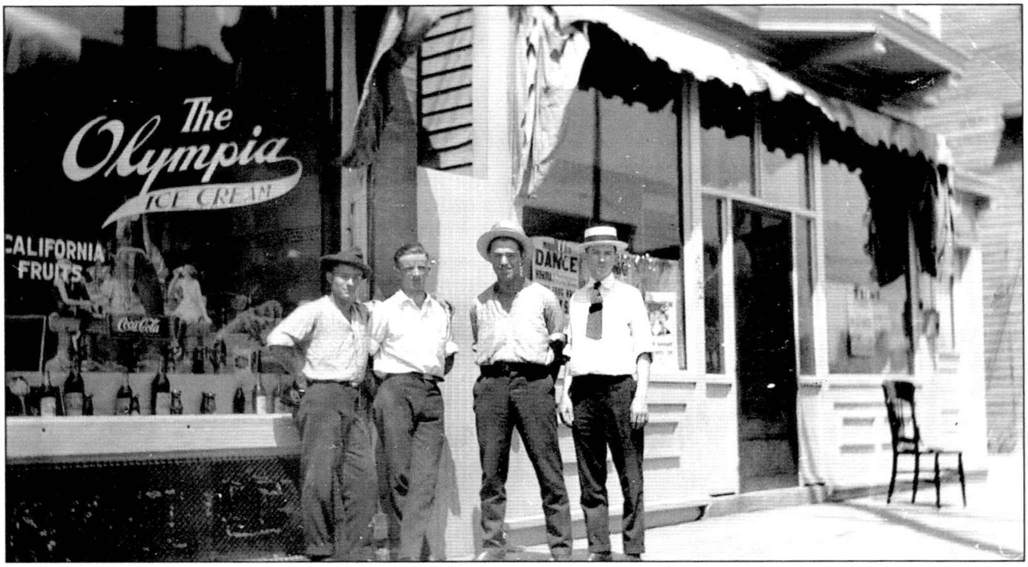

Out for a stroll on a sunny day, these four lads pose in front of the Olympia Ice Cream Parlor on Milwaukee Avenue.

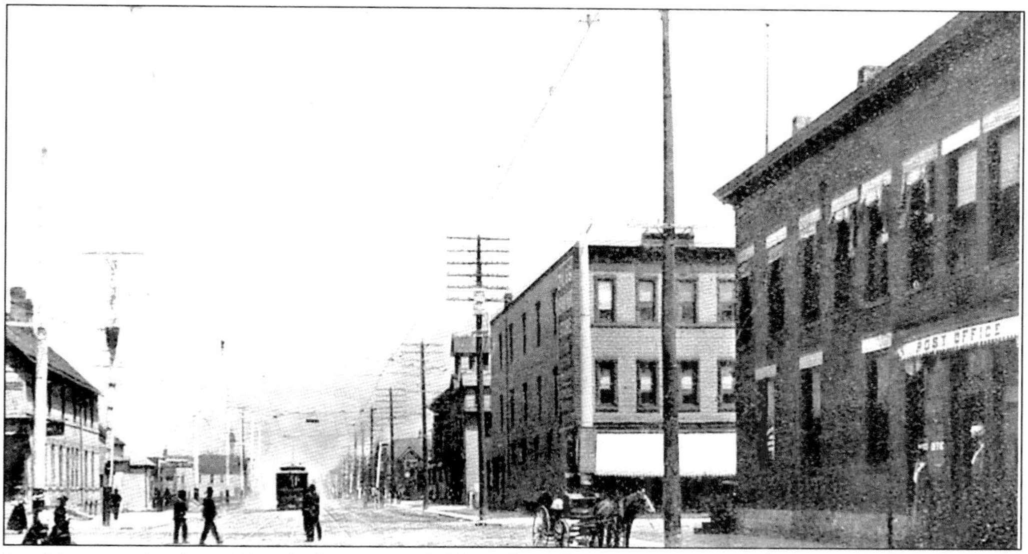

Looking north along Tenth Avenue at Milwaukee Avenue, *c.* 1902. The building in the right foreground is the South Milwaukee Bank and Post Office. Across Milwaukee Avenue from the bank is Zilg's Department Store, built in 1894. This building would become the Hotel Blatz, owned by Charles Franke. Notice the TMER&L streetcar as it approaches the intersection.

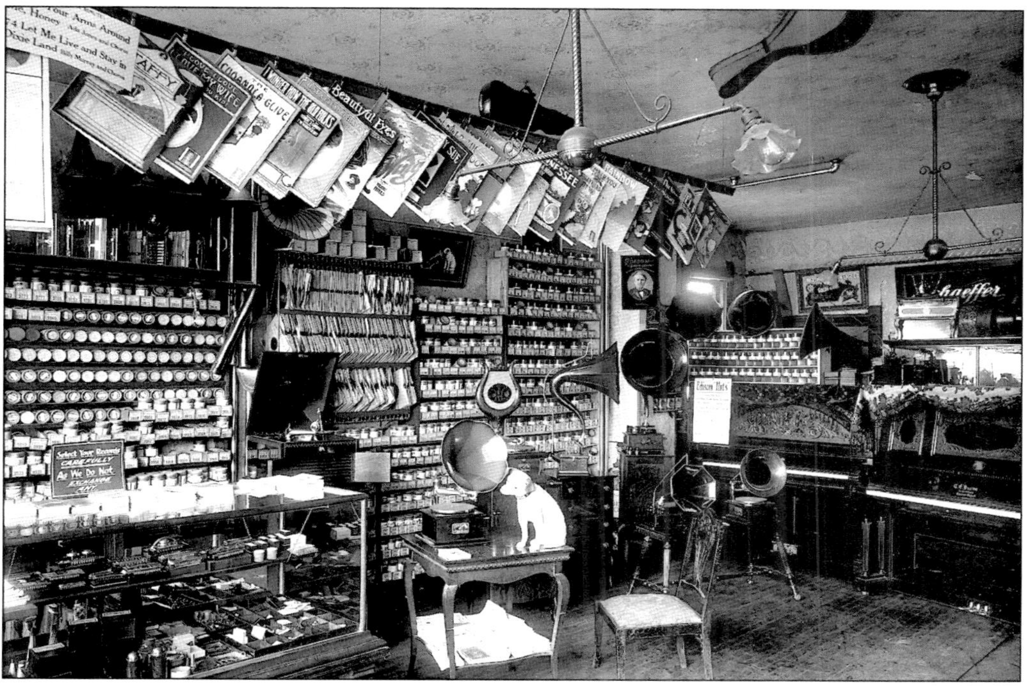

This 1910 photo shows the interior of August P. Wilde's Music and Jewelry store, located at 1015 Milwaukee Avenue. Note sheet music hanging from the ceiling. It was said that Wilde was the only man in Wisconsin "to have his heart located on the right side of his chest."

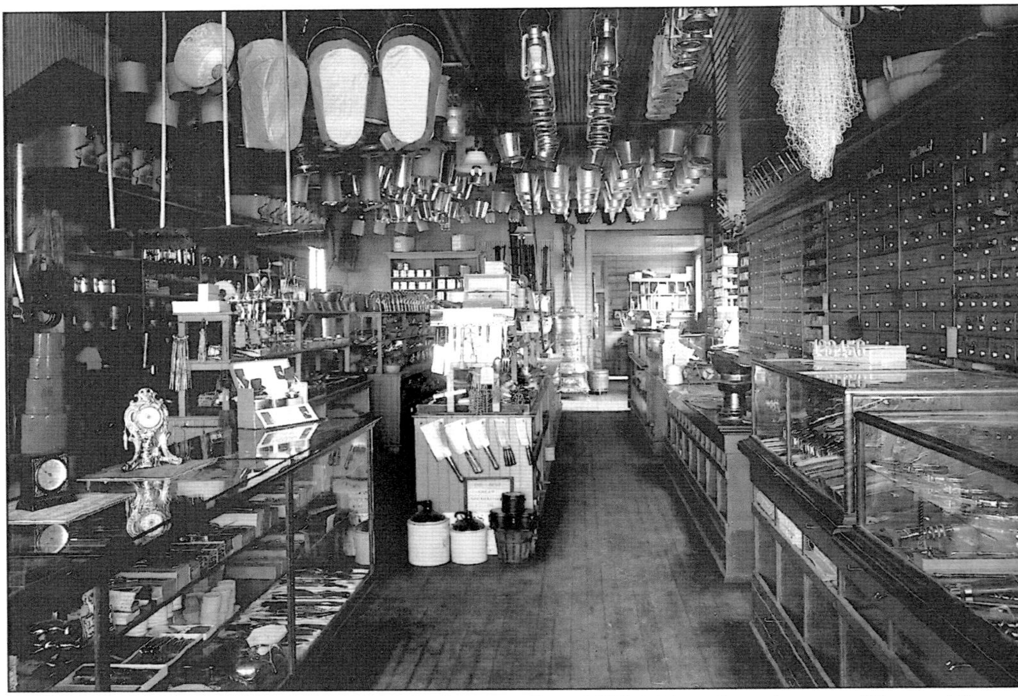

Fitzgerald's Hardware Store, *c.* 1911, was situated at 1021 Milwaukee Avenue. Fitzgerald's was South Milwaukee's premier hardware store for many years.

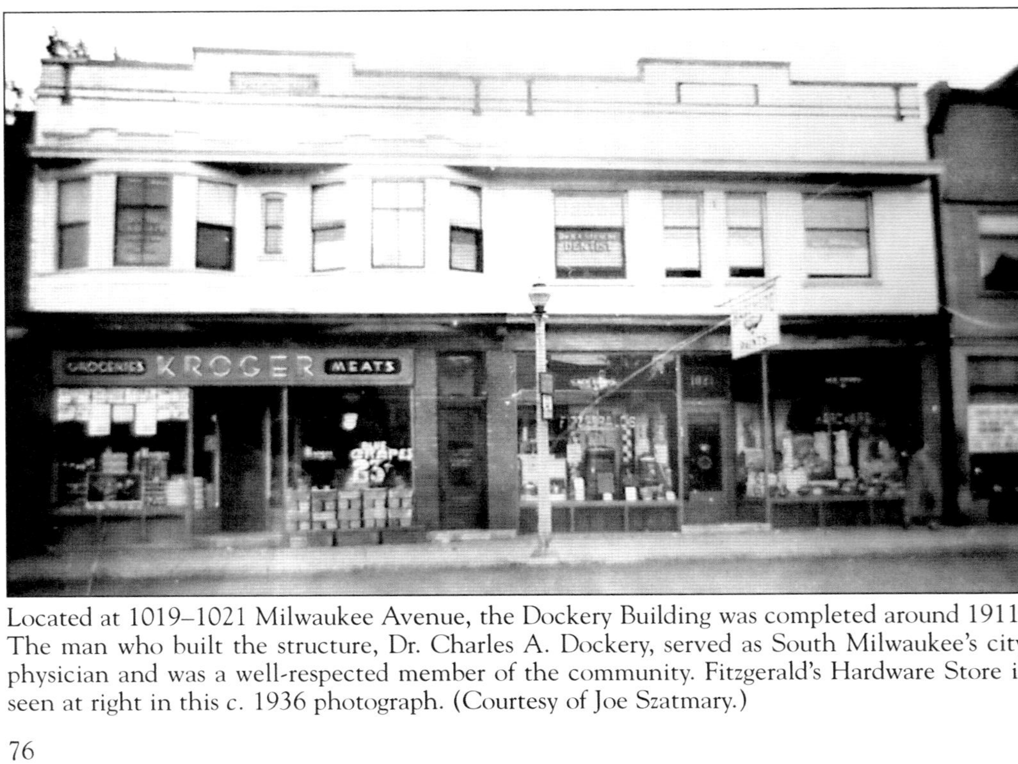

Located at 1019–1021 Milwaukee Avenue, the Dockery Building was completed around 1911. The man who built the structure, Dr. Charles A. Dockery, served as South Milwaukee's city physician and was a well-respected member of the community. Fitzgerald's Hardware Store is seen at right in this *c.* 1936 photograph. (Courtesy of Joe Szatmary.)

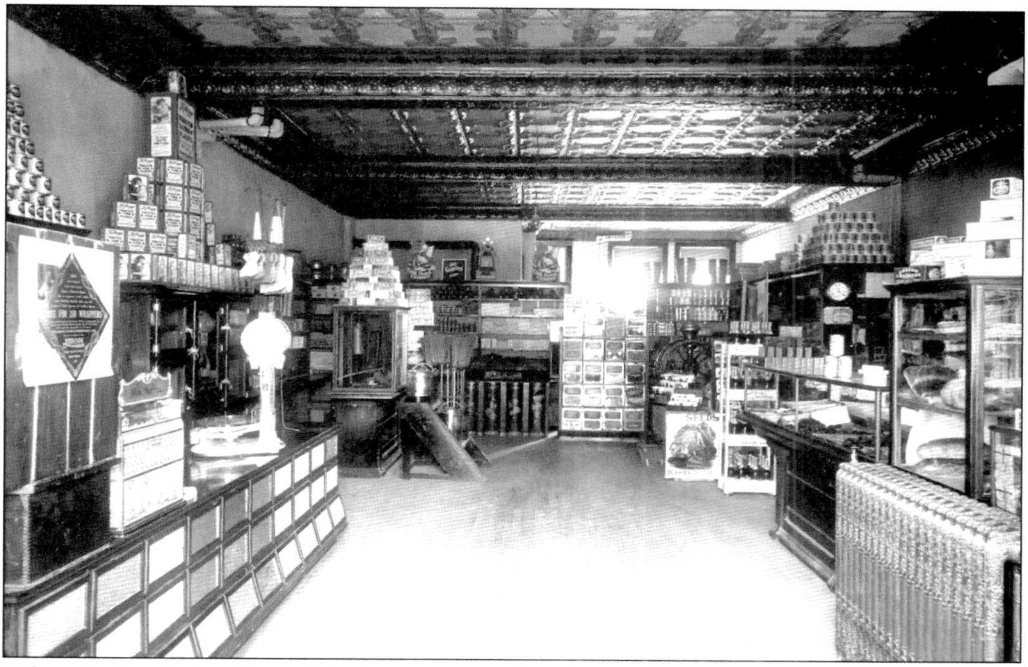

Advertised as being "a model of neatness and perfection," William Marren's grocery store was located at 1019 Milwaukee Avenue, next to Fitzgerald's hardware store. This photo was taken in 1911.

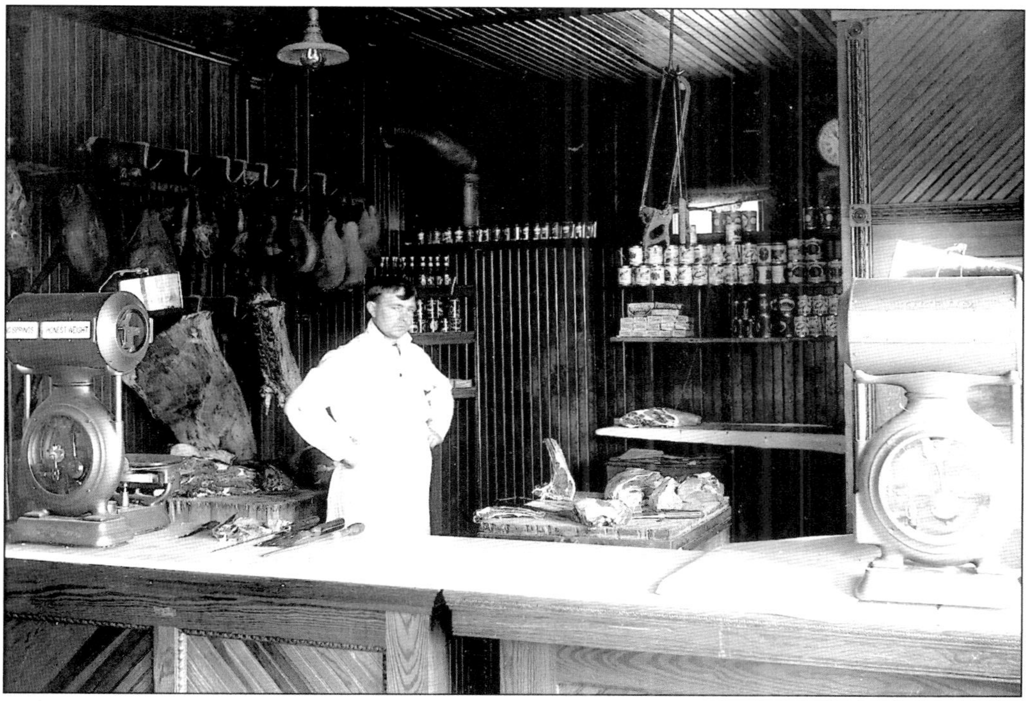

William A. Meyer's Meat Market was located at 1301 Madison Avenue.

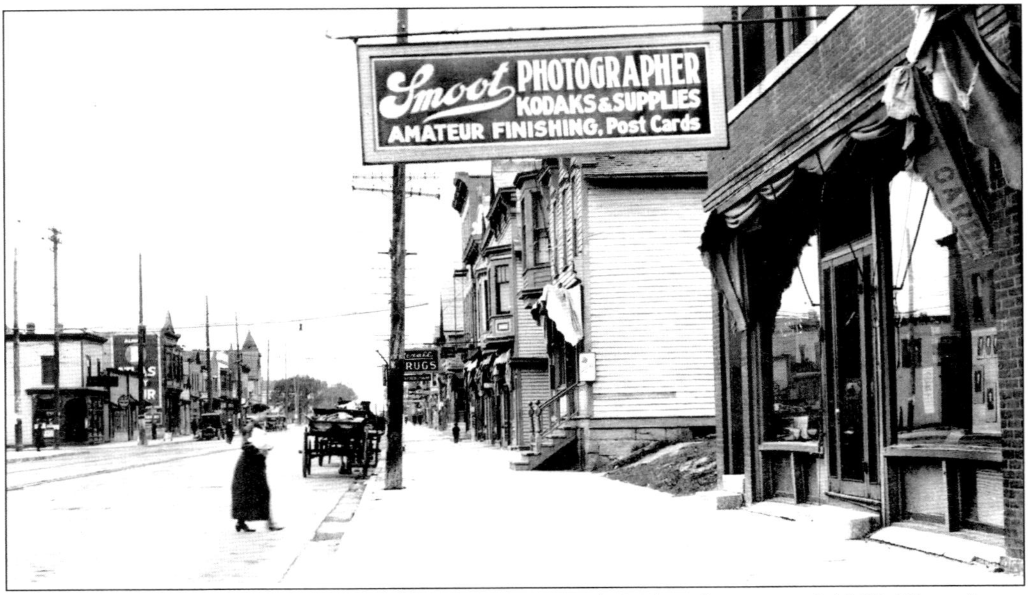

Warner Smoot opened a photography business in South Milwaukee around 1897. This photo, dated 1909, faces west and shows his studio at 914 Milwaukee Avenue.

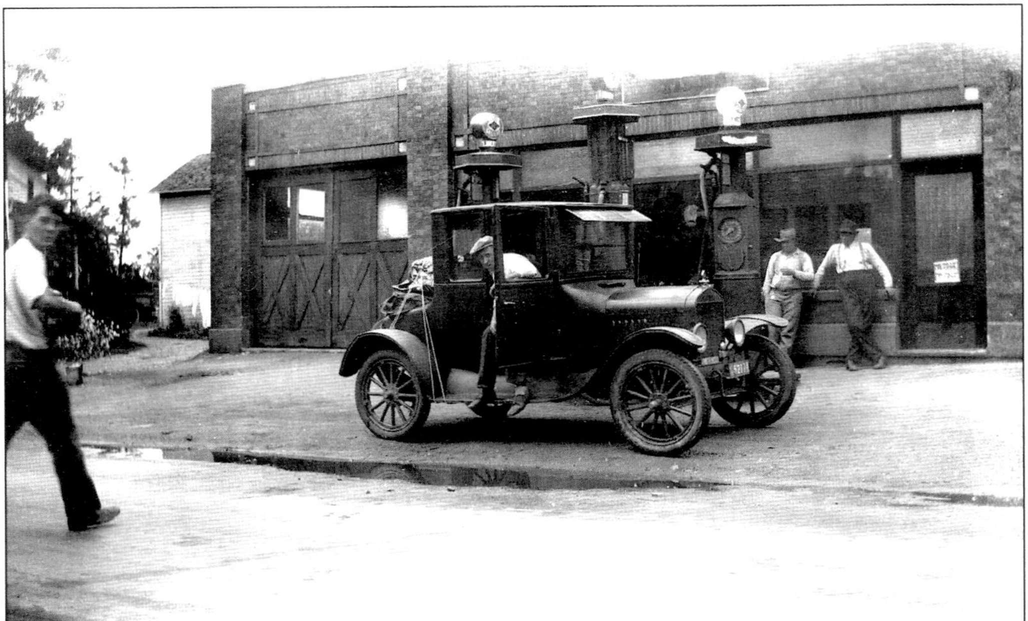

A Model T Ford stops for a fill-up in this undated photograph. This filling station is believed to have been on the 800 block of Milwaukee Avenue.

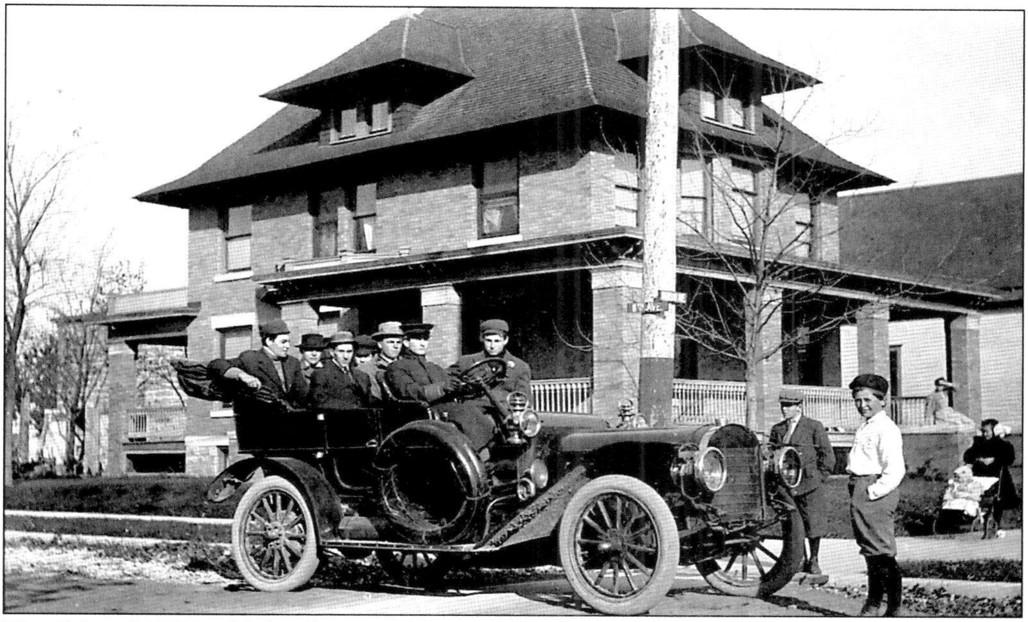

The Edward J. Petzold family poses in their touring car in front of the family home at 728 Michigan Avenue, c. 1917. Petzold was a well-known general contractor. Many of South Milwaukee's prominent businessmen lived in this part of the city.

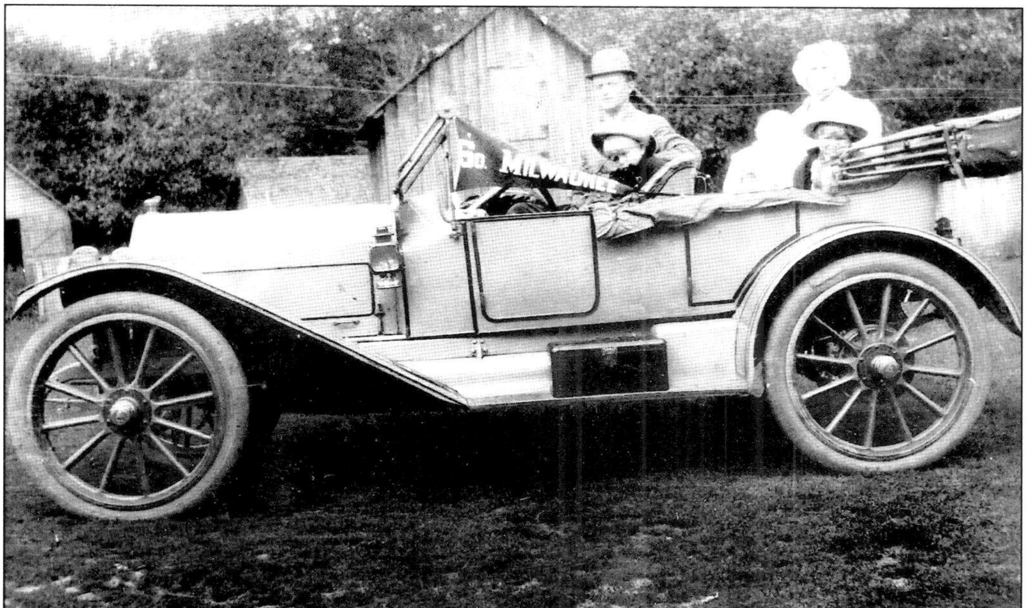

Another of South Milwaukee's leading families heads out for a drive—Louis Vogl with his wife Sophia and children, c. 1918. In 1919, the Vogls left South Milwaukee. After their return 10 years later, Vogl opened up a new bakery at 801 Milwaukee Avenue. After Vogl's death in 1936, his wife and son Andrew kept the business going until 1974.

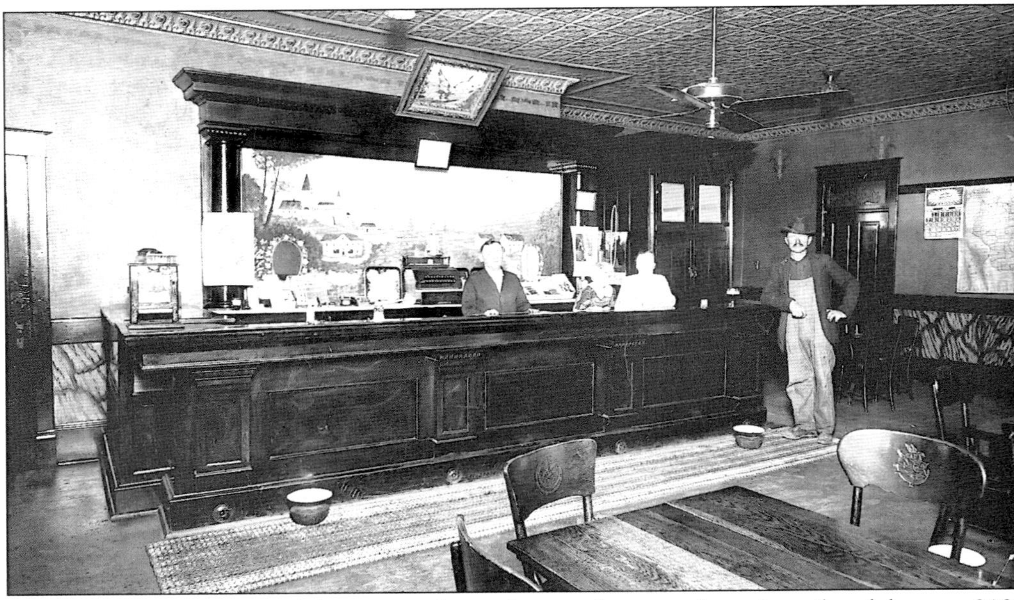

Andrew N. Weber operated this tavern, located across the street from the railroad depot at 2109 Eleventh Avenue. Weber and family are seen here behind the bar along with an unidentified customer in this c. 1923 photo. During Prohibition, taverns would become "soft drink parlors." The 1927 city directory lists 52 such establishments in South Milwaukee.

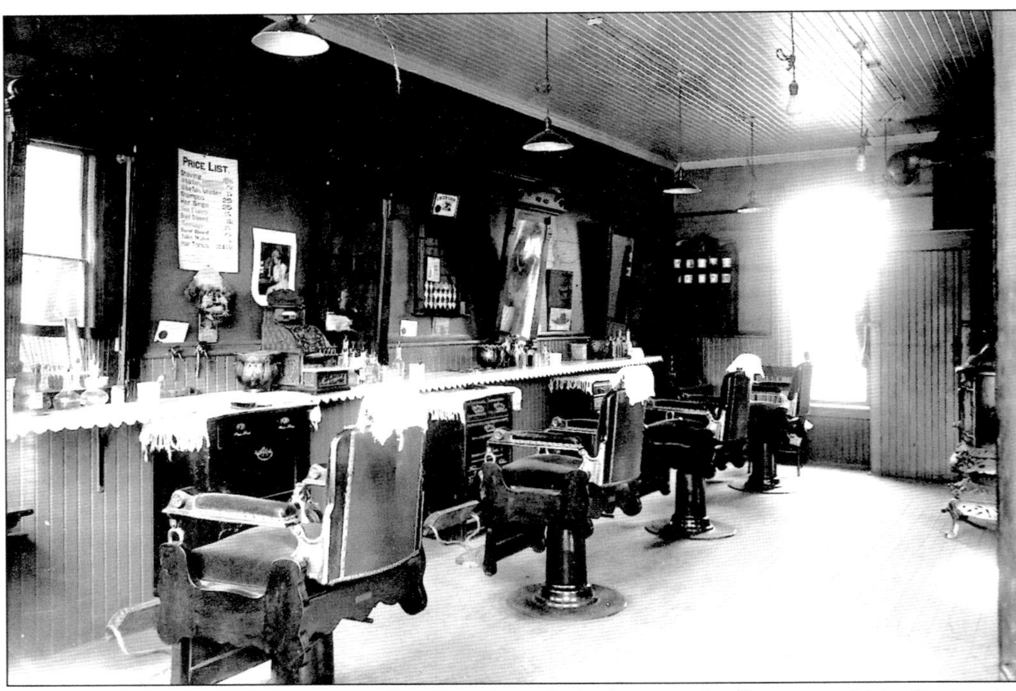

Joe Holt ran the barbershop seen here in this 1910 photograph. Because of his diminutive stature, Holt was nicknamed "The Little Shaver." Holt's Barber Shop was located at 1002 Milwaukee Avenue.

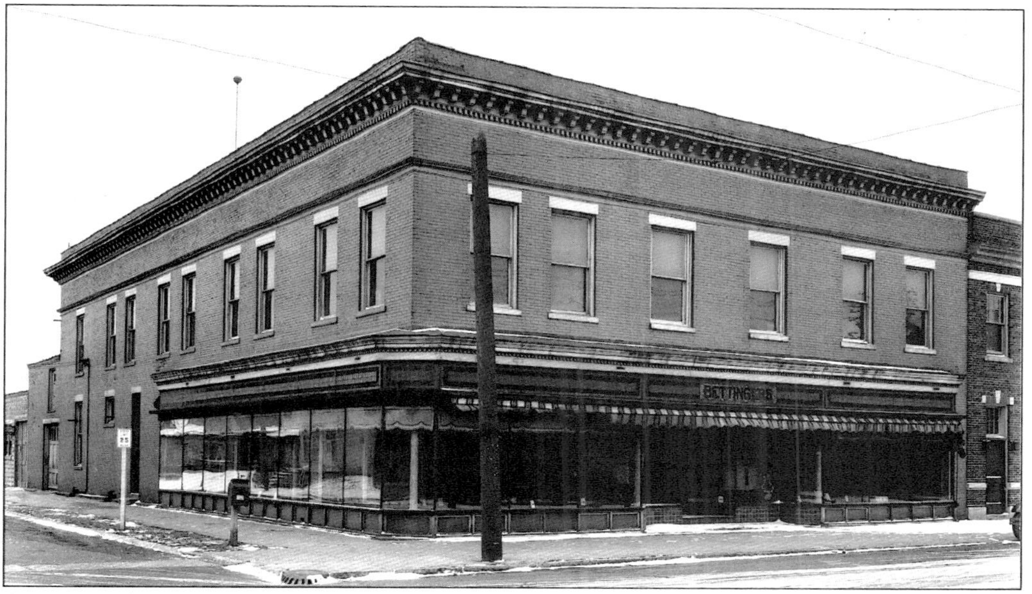

On December 23, 1902, Emil H. Bettinger opened a large new department store on the southeast corner of Tenth and Monroe Avenues. Bettinger & Sons was one of the city's finest mercantile store for many years. In 1904, Mr. Bettinger would become the first man to own an automobile in South Milwaukee. This photo was taken around 1935.

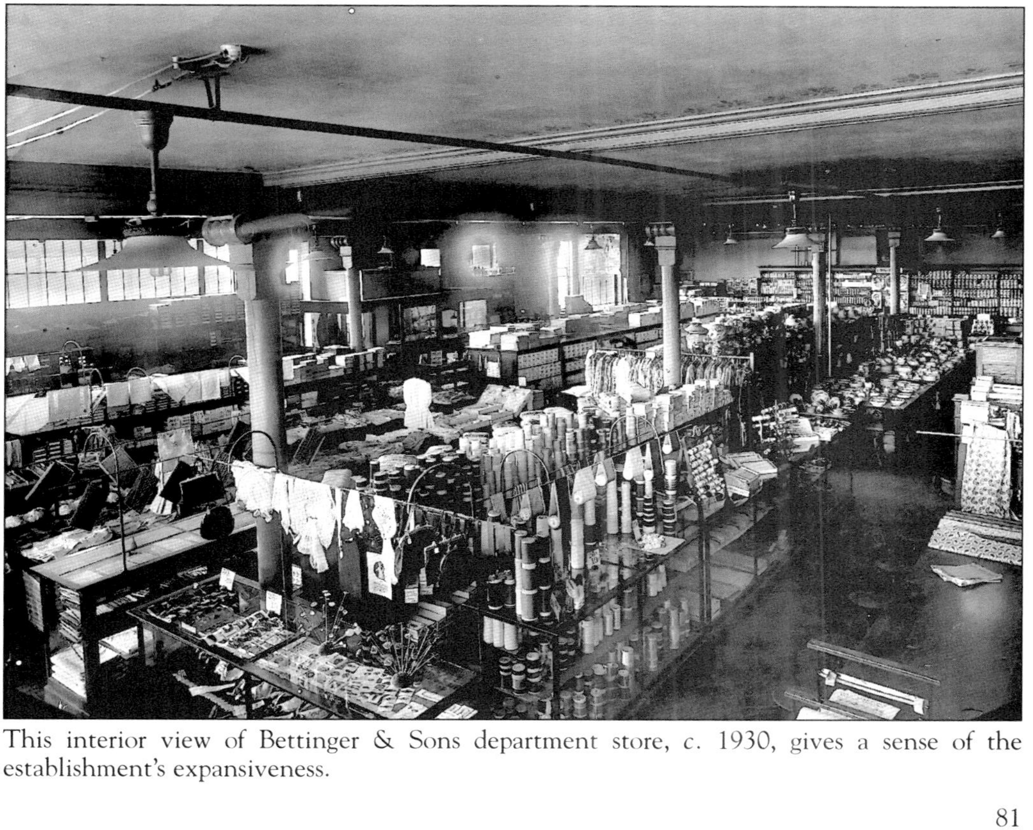

This interior view of Bettinger & Sons department store, *c.* 1930, gives a sense of the establishment's expansiveness.

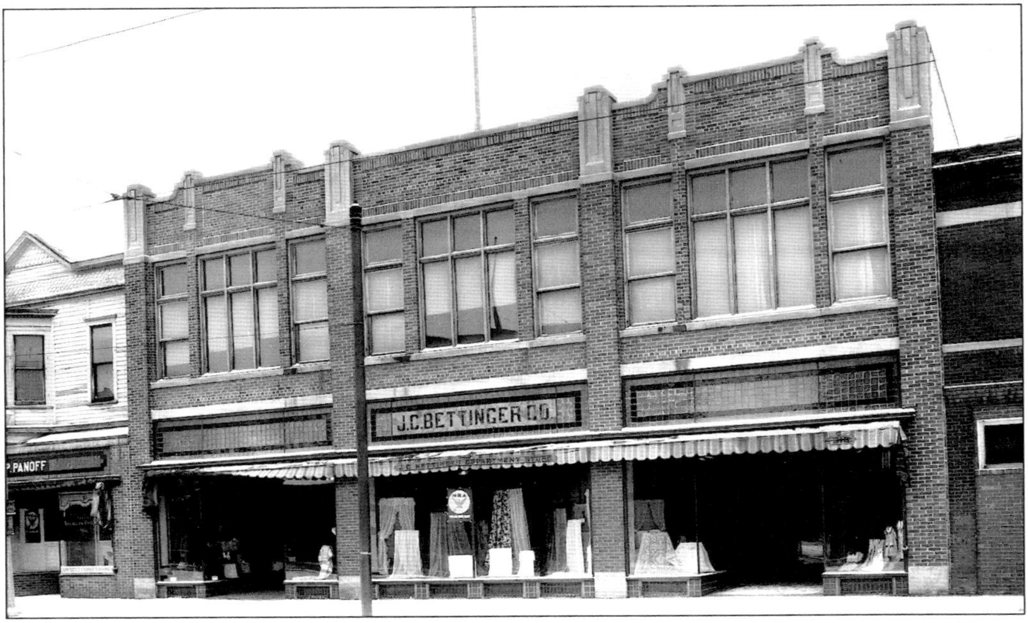

Emil's son, John C. Bettinger opened his own store at 916–918 Milwaukee Avenue in 1924.

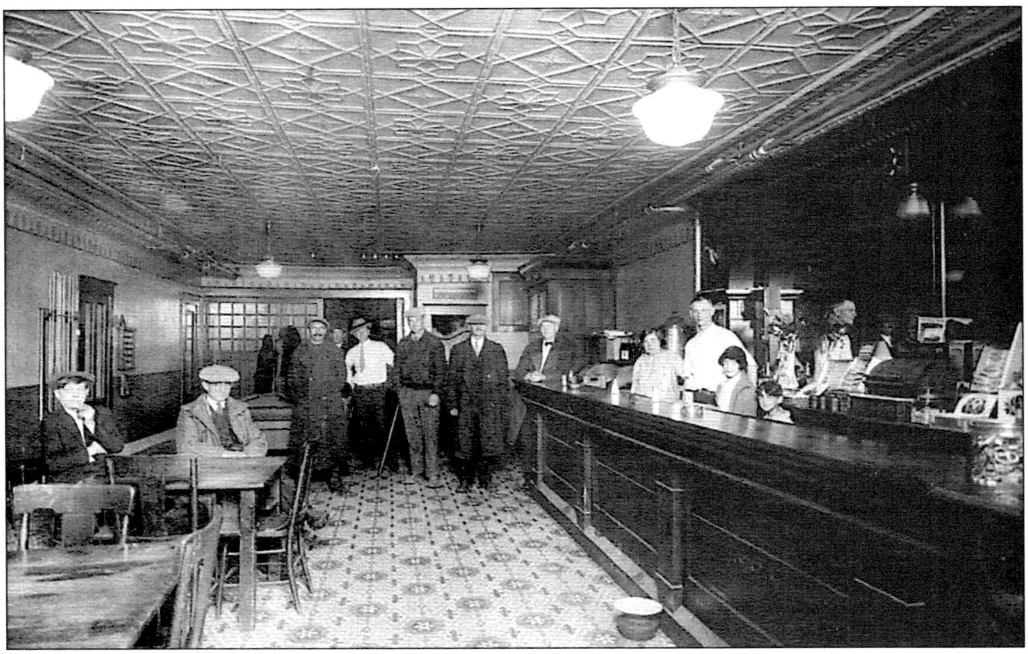

Frank Gestl operated the Orla Hotel at 1018 Milwaukee Avenue from 1926 to around 1932. The notorious Chicago gangster Al Capone was reported to have spent a night at the Orla. Pictured behind the bar in this *c.* 1927 image is Frank Gestl and his wife Rose, along with daughters Rosemary and Helen. (Courtesy of Fred Mitchell.)

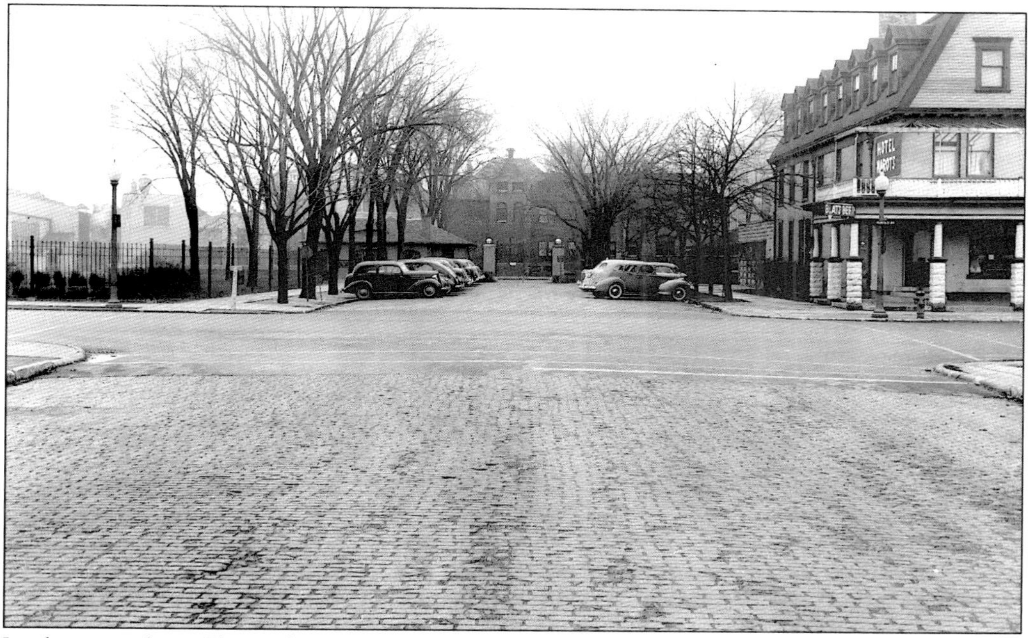

Looking north on Eleventh at Milwaukee Avenue, 1941. The grand old building on the right is the South Milwaukee (or Koch's) Hotel. It was also known during the course of its existence as Hotel Rogers, Hotel Marot's, and the South Milwaukee Inn. Badly damaged by a fire that claimed the top floors, the building was later bought by Bucyrus, and torn down in 1977.

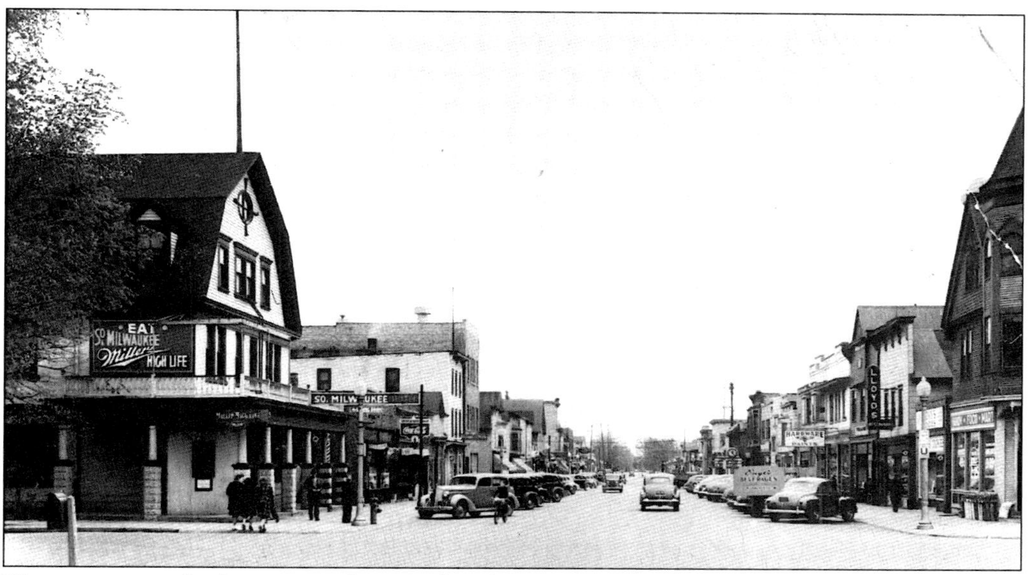

This is a view looking east along Milwaukee Avenue at Eleventh, c. 1945. The South Milwaukee Hotel is at left. In the 1927 city directory, this building was listed as the city's "Tourist Headquarters." Earlier, the old Yellowstone Trail Highway ran down this road, before turning north on Tenth and exiting the city via North Chicago Avenue.

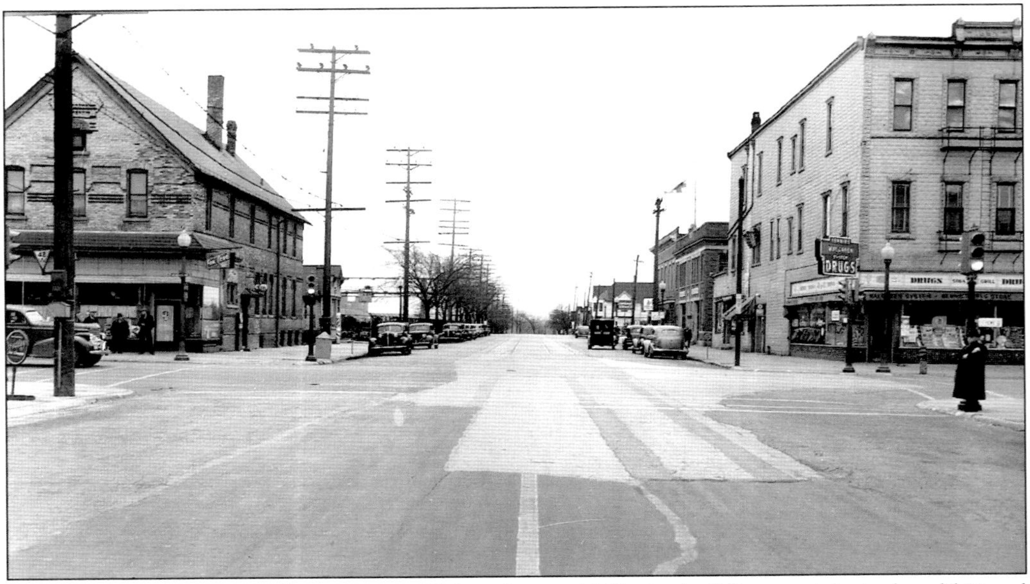

Looking north along Tenth Avenue at Milwaukee in 1941, the building at right is the old Hotel Blatz, then known as Dretzka's Pharmacy. This building also lost its top floors to a fire, though the lower level remains today. Next to that is the city hall (note the Red Cross flag). Bettinger & Sons is next to city hall. The building on the left corner was known as the Weber Building, which was built in 1892 and demolished in 1979.

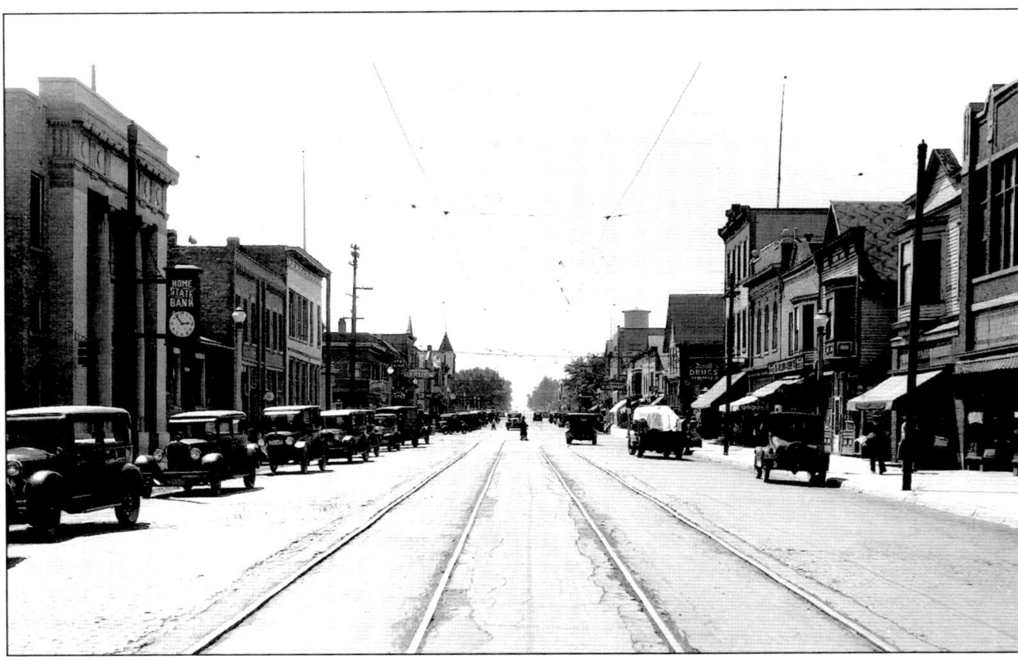

This c. 1925 view is west along the 900 block of Milwaukee Avenue. The Hotel Blatz can be seen at right center. East of that is another South Milwaukee downtown landmark, H. F. Bergmann's Drug Store. Note the TMER&L tracks, which continued east to Fifth Avenue.

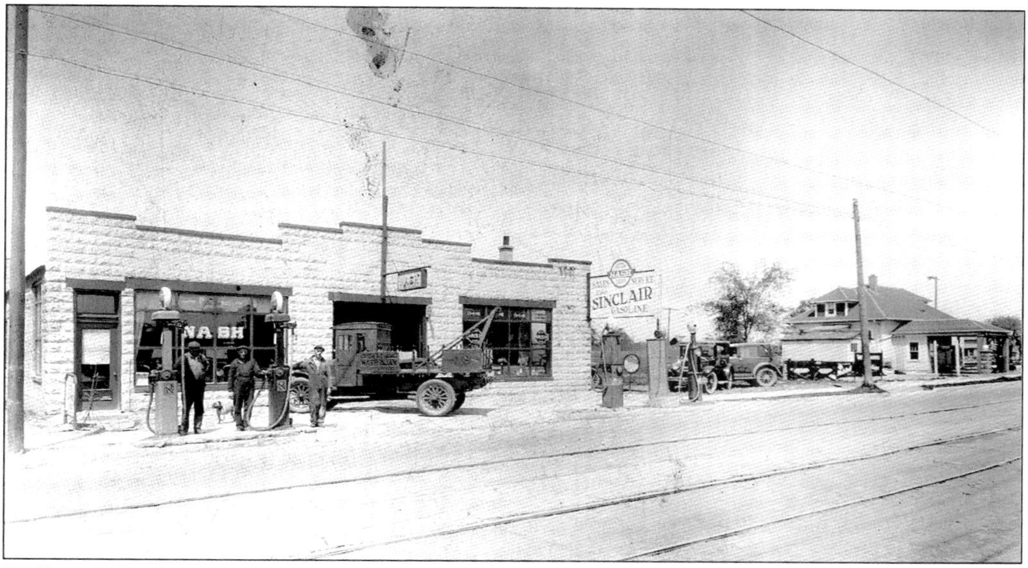

William F. Becker ran the College Avenue Garage at 106–112 North Chicago Avenue for many years. The family home was located across the street. By the 1950s, the Becker family had built a Buick dealership on the site. In this image, dated March 1928, we see William F. Becker, Ed Becker, and Lawrence E. Becker. John Violet's Filling Station can be seen at right.

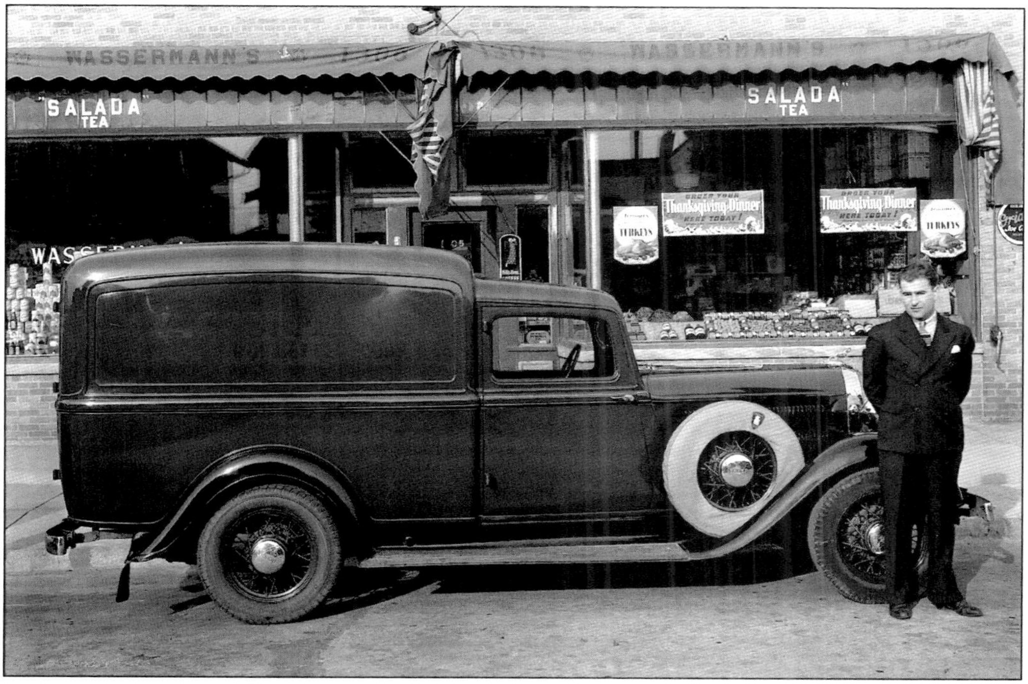

A dapper Harry Wasserman proudly stands alongside his new delivery truck outside his grocery store at 1304–1306 Milwaukee Avenue. The signs in the window are advertisements for Thanksgiving dinners.

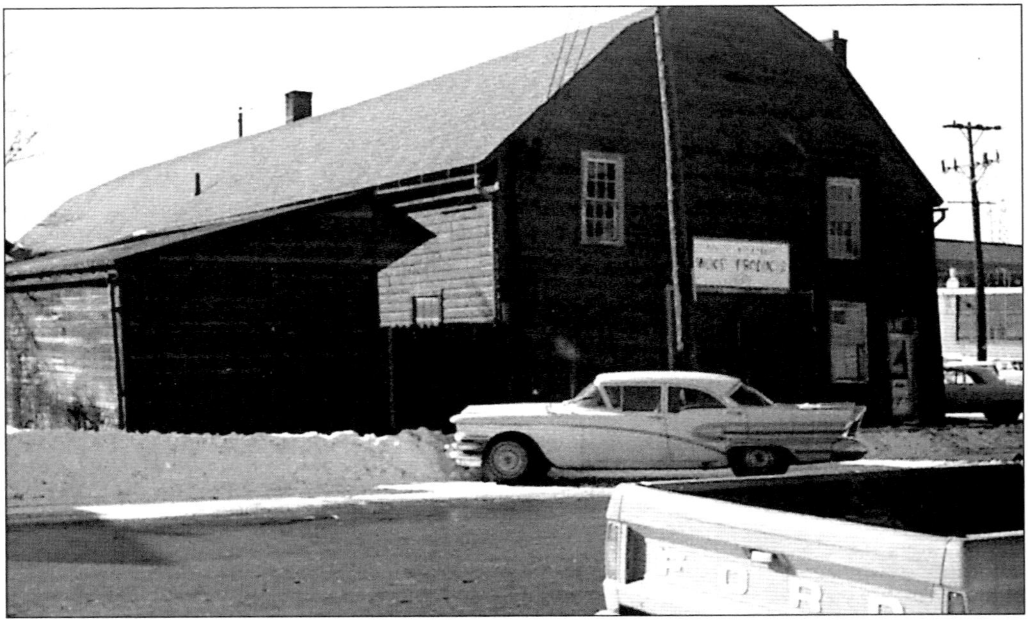

The South Milwaukee Wood Products Company was located at 1021 Madison Avenue. First opened in 1919, the company manufactured various wooden goods ranging from broom handles to bowling pins until the 1960s. (Courtesy of Joe Szatmary.)

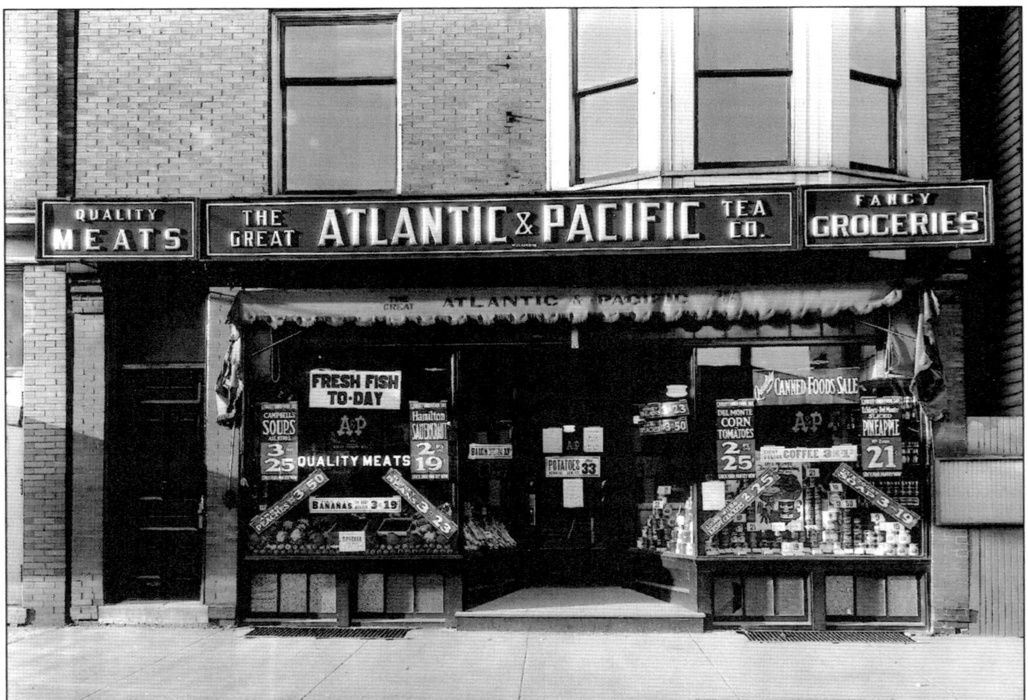

This A&P Tea Company store stood at 924 Milwaukee Avenue in 1930.

Astride their Harley-Davidson motorcycles, buddies Chester Jurkus (left) and Walter "Teeter" Shelenske pose on Milwaukee Avenue near the Mill Road in 1941. They are about to embark on a road trip to a motorcycle hill-climbing event in Muskegon, Michigan. Shelenske derived his nickname from "Lucky Teeter," a noted motorcycle daredevil of the day. (Courtesy of Walter Shelenske.)

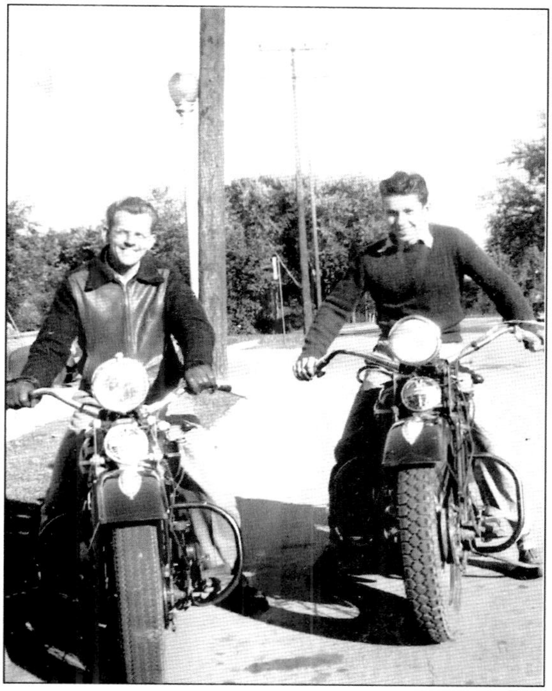

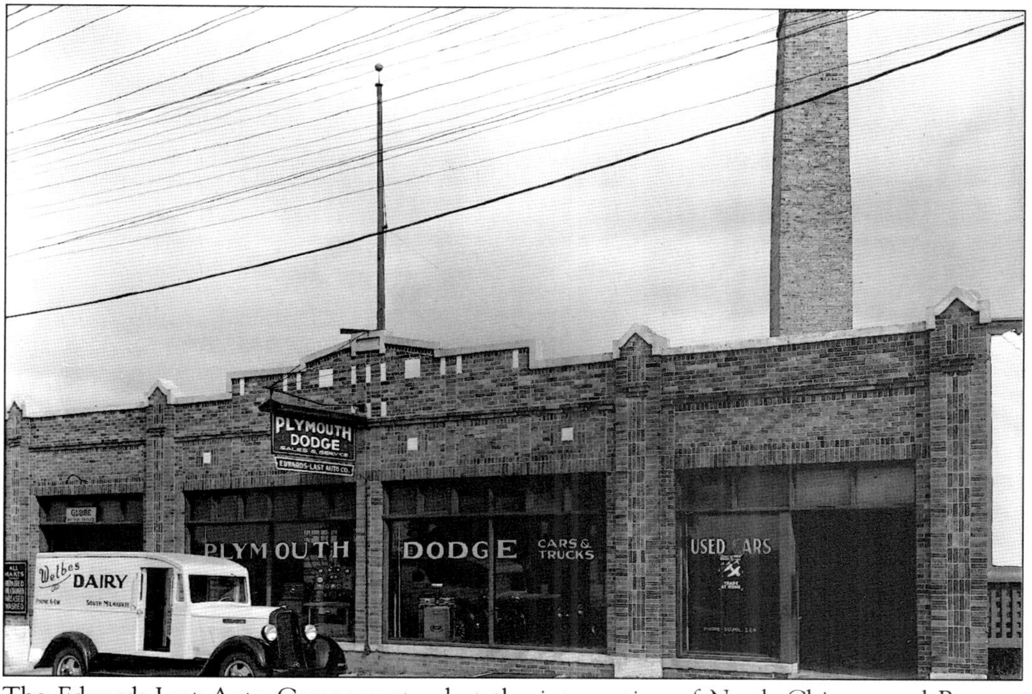

The Edwards-Last Auto Company stood at the intersection of North Chicago and Rawson Avenues. In this photograph we see a shiny new 1935 Dodge truck awaiting delivery to its new owner, Frank Welbes, who ran the local dairy until 1947.

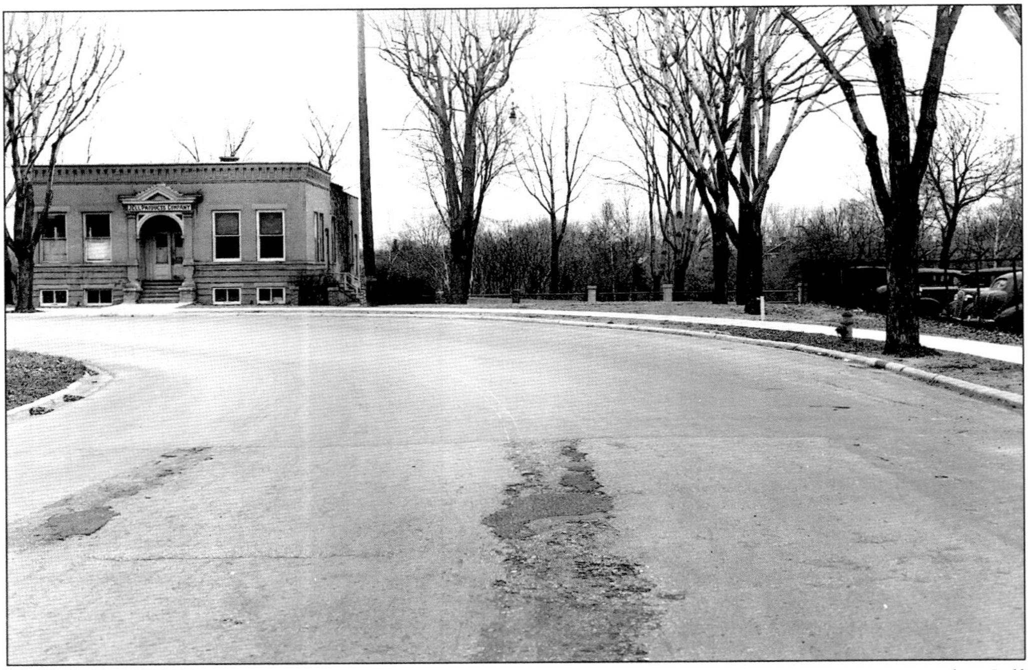

Looking north along Fifth Avenue at the east end of Milwaukee Avenue, 1941. The Jell Products Company manufactured various gelatin and pudding products here from 1930 to 1975. After that, the building was purchased by the Appleton Electric Company for use as a management club.

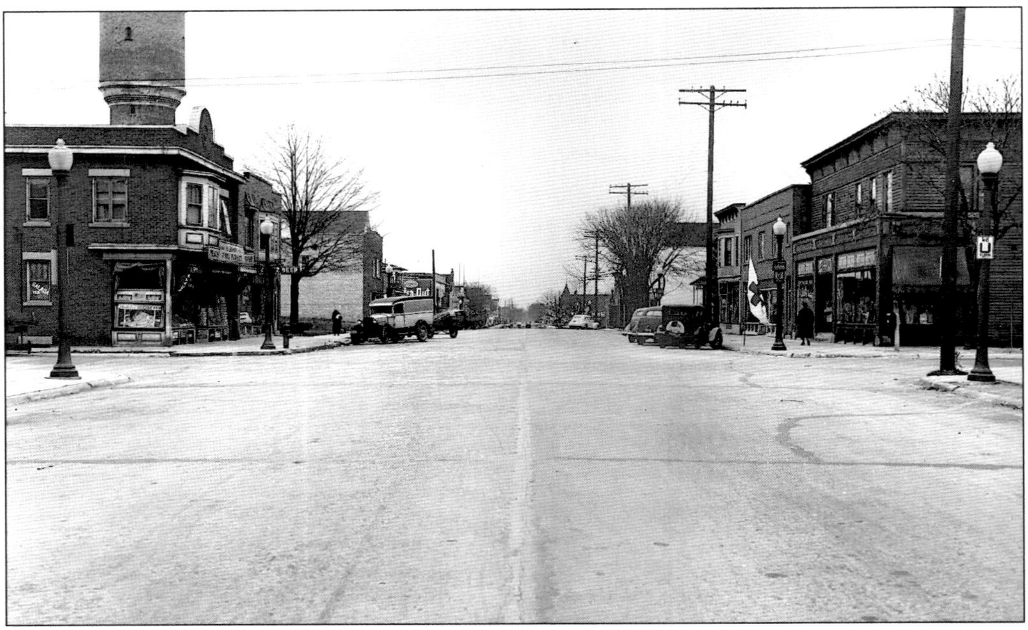

This is a 1941 view looking east along Milwaukee Avenue at Thirteenth. The Kleineider Building is seen in the right-hand corner.

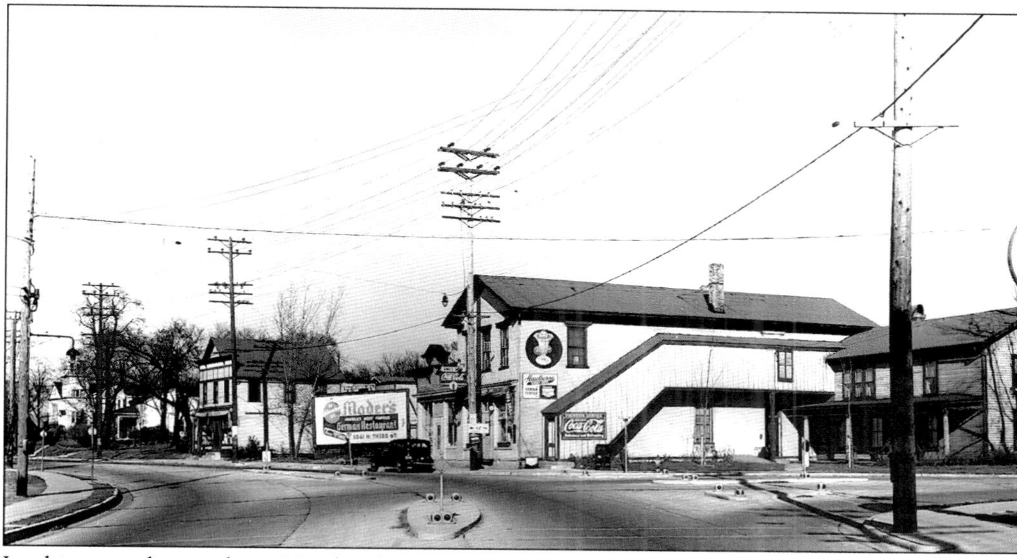

Looking northeast along North Chicago Avenue at the Hawthorne Avenue intersection. In 1882, Joseph E. Vollmer owned the large building in the foreground. Though the building changed owners many times over the years, old-timers always referred to it as "Vollmer's Hall." It was torn down in the 1960s. This intersection was the center of the community during the old Oak Creek Township days. In fact, Elihu Higgins' first log cabin once stood on the site of the smaller building at right.

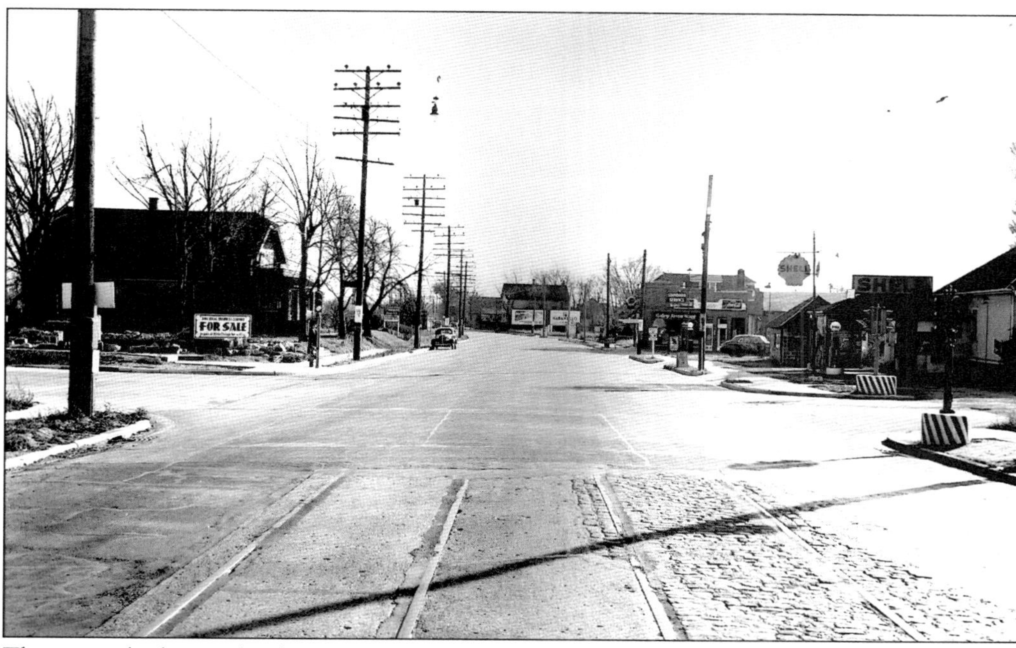

This view looks south along North Chicago Avenue at the College Avenue intersection, c, 1941. College Avenue forms South Milwaukee's northern border with the City of Cudahy. Violet's Filling Station as at the right hand corner of the intersection. W.F. Becker's College Avenue Garage is just south of it.

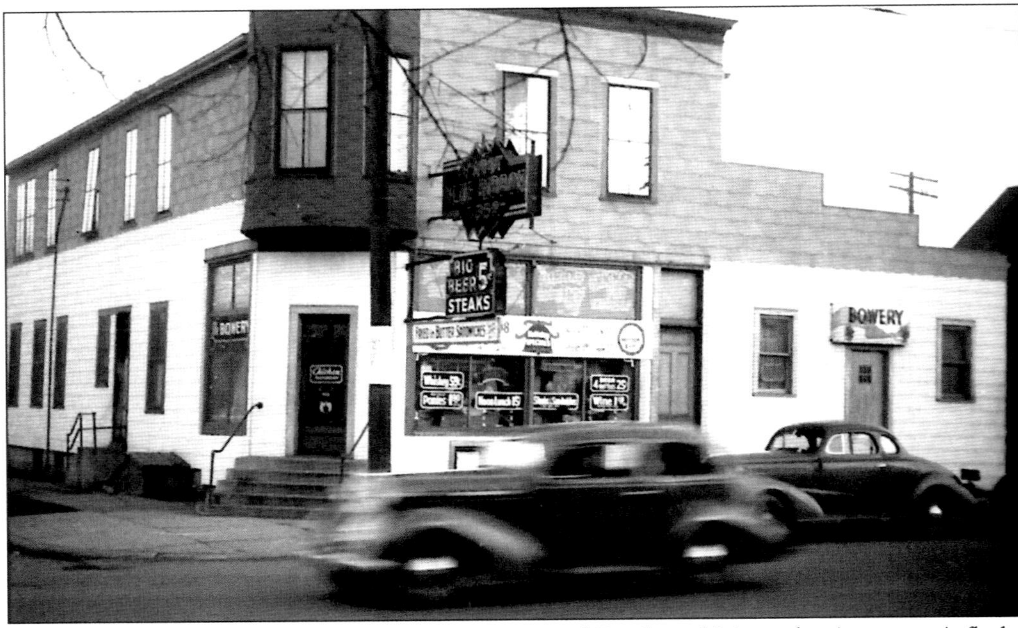

The Bowery Tavern stood on the southeast corner of Tenth and Manitoba Avenues. A flashy young piano player from West Milwaukee by the name of Wladzui (Walter) Liberace performed here in the early 1940s. In 1976, the building was destroyed by a fire that claimed two lives and injured several firefighters.

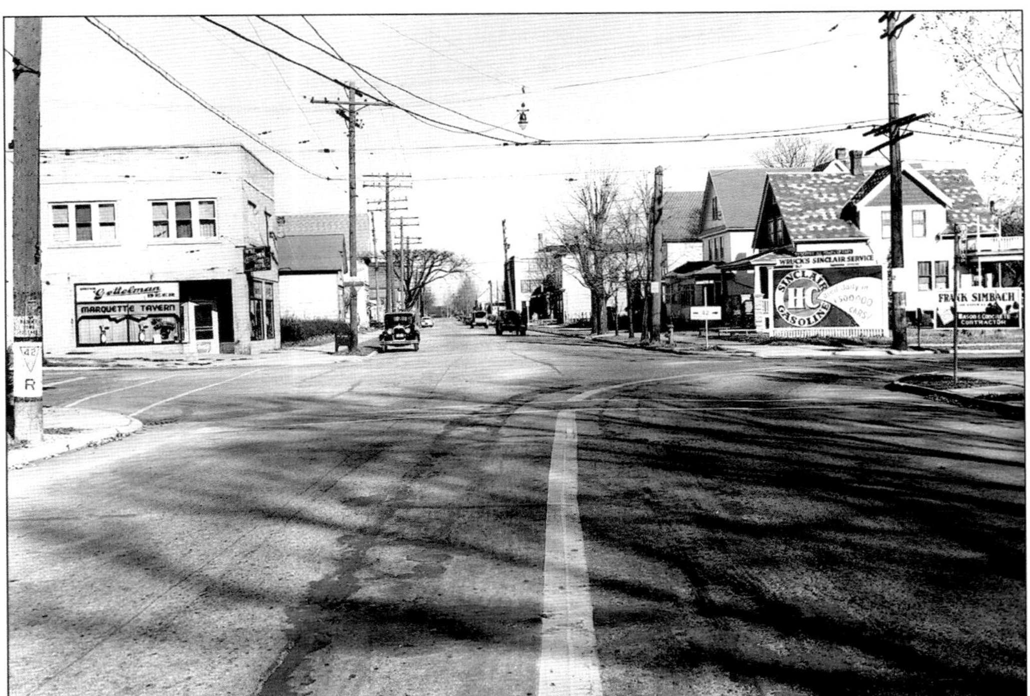

This view looks north along Twelfth Avenue at Marquette, *c.* 1941.

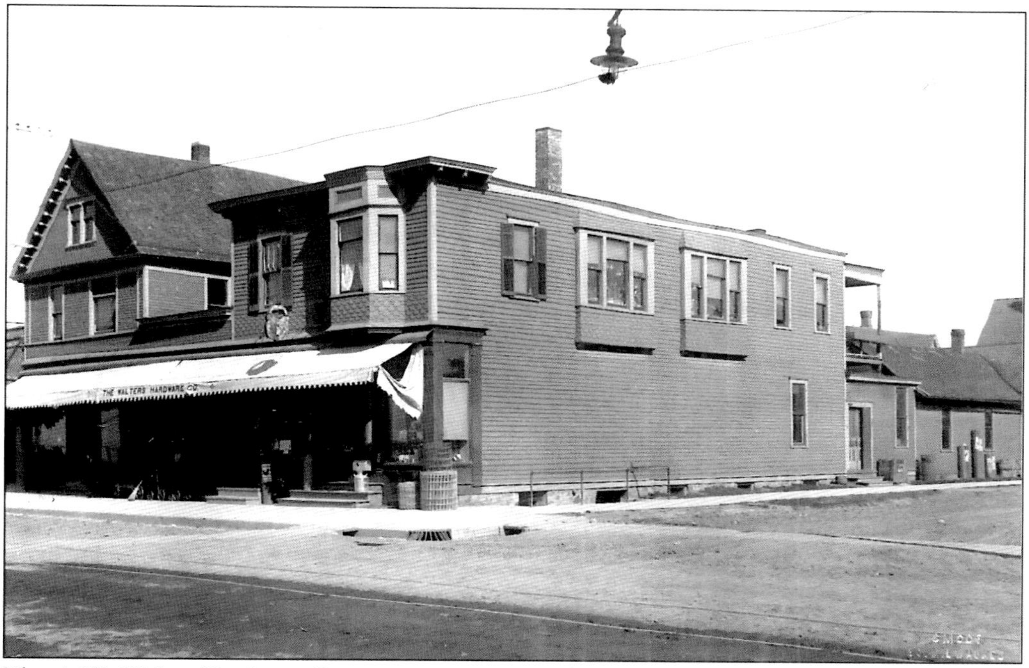

The A.W. Walter Hardware Store appears as it stood at 900–902 Milwaukee Avenue in 1910.

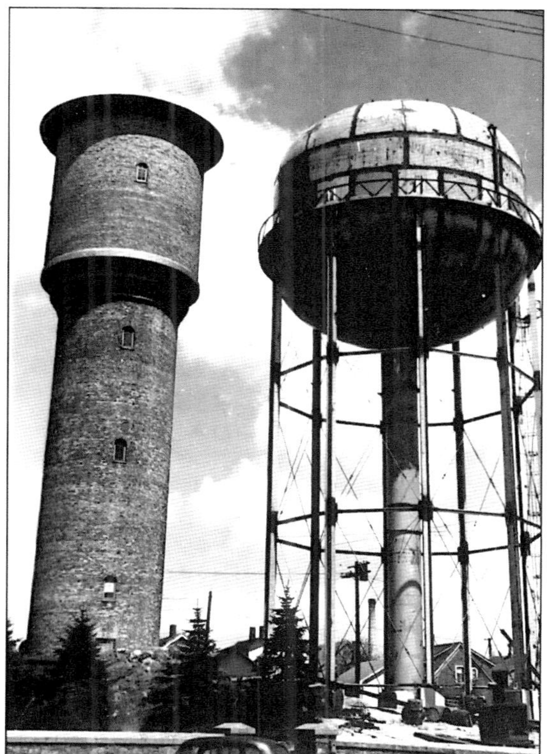

South Milwaukee built a new 500,000-gallon water tower in 1947. The old tower was dismantled brick by brick. This "new" water tower was torn down in July 2004.

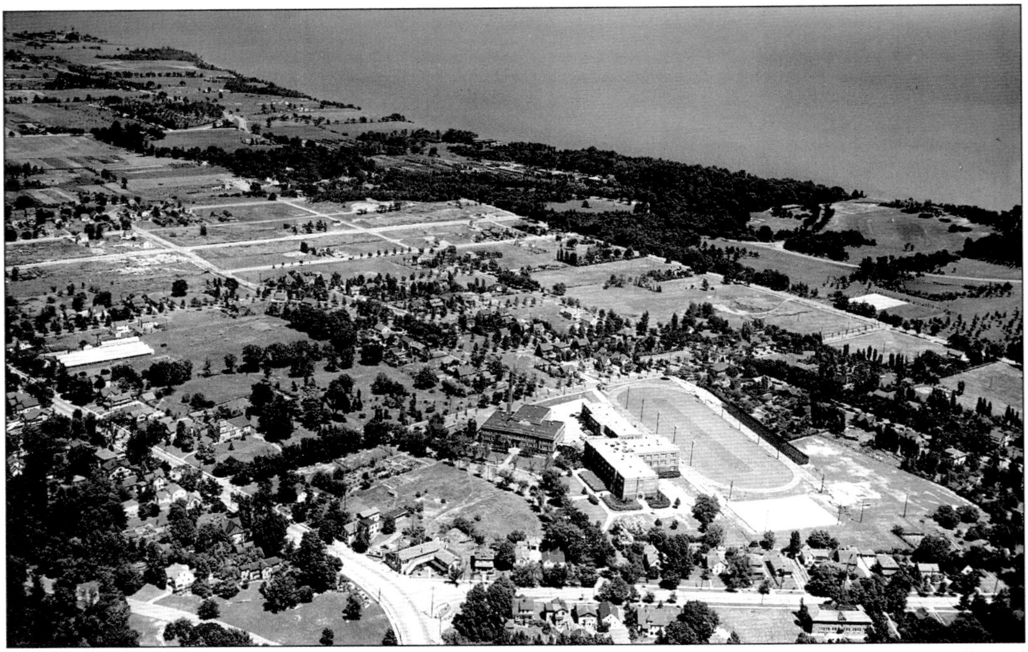

In this ariel view of the northeastern end of South Milwaukee, *c.* 1940, Vollmer's Hall and the Chicago Avenue intersection at Hawthorne are clearly visible. As late as the 1920s, this intersection was still referred to as "Old Town."

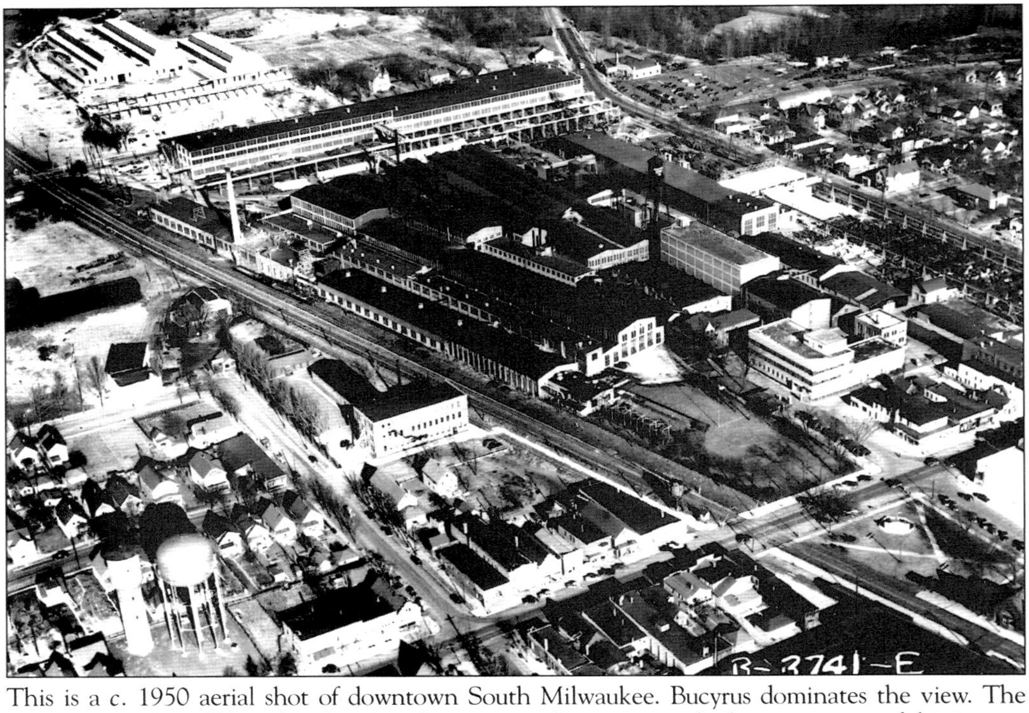

This is a *c.* 1950 aerial shot of downtown South Milwaukee. Bucyrus dominates the view. The intersection of Twelfth and Milwaukee Avenues can be seen near the bottom center of this image.

Six

Grant Park

Grant Park has always been one of South Milwaukee's greatest assets. Established in 1911, this 400-acre haven, located high above the shores of Lake Michigan, is a charter member of the Milwaukee County Park system. In 1920, the Grant Park Golf Course became the first county operated golf course.

One man who played a major role in the development of Grant Park was Frederick C. Wulff. A native of Germany, Wulff had received formal training in forestry and botany in Europe and was recruited and brought to America in 1914 by Milwaukee County to act as the park system's head of horticulture. As Grant Park's first superintendent, Wulff and his family would live in a cottage that was built in 1916 and still stands today.

Characterized by a hard-working nature and an extraordinary devotion to detail, Wulff energetically set about transforming Grant Park from an under-utilized parcel of second-rate farmland studded with ravines and woodlots, to a popular recreation area that continues to draw tens of thousands of visitors annually.

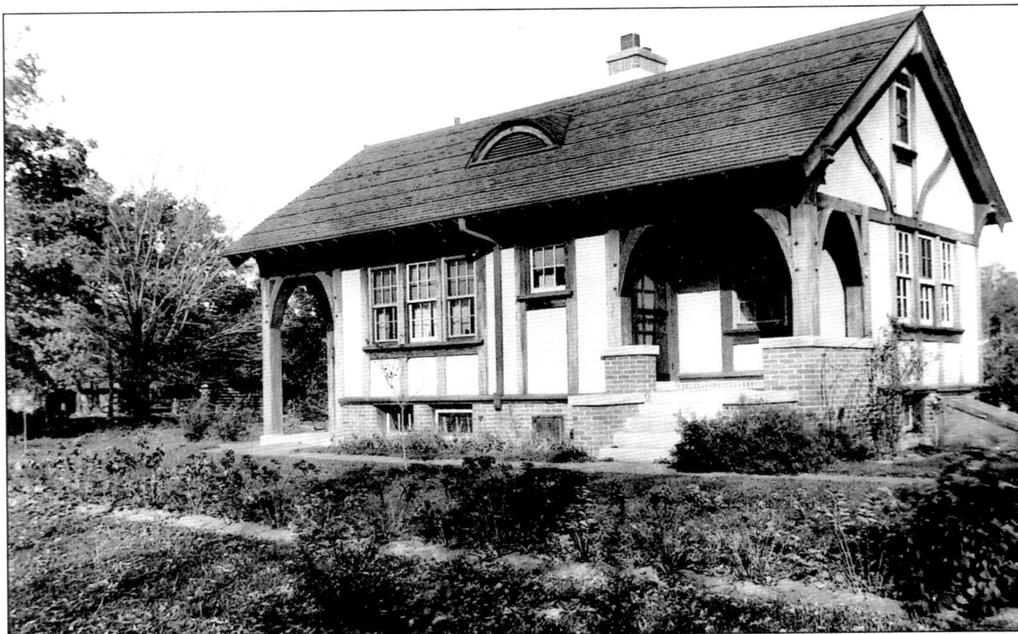

The residence of Grant Park superintendent Frederick C. Wulff and family is seen here in this photograph dated 1921. The building is still used by the Milwaukee County Park System.

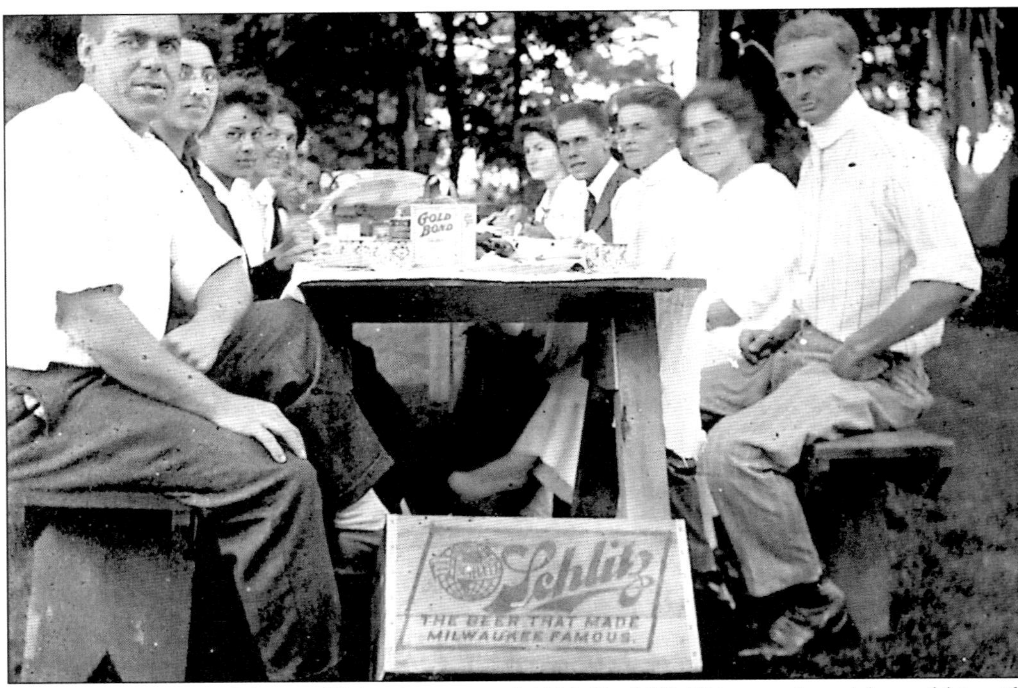

In this photograph of the Wulff family picnic of 1923, Fred Wulff is seated at right and his wife Dorothy is next to him. What picnic is complete without a box of Gold Bond powder? Note too, the wooden case of Schlitz Beer, none too discreetly displayed during the days of Prohibition.

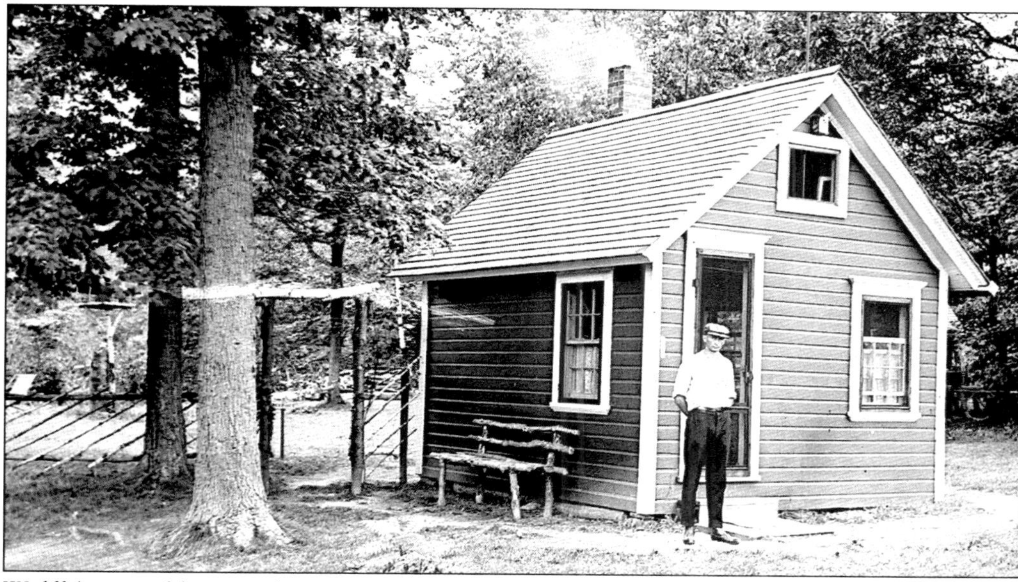

Wulff (pictured here in this 1916 image) used this small office, located near his residence, to conduct the affairs of the park's campground.

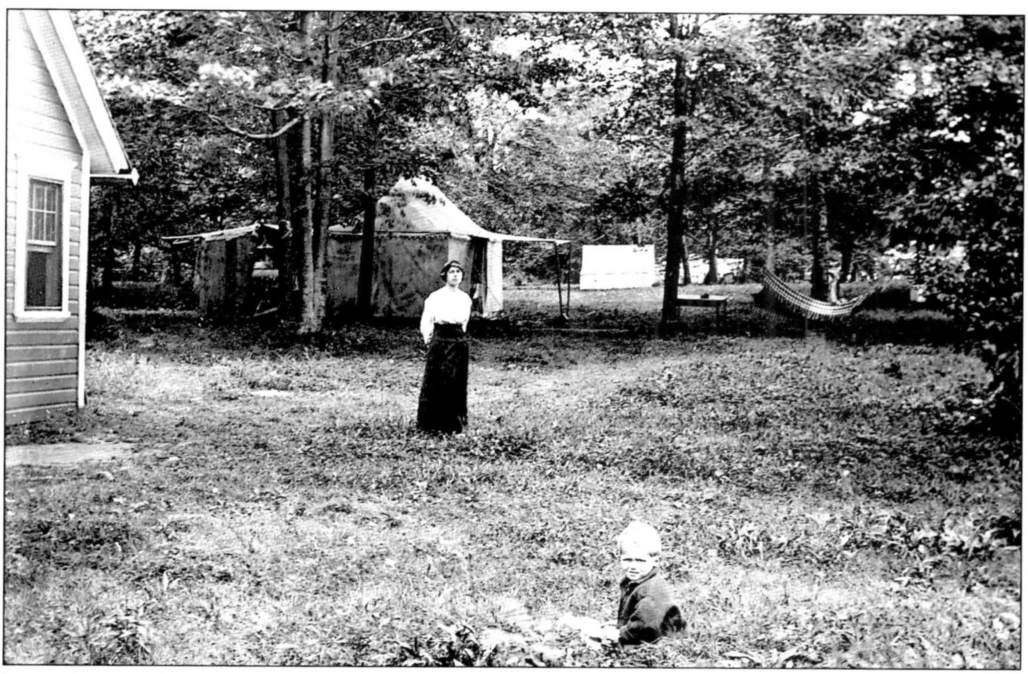

Dorothy Wulff and child pose next to the office building in 1916. The "Family Camp" is seen in the background. Used mostly by youth groups, this campground would become the Grant Park Tourist Camp in 1921, used to handle the large numbers of automobile travelers passing through the area via the Yellowstone Trail. Attendance peaked in 1929 with 2,502 registered guests. The camp remained in operation until around 1947.

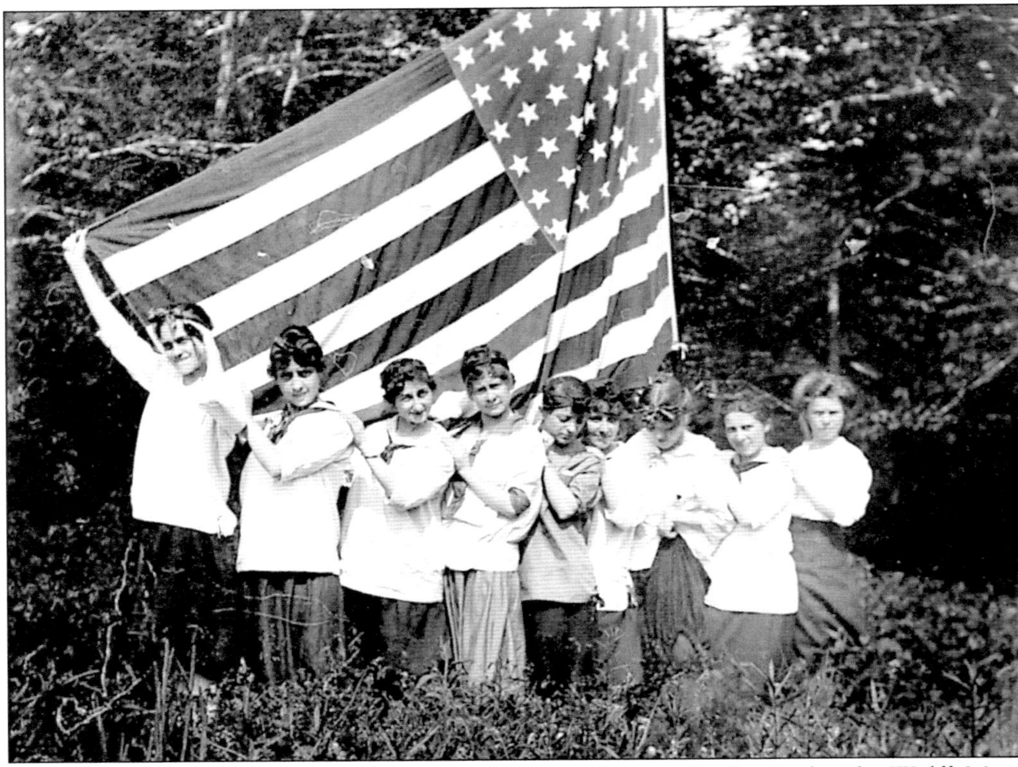

The "Campfire Girls," a YWCA youth group, pose for this 1916 photo taken by Wulff. Many of his photographs had captions on the back in handwritten German. This one was translated as saying "The girls in bloomers."

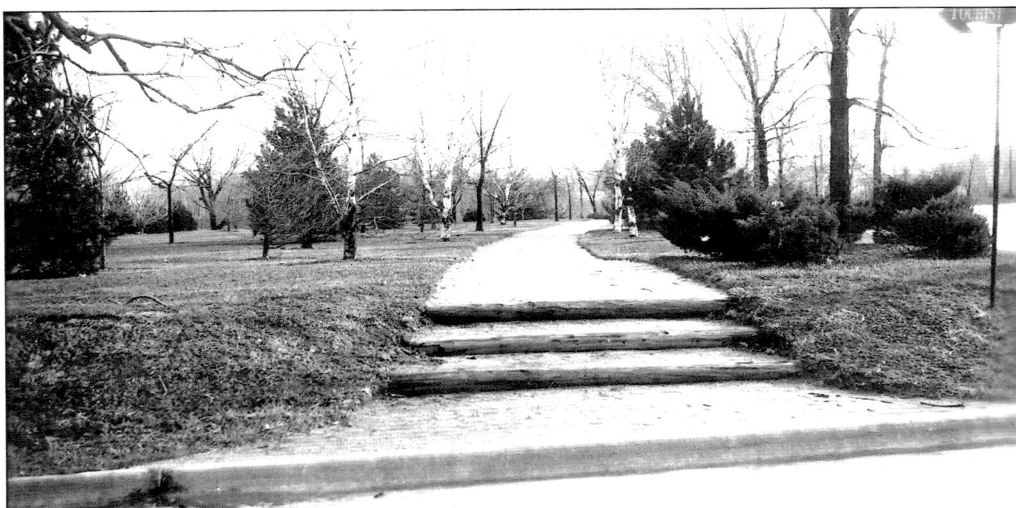

This 1931 photograph was taken near the park entrance at Lake Drive and Park Avenue. The arrow shaped sign at upper right guides travelers north along Lake Drive towards the Grant Park Tourist Camp.

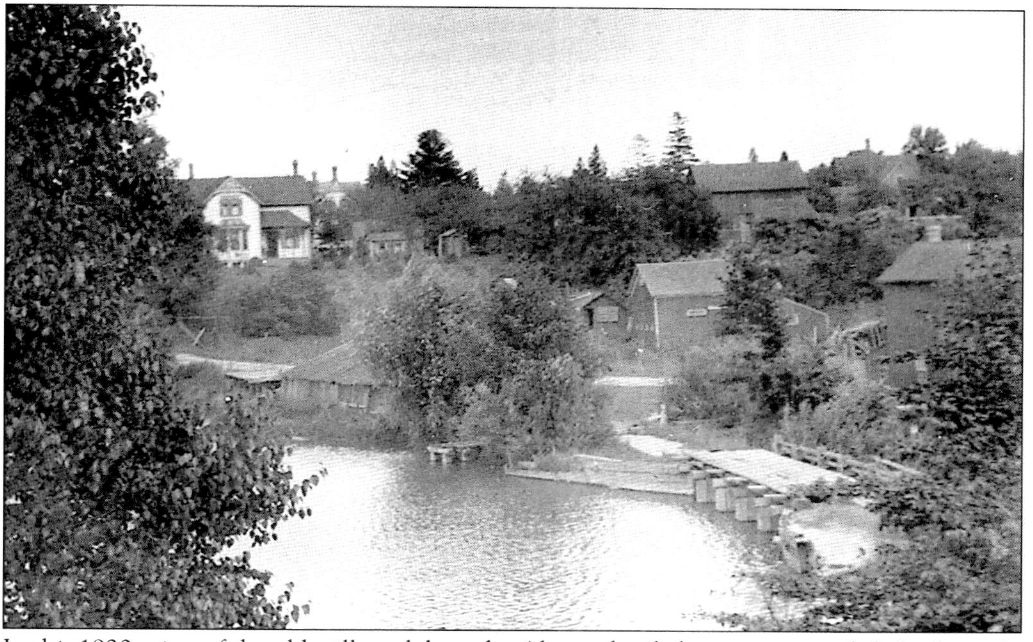

In this 1920s view of the old millpond dam, the Ahrens family home is seen at left. In the early 1930s, this land was transferred to the Milwaukee County Park System. A program named "Project 60" was created to construct the Oak Creek Parkway, which would reconfigure the intersection at the bottom of the Mill Road and build a new road leading to the lakefront.

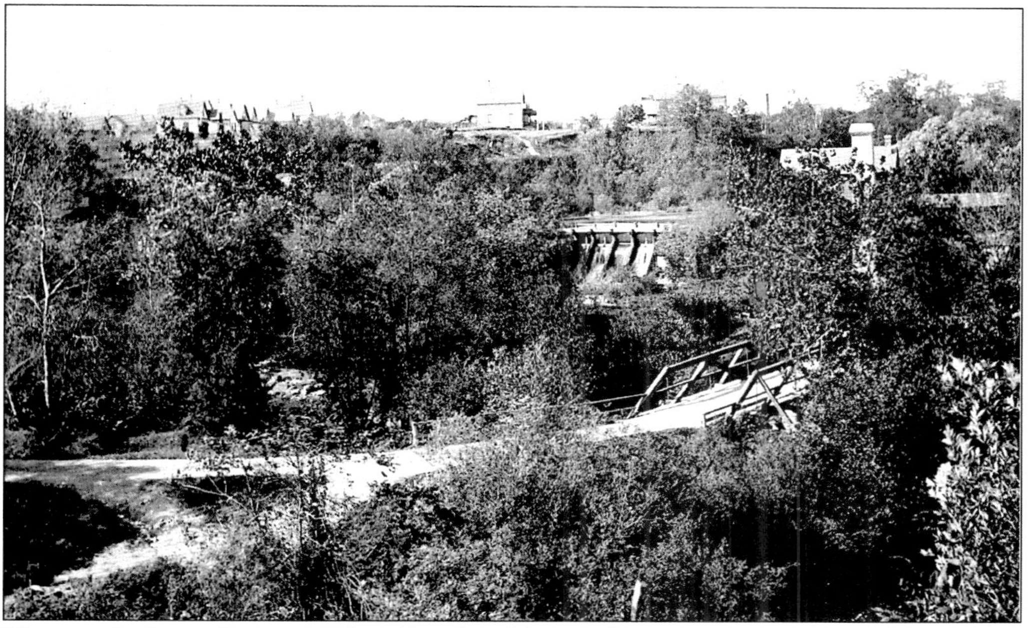

This view looks southwest over the old mill and dam. Before Project 60, one taking the Mill (or Lake) Road south from Hawthorne Avenue would have to turn east at the mill and cross over the first bridge before turning south again, following the road up the hill and intersecting with Milwaukee Avenue near Fifth Avenue.

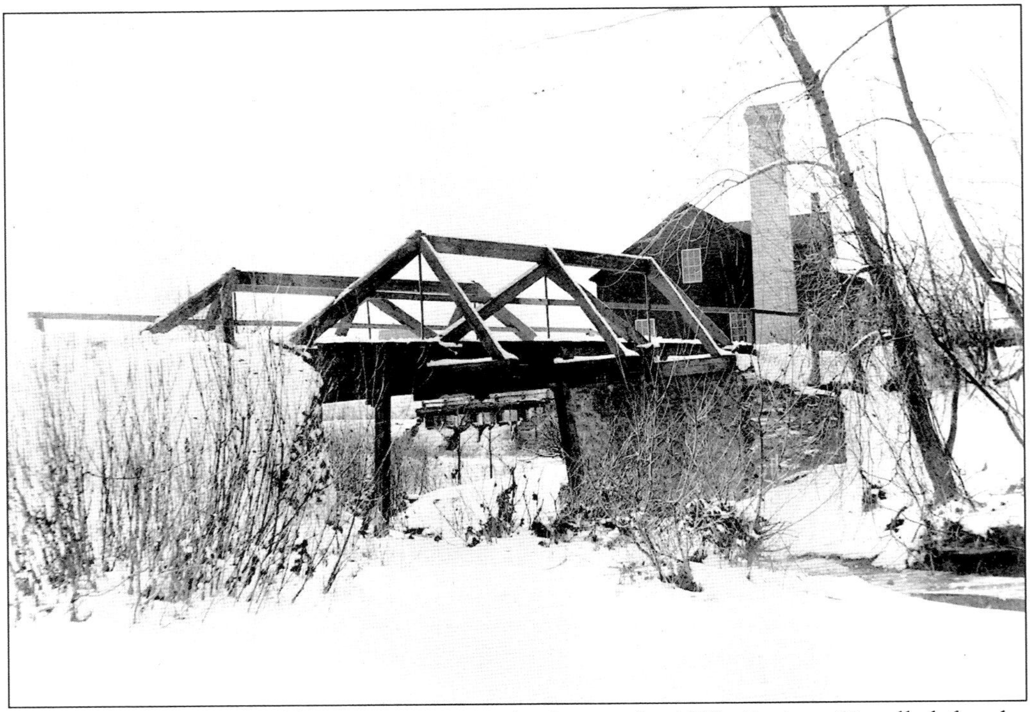

The old mill is pictured here in a wintery landscape. In 1933, Project 60 called for the demolition of this historic landmark, a move that was hotly debated at the time. The chimney remained standing until the late 1960s.

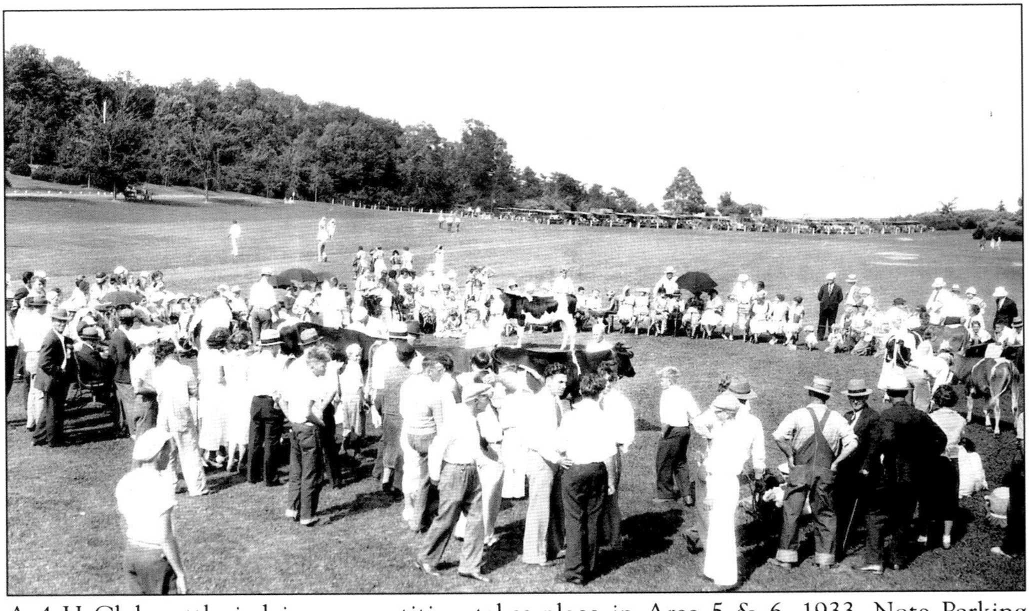

A 4-H Club cattle judging competition takes place in Area 5 & 6, 1933. Note Parking Station 2 in the background.

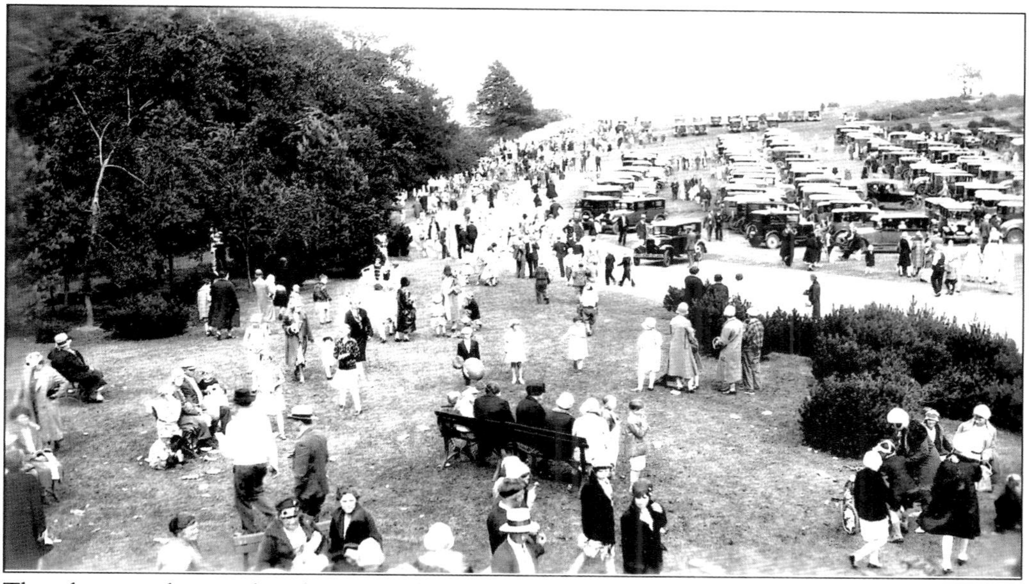

This photograph was taken from atop the pavilion at Area 5 & 6 during the city's Independence Day activities in 1931. Superintendent Wulff dutifully recorded that no less than 40,458 people, along with 6,743 vehicles, entered Grant Park that day.

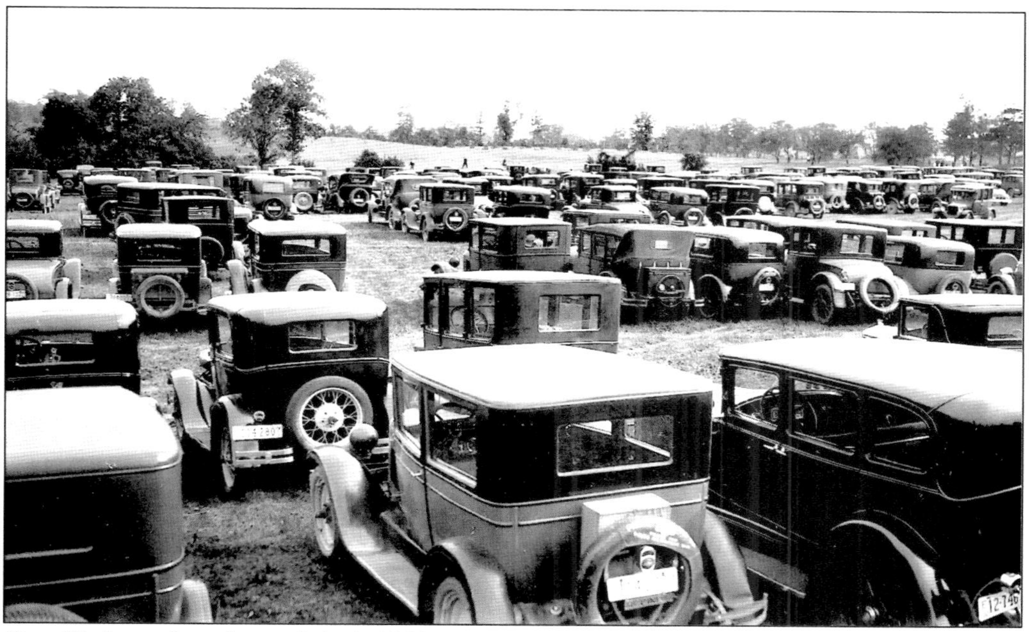

Cars fill the parking lot on July 4, 1930.

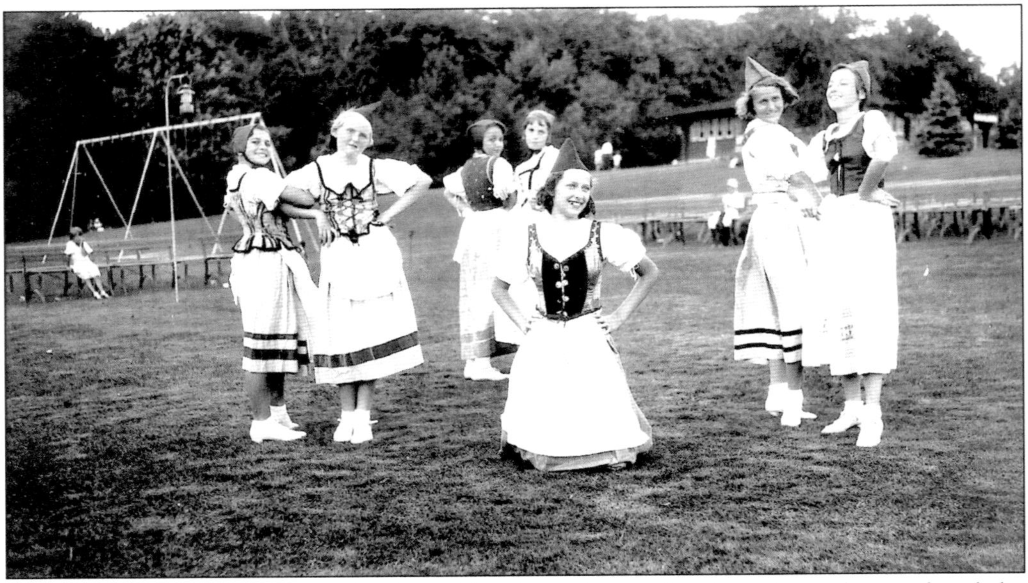

This 4-H Club folk dance was held in 1933. Note the pavilion in right background and the lantern hanging from a hook for evening performances at left.

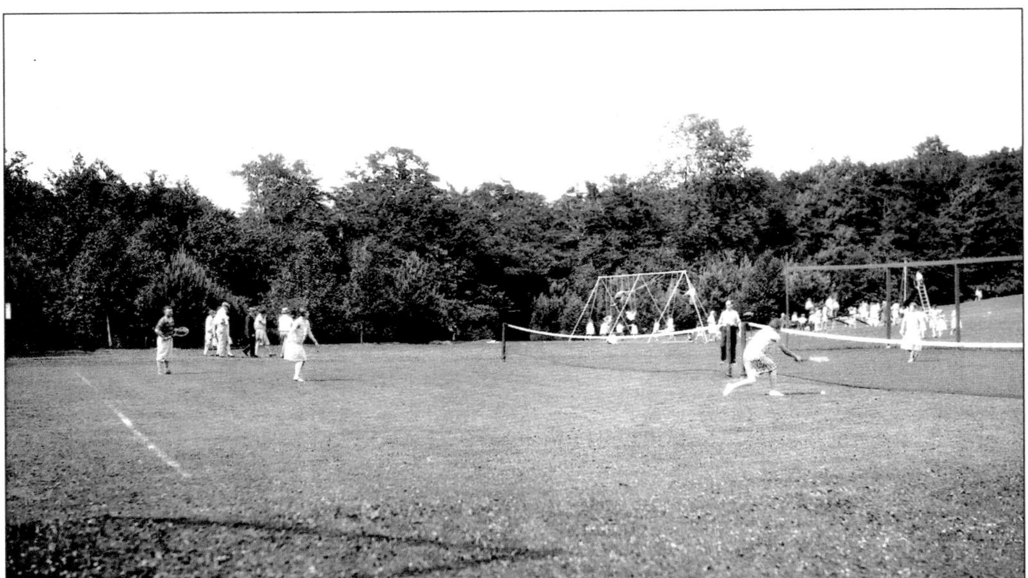

Many park-goers enjoyed a game of lawn tennis. In 1929, people were charged 20¢ per game. The pavilion is just out of view on the right.

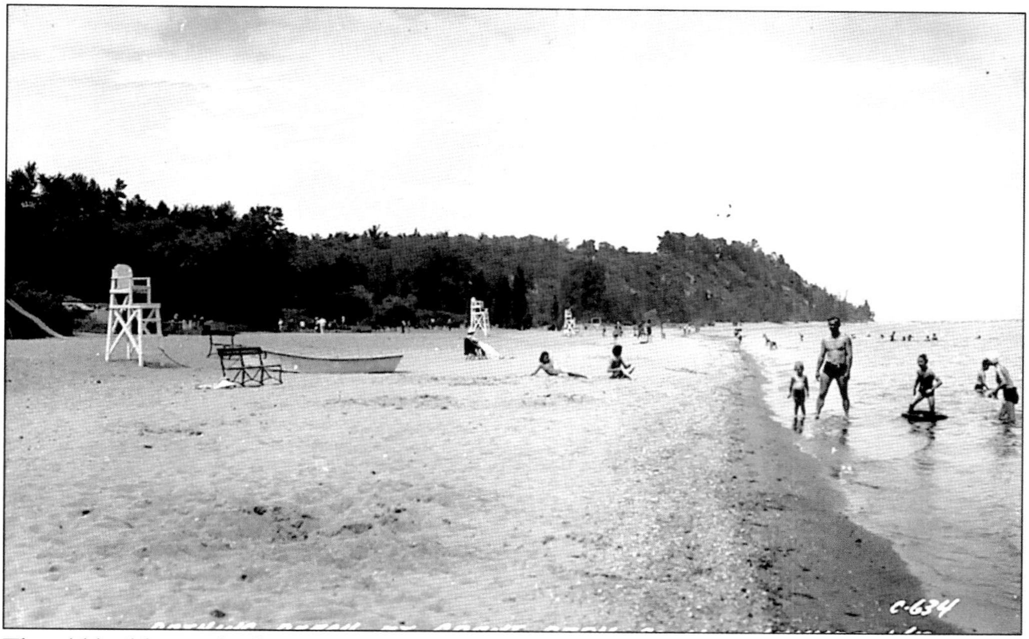

The old bathhouse, built in 1935, can barely be seen in the left background of this view of the Grant Park Beach, *c.* 1940.

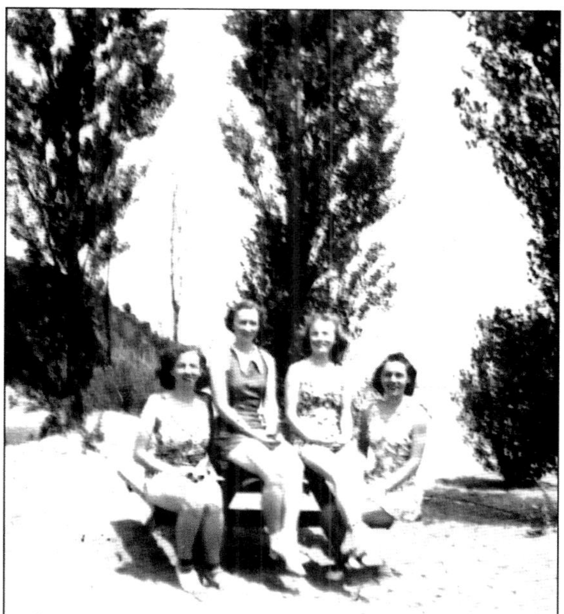

Local teenagers Anne Jurkus, Mabel Pauline, Mary Emer, and Bernice Shelenske enjoy a day at the Grant Park Beach in this *c.* 1936 photograph.

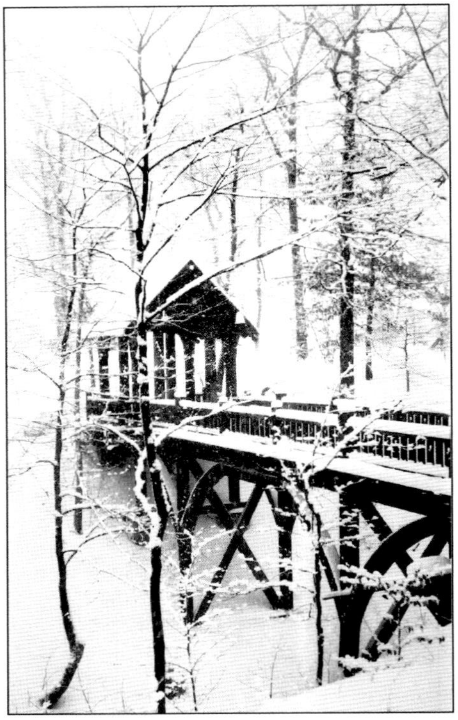

A beautiful 1933 winter view shows the bridge leading from Parking Station One to the "Seven Bridges" area. Carved overhead on the entryway arch are the words, "Enter This Wild Wood and View the Haunts of Nature."

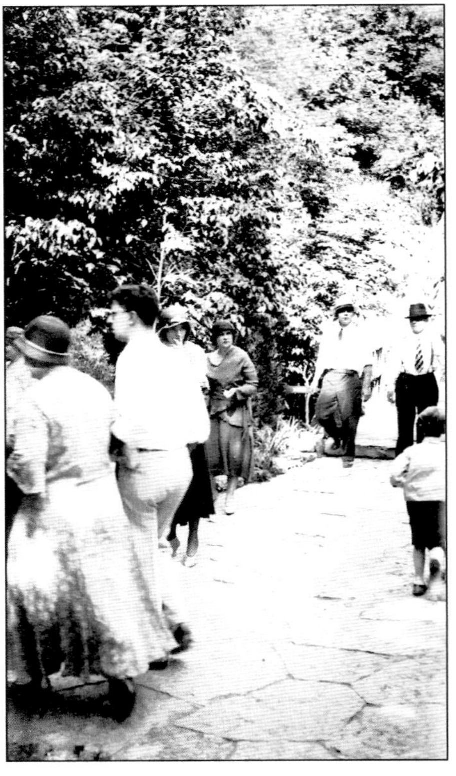

The Seven Bridges area, winding through the ravine in Grant Park, is always a popular spot, as evidenced by this 1931 photograph.

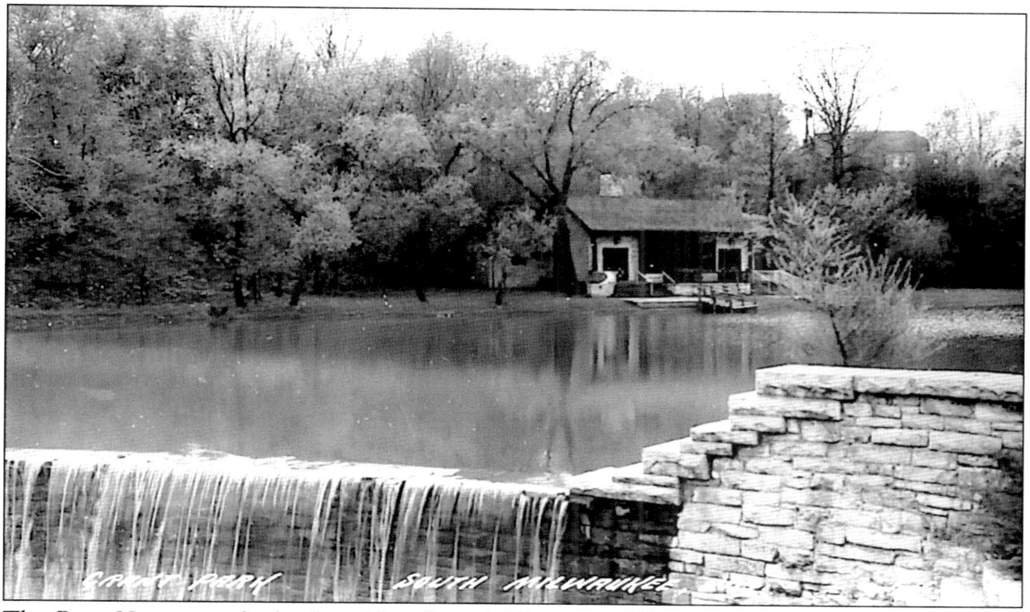

The Boat House overlooks the old millpond. The waterfalls are in the approximate location of the old dam. The millpond, also known as the "lagoon," was a popular recreation spot, with summer boat rentals and ice skating in the winter.

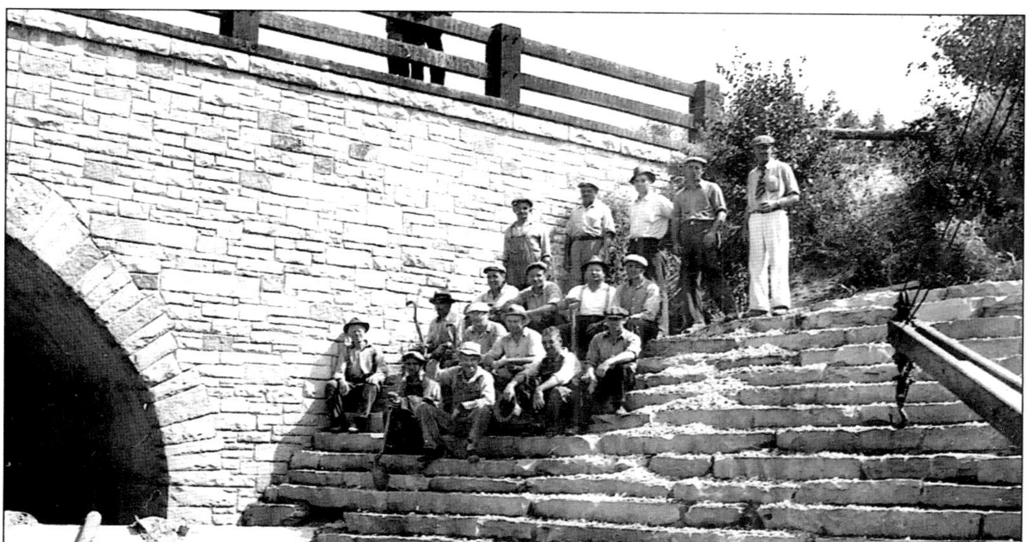

WPA and CCC workers were used extensively during Project 60 construction. Here, a crew takes a break at the new bridge at the mill site. Frederick Wulff is seen standing to the right of this 1934 photograph.

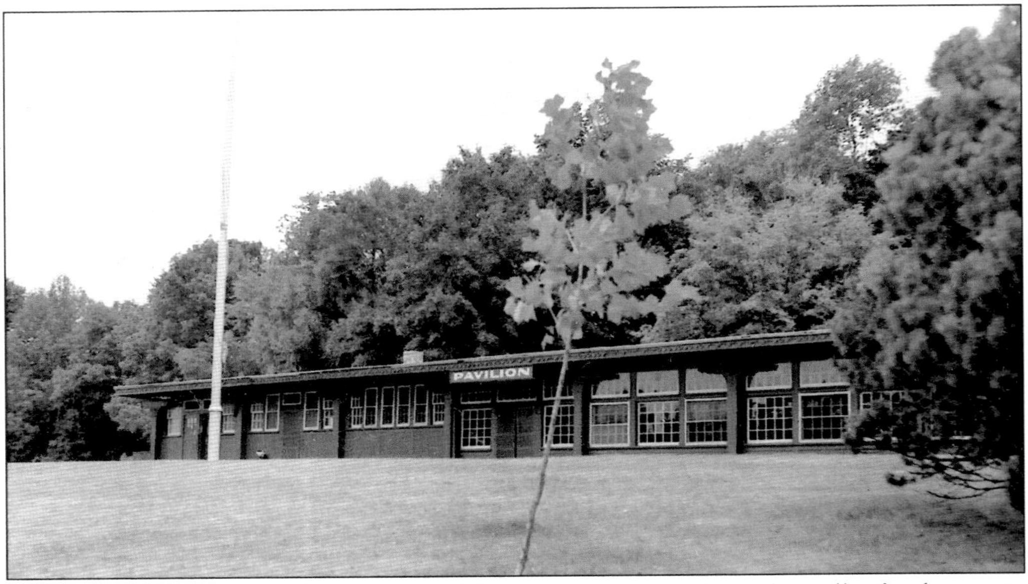

The pavilion at Area 5 & 6 was built by WPA labor around 1929 and is still a focal point in South Milwaukee's Independence Day activities.

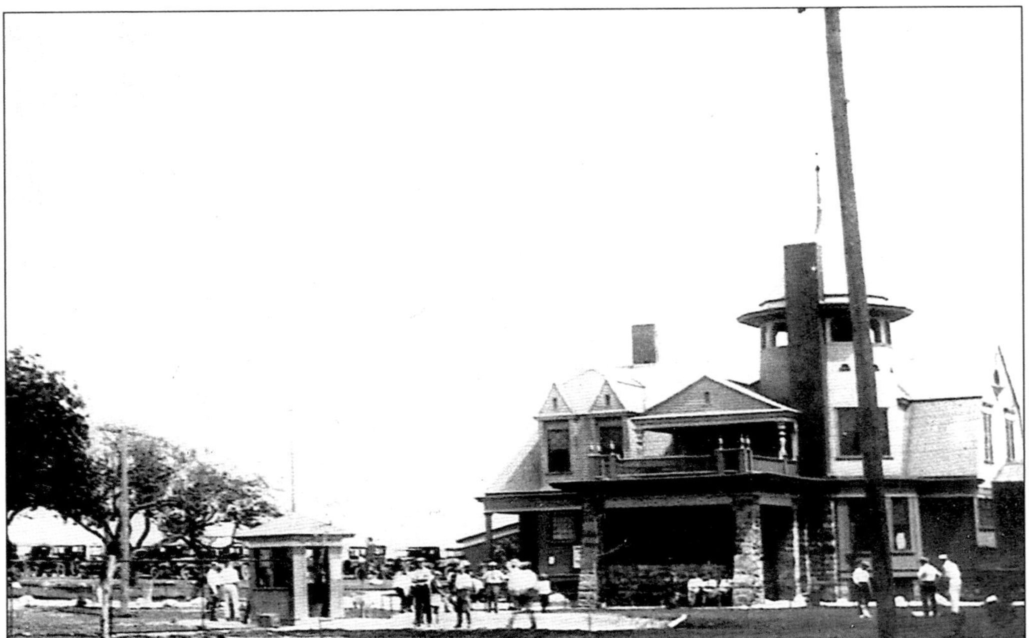

When the Grant Park Golf Course opened on August 14, 1920, it became the Milwaukee County Park System's first golf course. This early 1920s photo shows the action at the starter's hut on the first tee. The beautiful Queen Anne style clubhouse, built in 1892, was originally the home of Horace N. Fowle. (Courtesy of Joe Szatmary.)

Seven

Events That Shaped Us

Any real municipality needs to be characterized as something more than a simple conglomeration of people, bricks, and mortar. It is the collective experience of events and happenings, combined with the efforts of people with vision and foresight, that truly shapes and defines a community. South Milwaukee's long and colorful past, along with a generations-old spirit of self-reliance, has created a tradition of civic pride and well-being that remains strong to this day.

Additionally, it must be said that the people of South Milwaukee have always made good use of their spare time. Whether it was under the big tops of famed circus-man P.T. Barnum, who "set up shop" along Hawthorne Avenue on July 2, 1850, or in attendance at the nationally renowned Spectacle of Music festivals one hundred years later, South Milwaukeeans have always enjoyed a good show. . . .

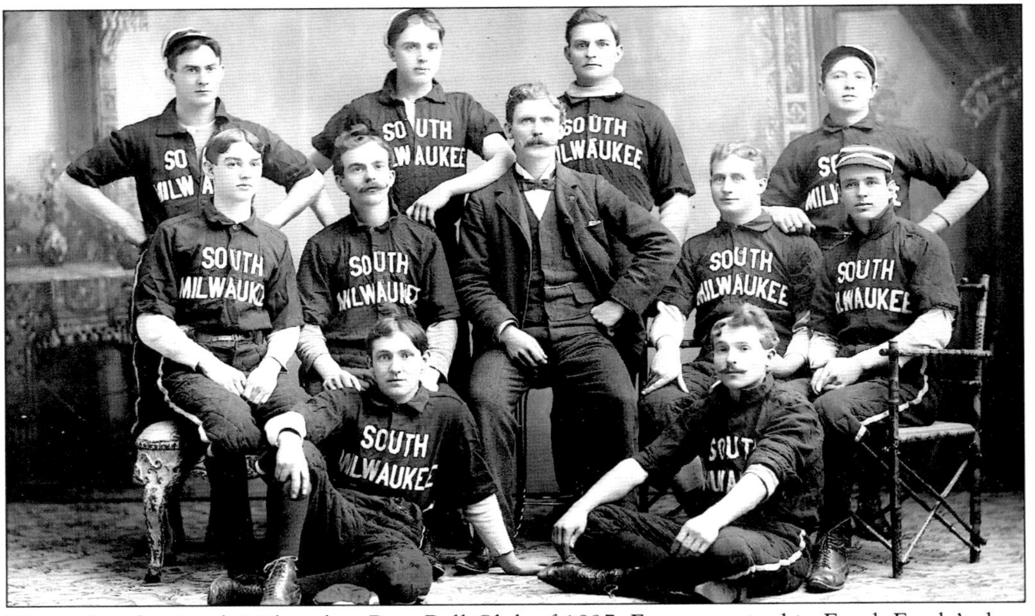

Pictured is the South Milwaukee Base Ball Club of 1897. First organized in Frank Fowle's shoe store in March 1893, the club was put together by local businessmen and stayed active until the 1920s. The first baseball park was located southeast of Tenth and Madison Avenues. It would later be moved to Eleventh and Oak.

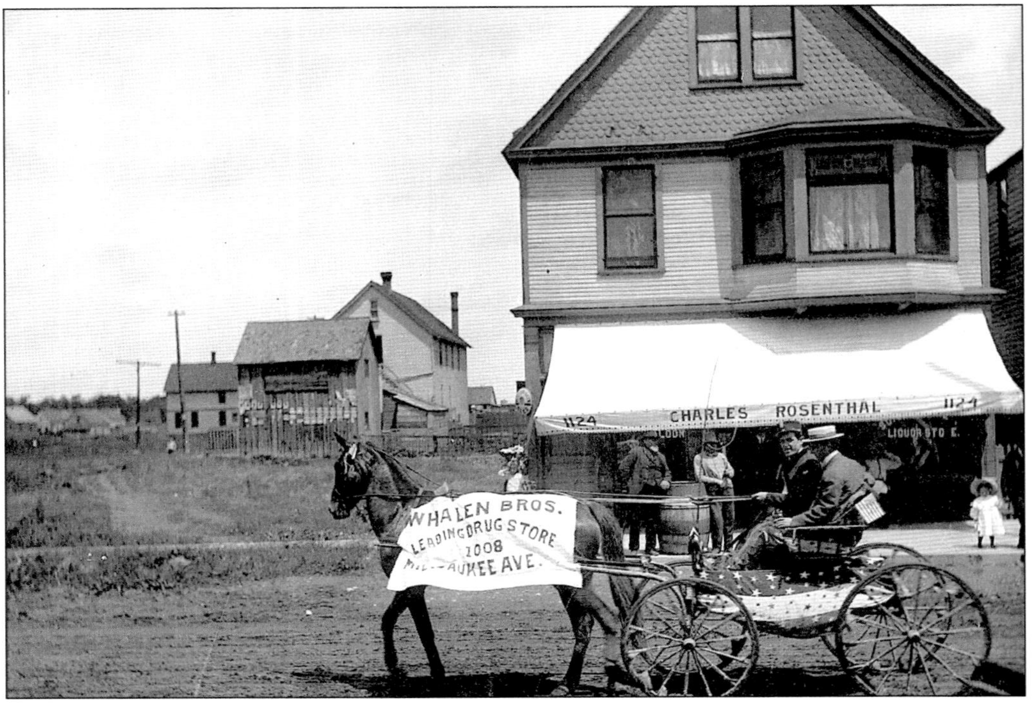

A humble Independence Day parade is captured in this photograph of 1905. The carriage is seen passing the Charles Rosenthal's saloon, which was located at 1124 Milwaukee Avenue.

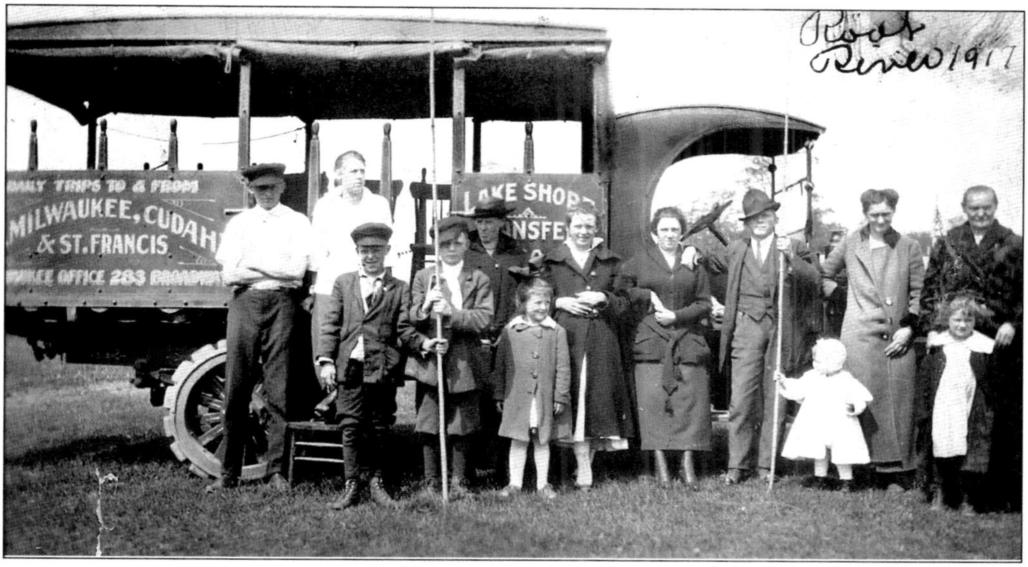

This 1917 photograph was taken at the company picnic for the Lake Shore Transfer Company. Located for many years on Milwaukee Avenue, the company's slogan was "We Deliver the Goods." The truck seen in the background was manufactured in South Milwaukee by the Stephenson Motor Company.

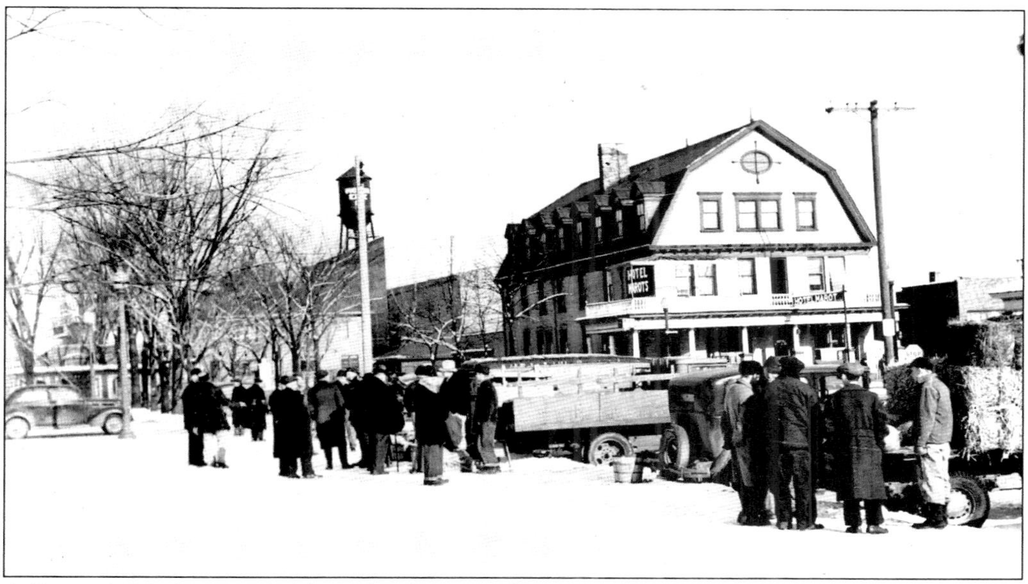

A Farmer's Market was held on the first Tuesday of each month at Eleventh and Milwaukee Avenues. This photograph, taken around 1940, shows the Hotel Marot's in the background.

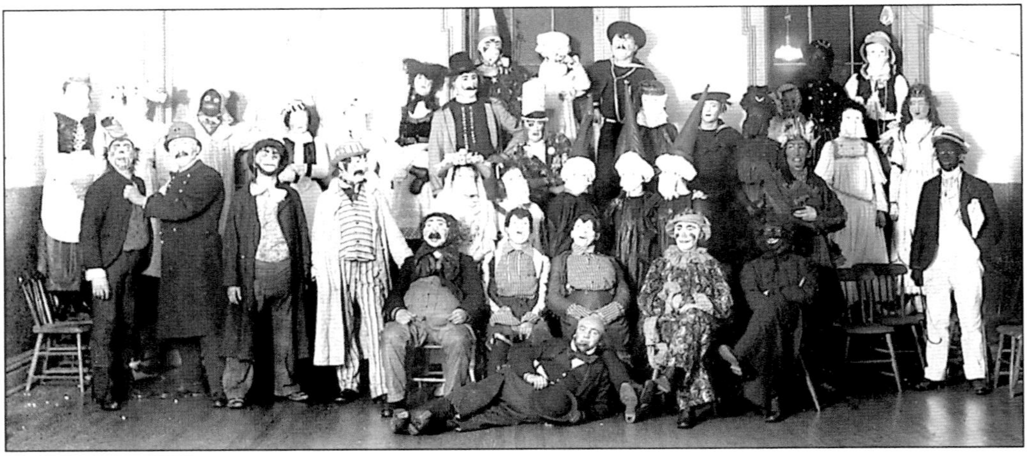

This masked ball was held in Vollmer's Hall, c. 1915.

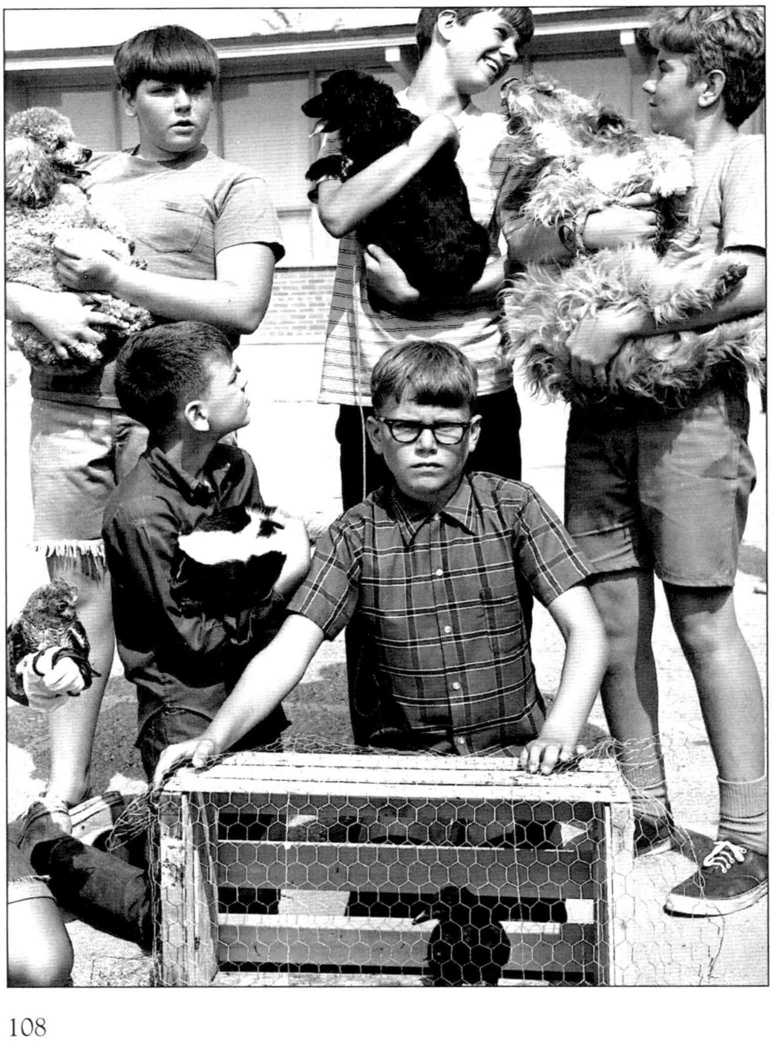

Since 1947, the South Milwaukee Recreation Department has sponsored youth activities, ranging from athletic programs to musicals. They also provided an open playground program at the elementary schools each summer. Many a South Milwaukee youth spent time playing games like Nock-Hockey, Caroms, and Ping-Pong. Here we see a pet show held at Parkway Playground, c. 1967. Shown standing, from left to right, are Scott Menningen, Tim Repa, and Rob Tosic. Tim Nelson kneels next to his pet crow. The others are unidentified.

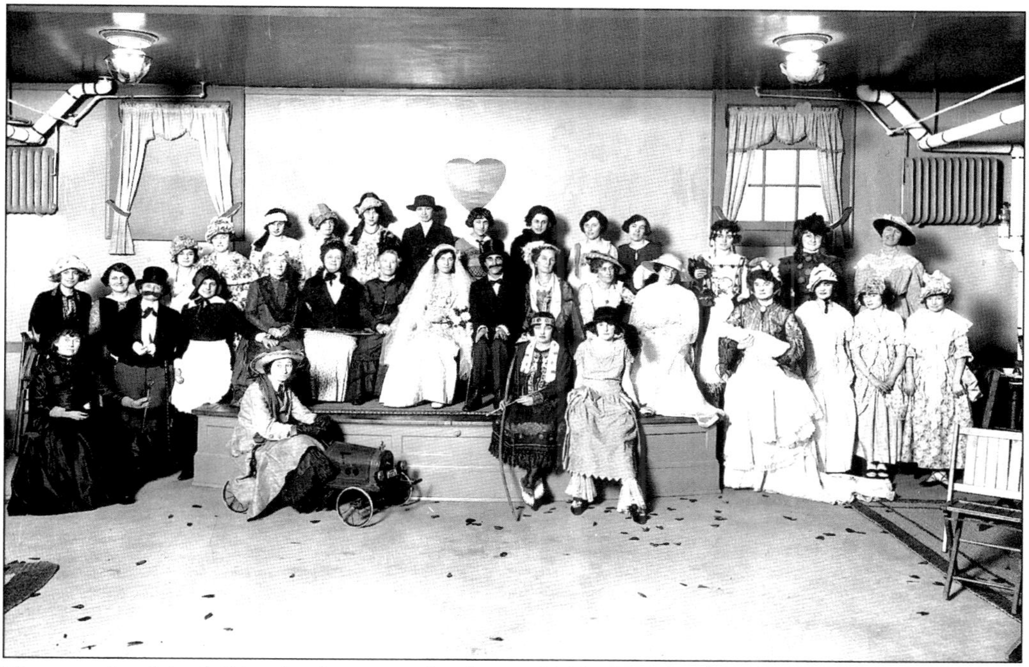

The cast for this children's play poses for this *c.* 1910 photograph, taken at Bergmann's Hall. The hall was located on the second floor of Henry F. Bergmann's Drug Store at 926 Milwaukee Avenue. Bergmann's Hall was also the home of one of South Milwaukee's first movie theaters.

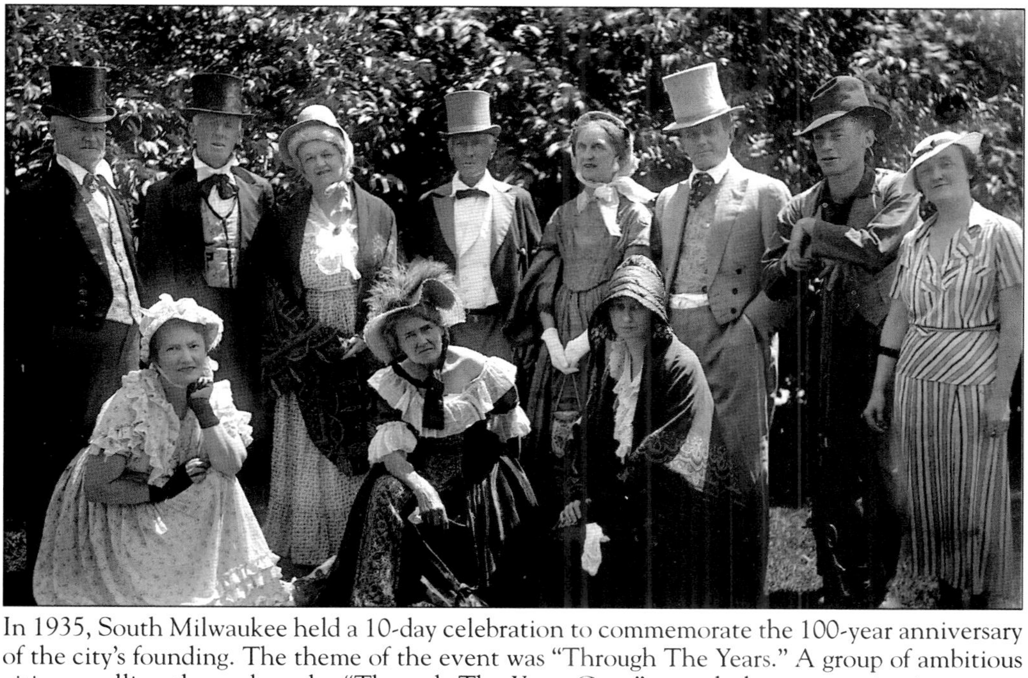

In 1935, South Milwaukee held a 10-day celebration to commemorate the 100-year anniversary of the city's founding. The theme of the event was "Through The Years." A group of ambitious citizens calling themselves the "Through The Years Gang" staged plays reenacting important events in South Milwaukee's past. These plays were held on the high school athletic field.

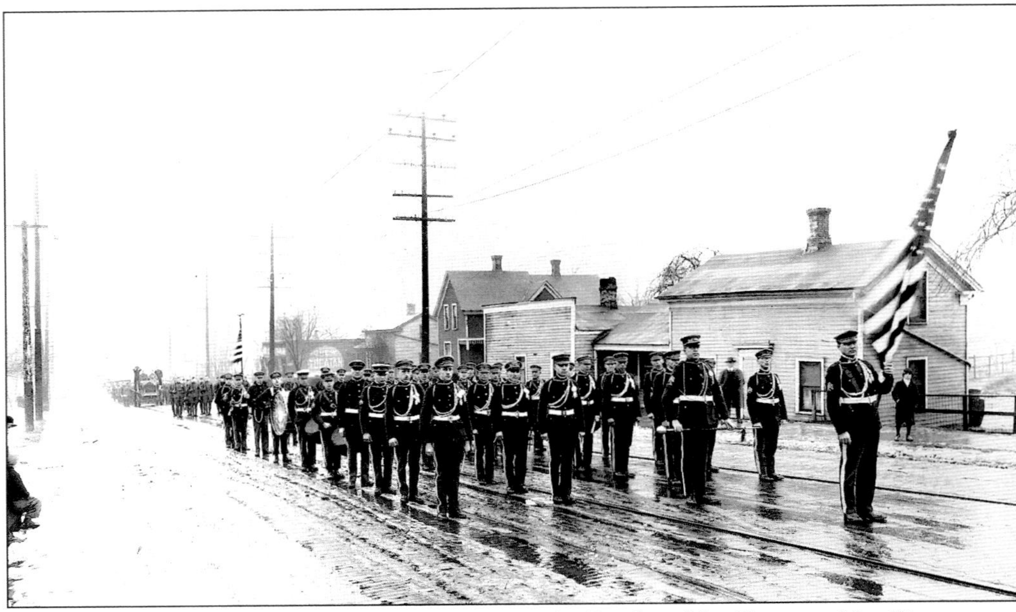

Pictured is the January 1, 1921, funeral procession for Everhart Van Eimeren. Van Eimeran was the first South Milwaukee casualty during World War I, killed in France in August 1918. His body was later returned to South Milwaukee for burial. The Bucyrus Fife, Drum & Bugle Corps (complete with muffled drums) led this solemn procession, followed by an honor guard and the motorized hearse.

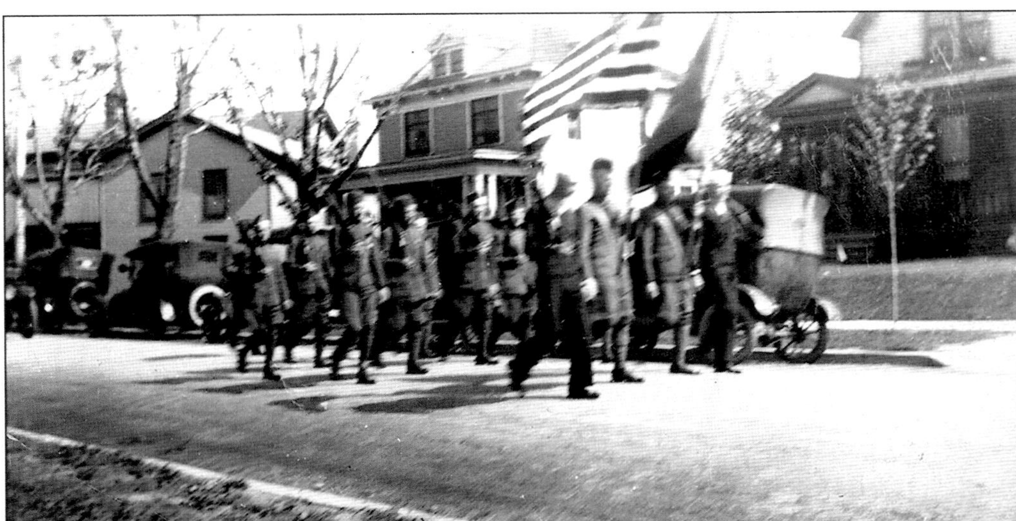

Taken during a 1920s Memorial Day Parade, a color guard of WW I veterans march along Hawthorne Avenue. Vollmer's Hall is visible at the extreme left.

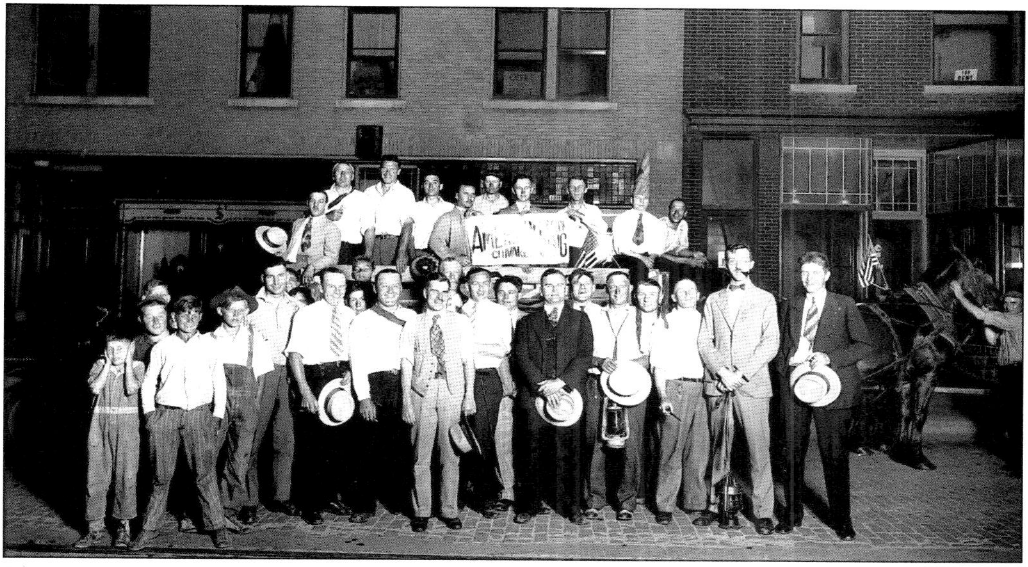

The American Legion "Chivaree Gang" poses along Milwaukee Avenue, *c.* 1928. "Chivarees" were an old wedding custom where friends of the groom would pay a "surprise" visit to the newly wedded couple on their honeymoon night. By clanging pots and otherwise making a racket outside, the revelers would force the flustered groom to emerge and offer "refreshments" to the miscreants to help speed them along their way. (Courtesy of Leo M. Broskowski.)

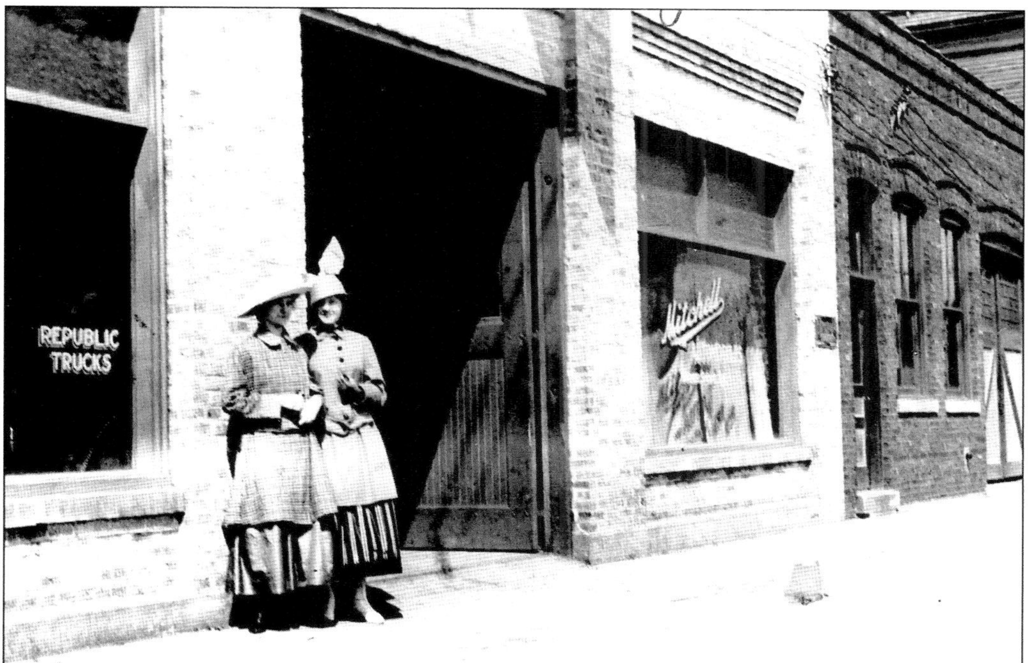

Two young women strike a pose in front of Nirschl's Garage at 906–908 Milwaukee Avenue, *c.* 1918. The Lake Shore Transfer Company building is seen at right.

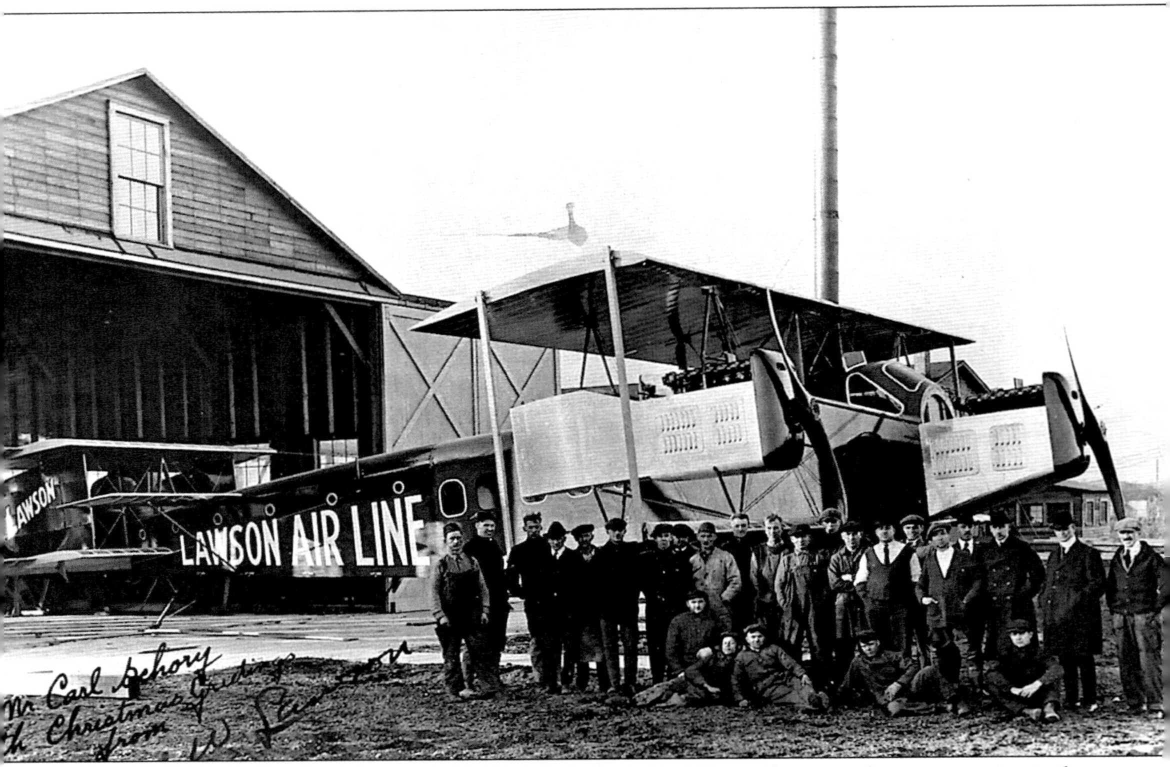

The Lawson Air Line Company is South Milwaukee's best claim to the aeronautics industry. Born in London, England, Alfred W. Lawson moved to America at an early age where he developed a passion for flight. In 1920, he would rent a vacant building at Ninth and Menomonee Avenues, where he continued the development of an "Air Liner" that he believed would revolutionize the industry. With its 124-foot wingspan and three "Liberty" engines, the airplane built in South Milwaukee was believed to be the largest in the world at the time. This photograph, taken around December 1920, shows the nearly completed plane along with the men who built it. (Courtesy of Beverly Rayeske.)

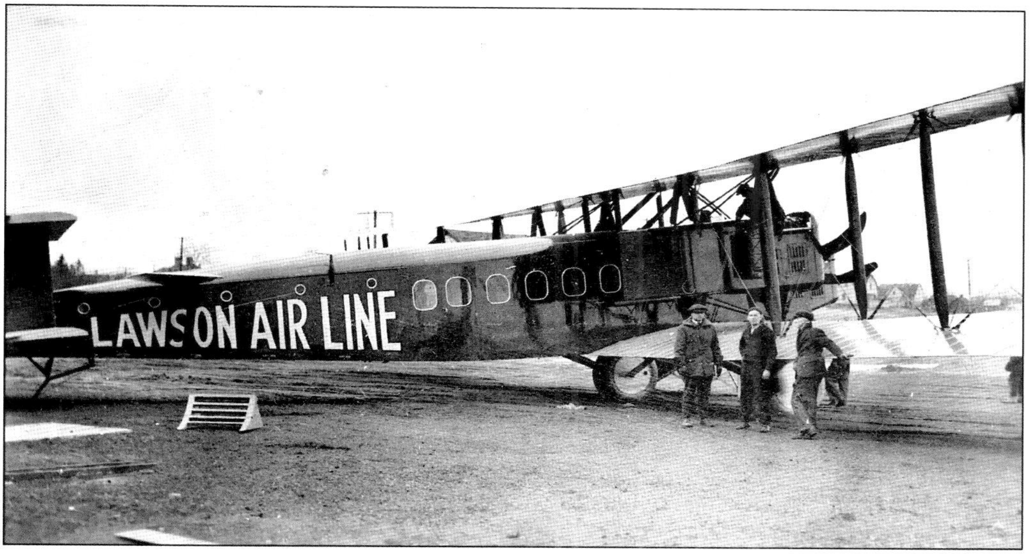

Under intense pressure from the company's stockholders, Lawson scheduled the test flight of his ponderously bulky, green-painted "Midnight Airliner" on Sunday, May 8, 1921. The weather conditions were less than ideal. A three-acre field south of the hangar would serve as the runway. Many of Lawson's associates felt that more room would be required for takeoff, so Lawson got permission from farmer John Hughes to use his field for additional room. (Courtesy of Beverly Rayeske.)

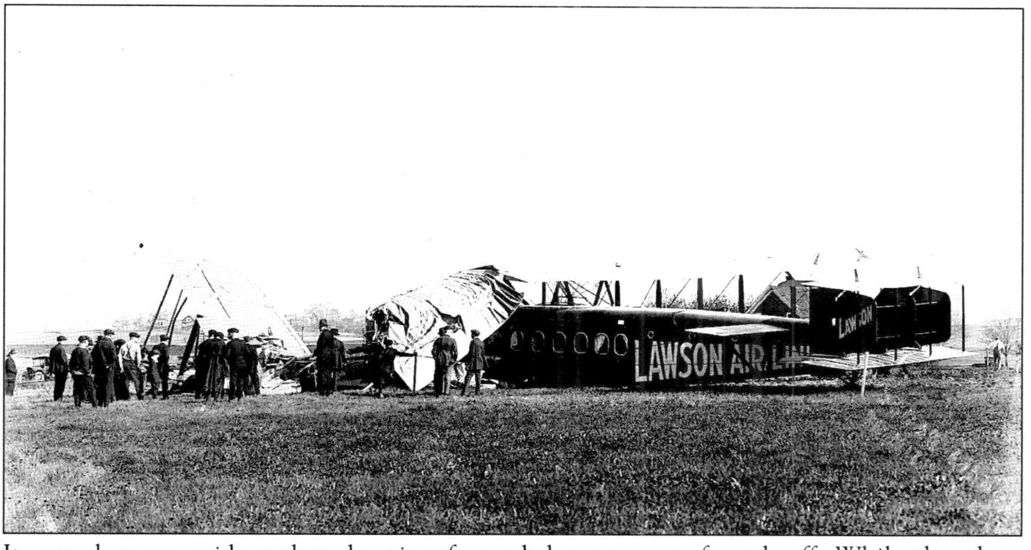

It soon became evident that the aircraft needed more room for takeoff. While the plane struggled to gain speed, progress was slowed by the furrows ploughed in farmer Hughes' field. At the altitude of 10 feet, pilot Charles Wilcox, swung the plane to the left to avoid hitting Hughes' home. The plane struck an elm tree and clipped a telephone pole before spinning ignominiously into the ground. In 1922, the Lawson Air Line Company declared bankruptcy.

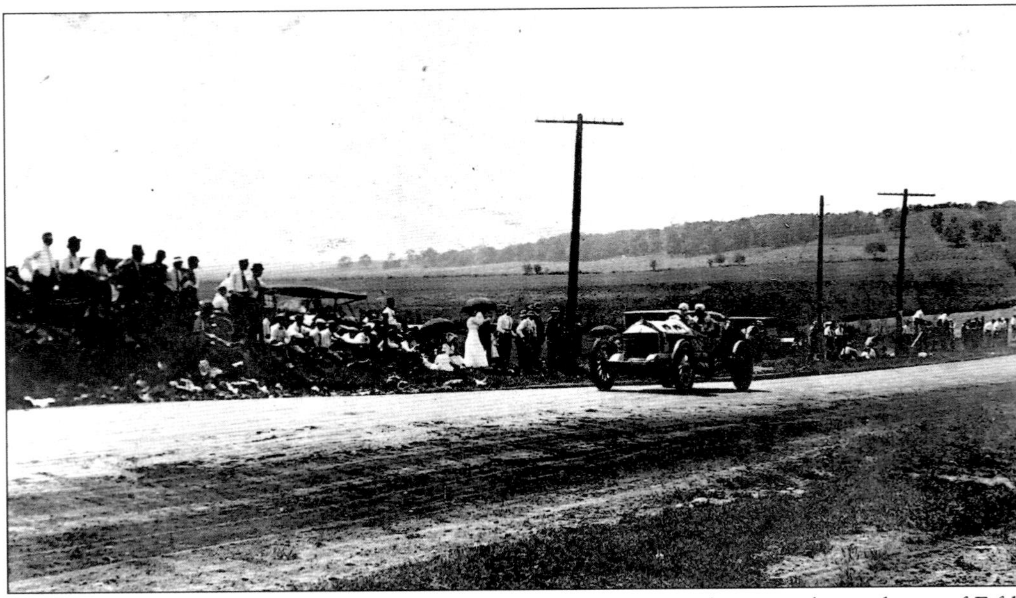

First opened in August 1928, the South Milwaukee Motor Speedway was located east of Fifth Avenue near Puetz Road. This non-sanctioned track was a five-eighths-of-a-mile, graded and oiled oval, with heavily banked turns. A grandstand and bleachers provided seating for 15,000 spectators. The speedway closed around 1934.

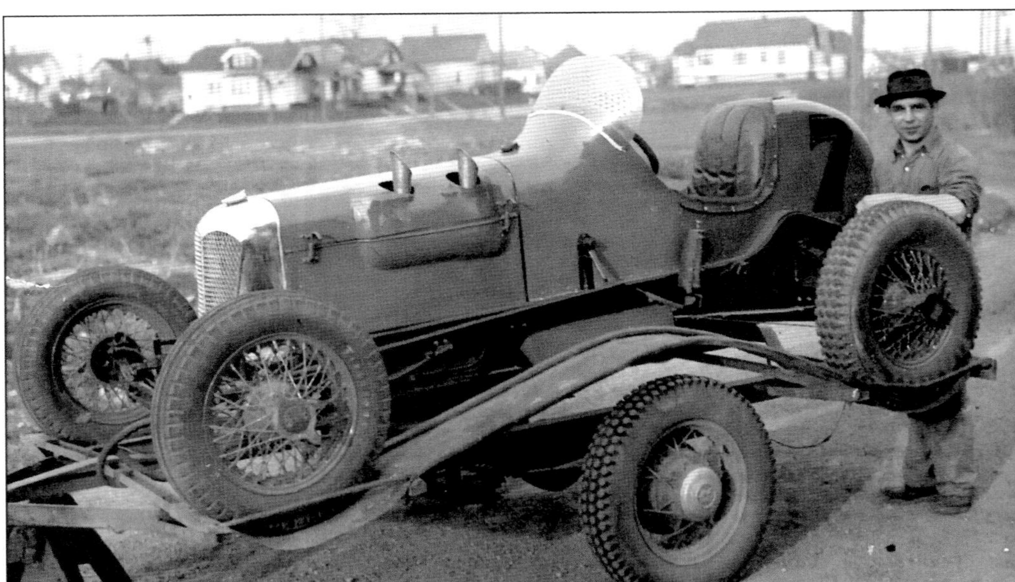

South Milwaukee resident Tony Willman was a familiar face at the South Milwaukee Speedway. In fact, Willman's skill in midget racing earned him a National Championship. So great was Tony Willman's fame that this quiet and soft-spoken man was named honorary mayor of South Milwaukee in 1939. On October 12, 1941, Willman was tragically killed in a racing accident in Thompson, Connecticut. The "Great Tony Willman" was named to the National Midget Auto Racing Hall of Fame in 1996.

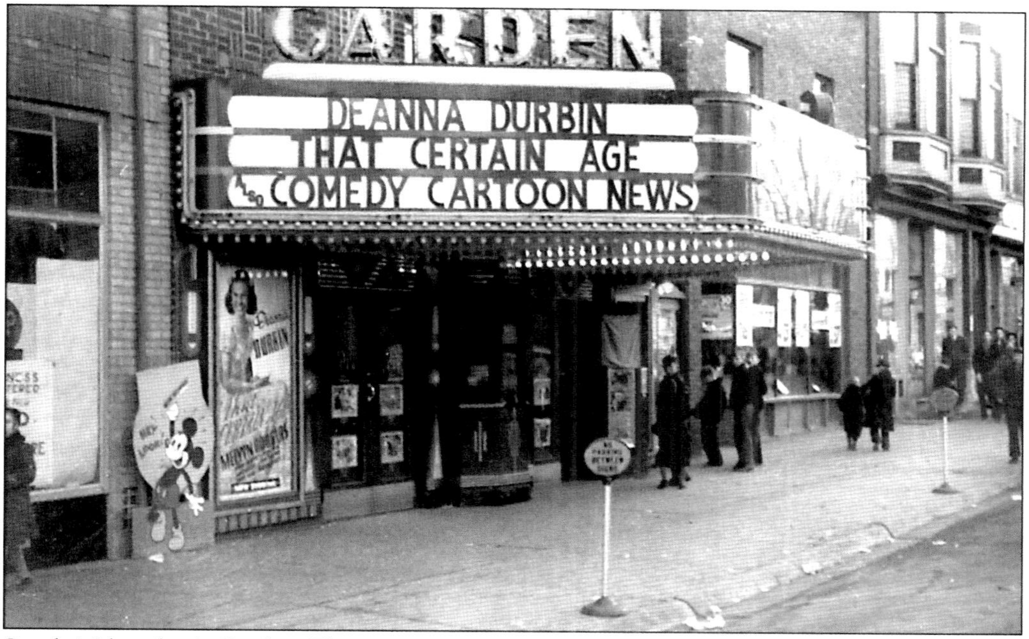

South Milwaukee's Garden Theater appears as it stood, in all its glory, in a photograph taken in January 1939. Located at 1005 Milwaukee Avenue, the Garden opened in December 1922 and closed its doors in 1976.

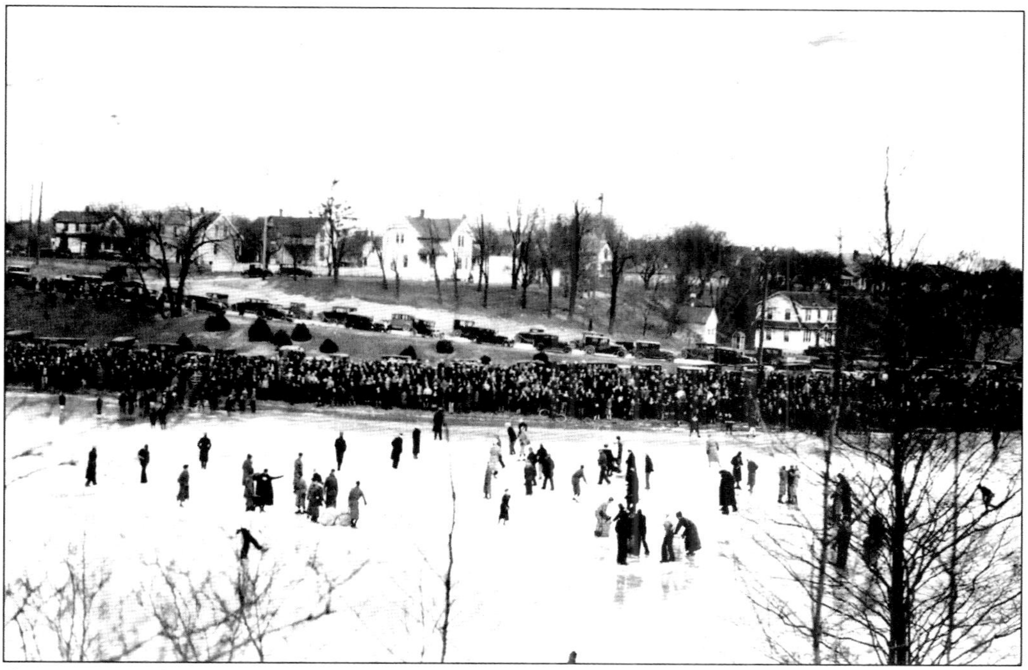

Quite a crowd is gathered at the old Mill Pond to watch ice skaters in action at an "Ice Carnival" in this c. 1932 image. Known locally as the "lagoon," the pond still continues to serve as a venue for skaters young and old alike.

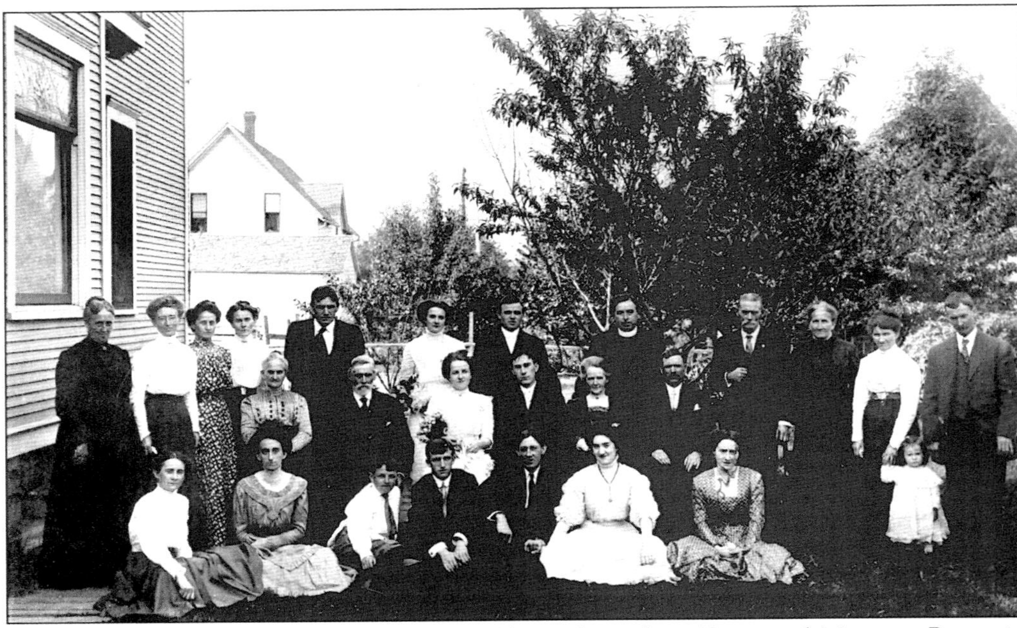

This family portrait was taken after the wedding of Matthew Keese and Margaret Rouse in 1910. The bride and groom are seated in the middle row, flanked by their proud parents. The photo was taken at the home of the bride's parents at 716 Madison Avenue.

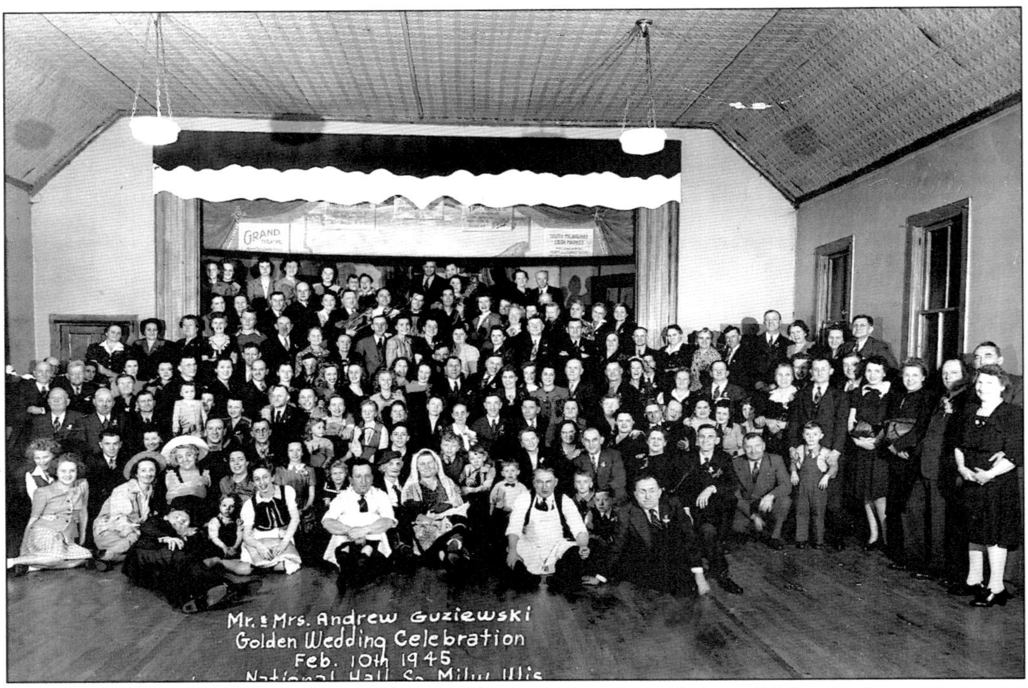

Family and friends celebrate the golden wedding anniversary of Mr. and Mrs. Andrew Guziewski at National Hall in 1945. Located on the southwest corner of Fourteenth and Milwaukee Avenues, National Hall was popular with South Milwaukee's many Polish residents.

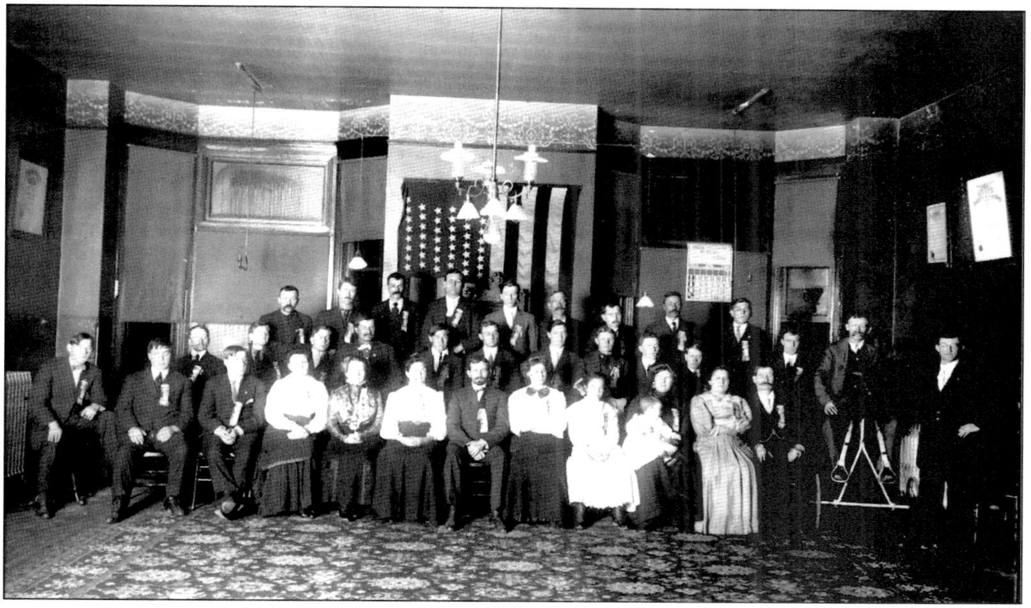

The United Order of Foresters, Oak Creek Camp No. 146, pose in Donsing's Hall in 1911. Around 1922, Henry Donsing sold this building to William Smith, who continued operating the meat market and hall until sometime around 1947.

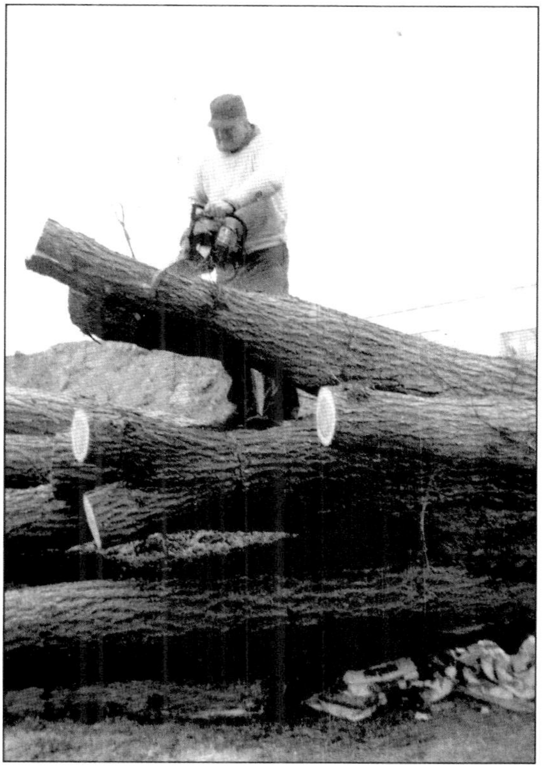

Merle Monson began his tree-cutting service in South Milwaukee around 1948. He remained active in the business for the next 45 years and was still climbing and felling trees when he was well into his 70s. Here, we see him at work cleaning up after a 1952 storm that toppled many trees and caused considerable damage in the city.

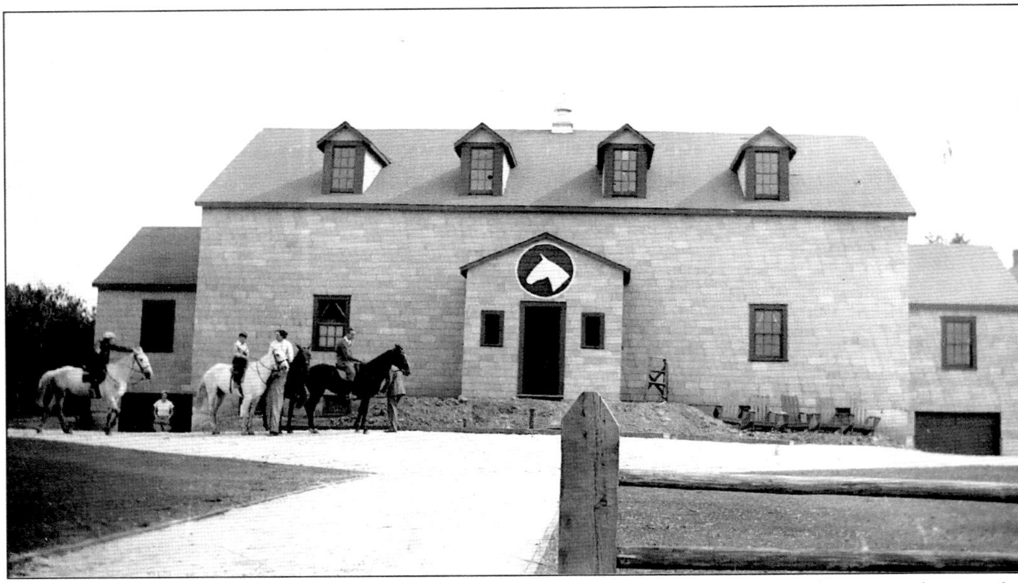

The Shamrock Riding Stables were located at 305 Michigan Avenue. In business during the early 1930s, the stable had established bridal paths throughout Grant Park.

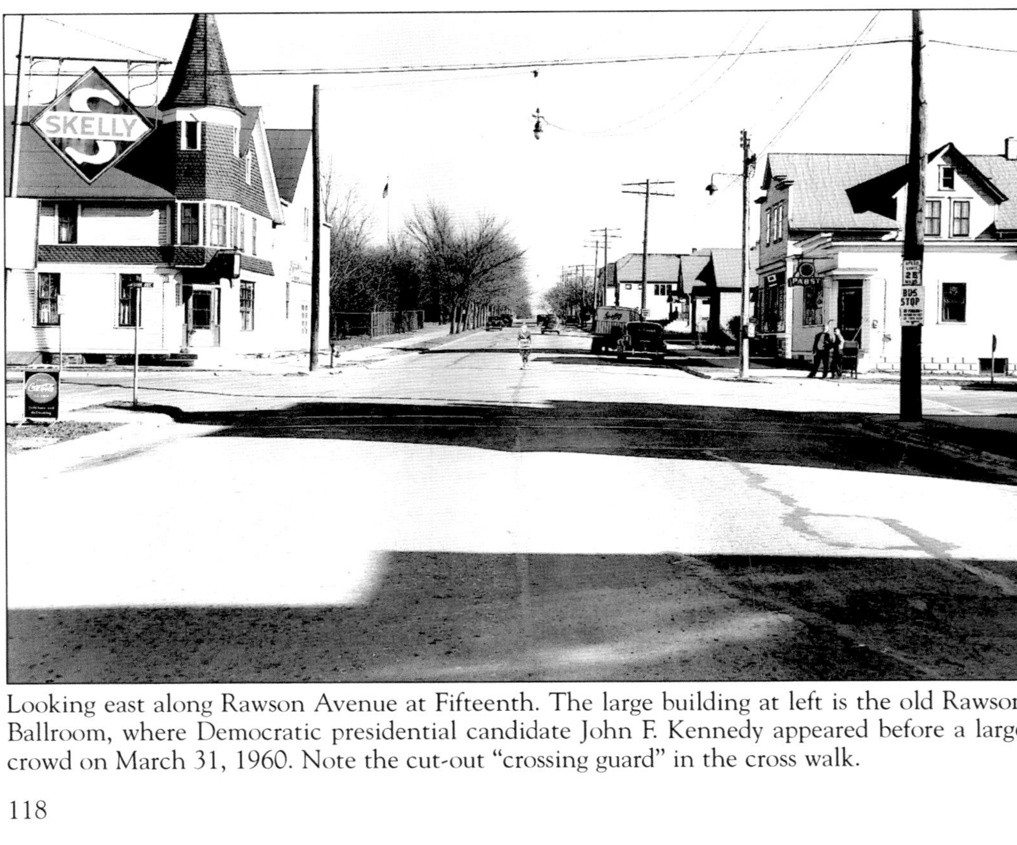

Looking east along Rawson Avenue at Fifteenth. The large building at left is the old Rawson Ballroom, where Democratic presidential candidate John F. Kennedy appeared before a large crowd on March 31, 1960. Note the cut-out "crossing guard" in the cross walk.

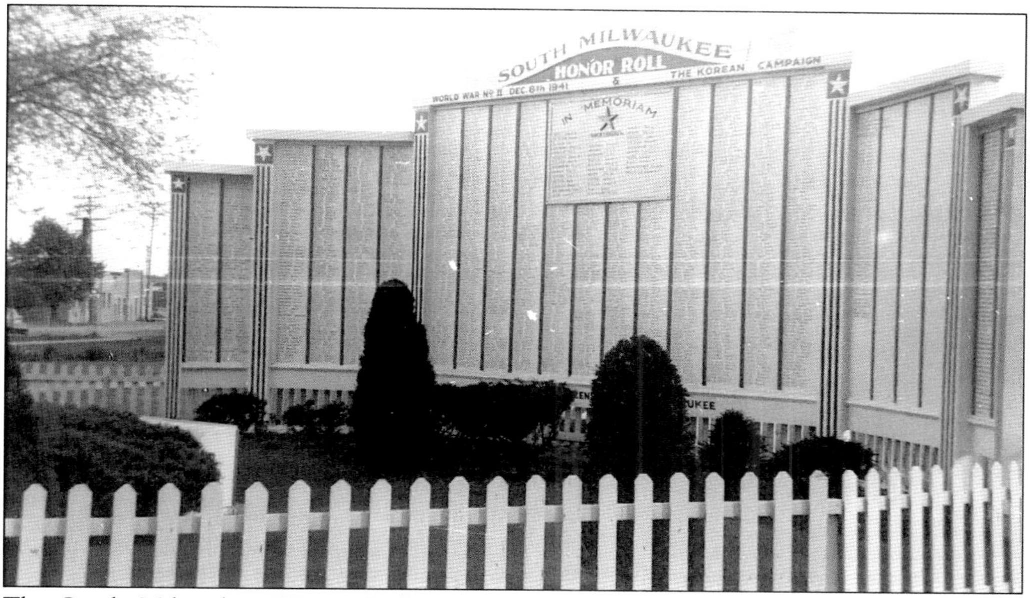

The South Milwaukee "Honor Roll," commemorating those who served America's cause during WW II and the Korean War. This monument was located near the southwest corner of Eleventh and Milwaukee Avenues, in what was then known as Depot Park. The Honor Roll also sat for a time in front of the Carnegie Library on Tenth Avenue.

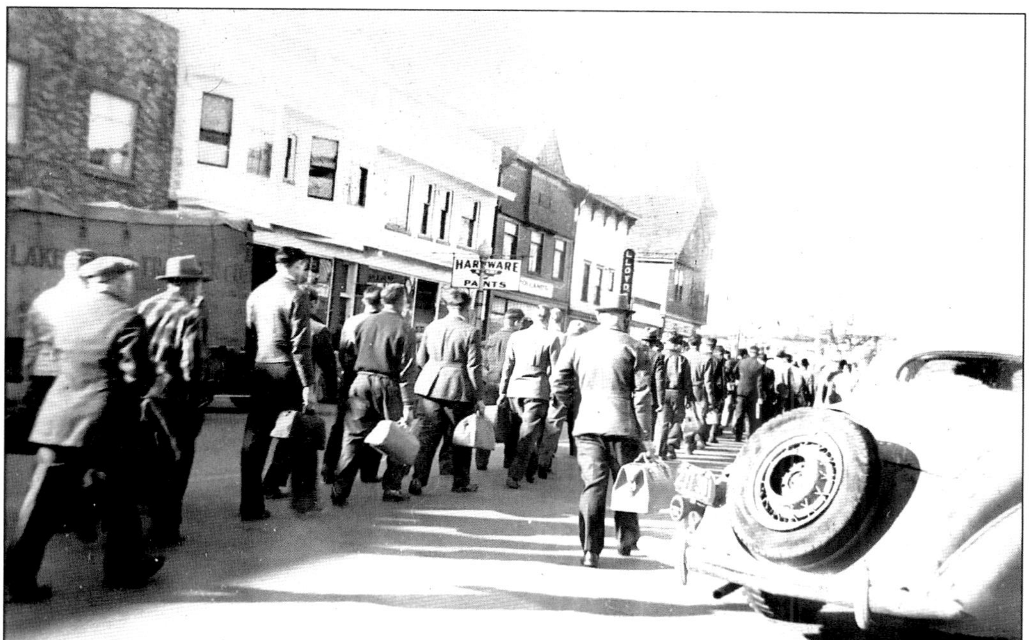

This photograph, taken around April 1943, shows a column of new enlistees marching from city hall down Milwaukee Avenue towards the railroad depot. There, they would board the train to Fort Sheridan, Illinois, and off into the history books. Fitzgerald's Hardware store can be seen in the background. (Courtesy of Joe Hosmanek.)

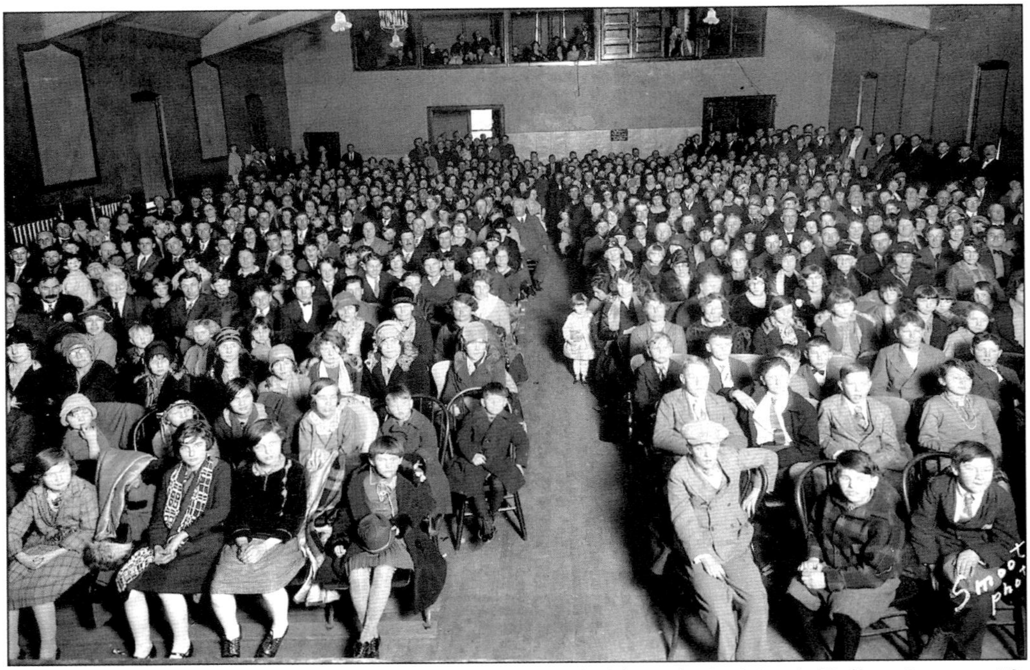

This photo shows a "Rural Play and Music Contest," held inside St. Mary's Hall on January 13, 1927. (Courtesy of Bruce Rayeske.)

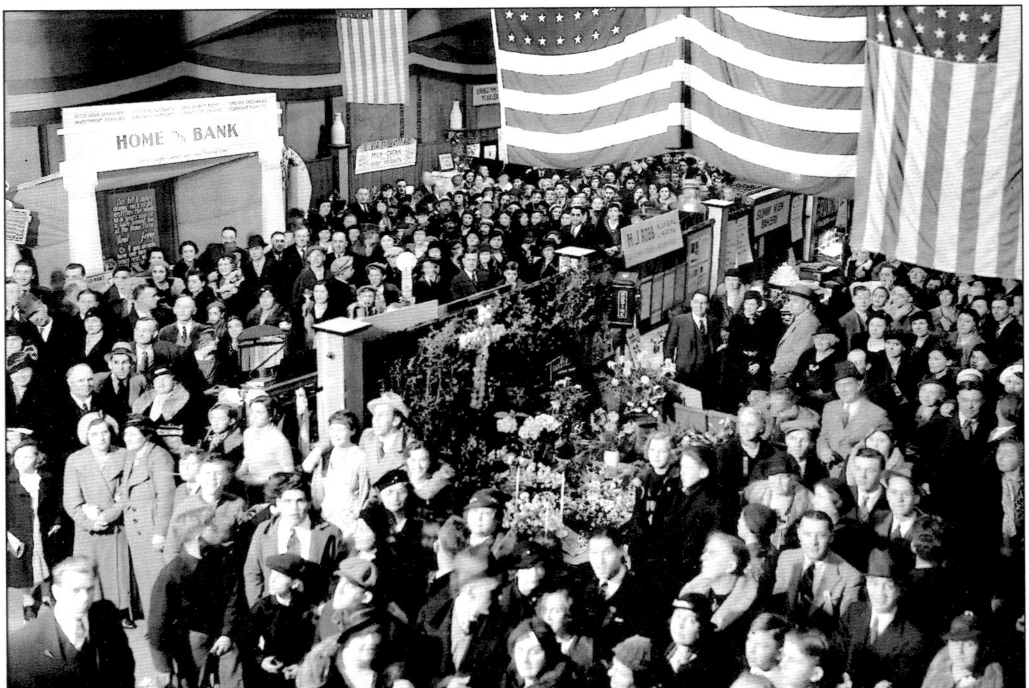

Local merchants show off their wares at the South Milwaukee Home show, *c.* 1940. The event was held in St. Mary's Hall. (Courtesy of Bruce Rayeske.)

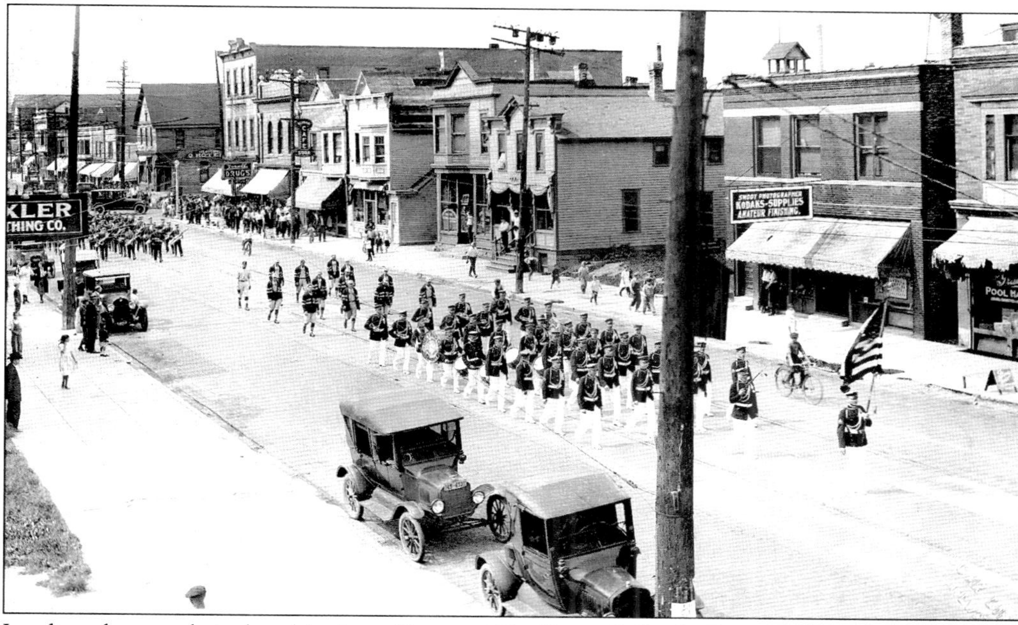

Leading the parade is the ubiquitous Bucyrus Fife, Drum & Bugle Corps, followed closely by the company's baseball team in this c. 1923 image, taken from the upper floor of the Saxler building at 911–915 Milwaukee Avenue.

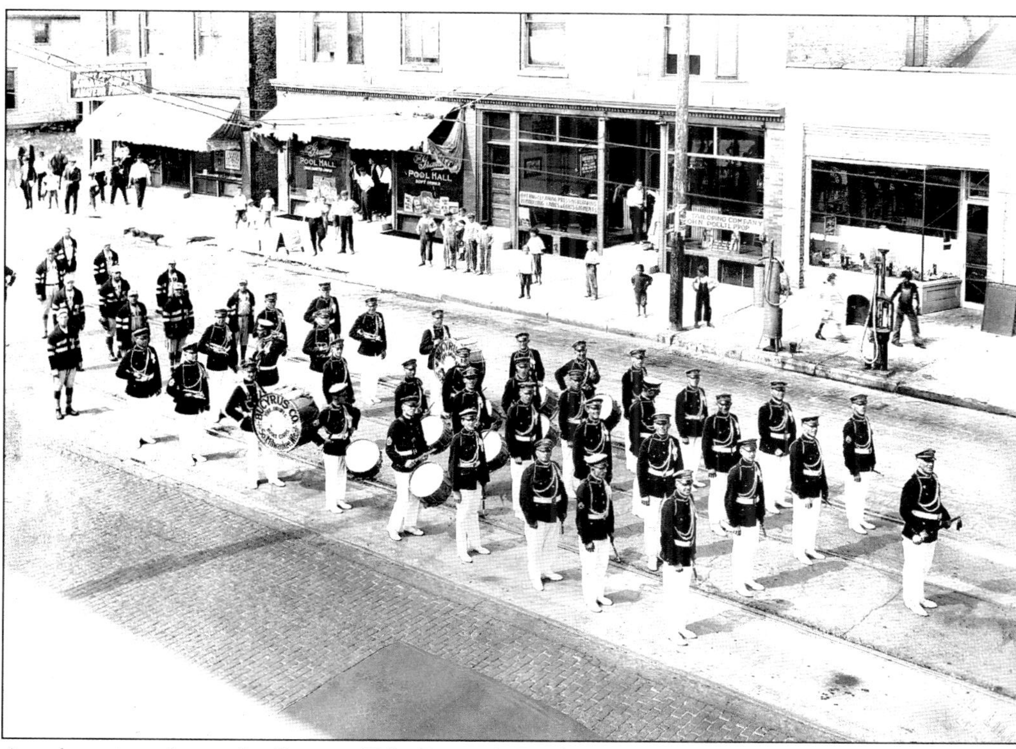

Another view shows the Bucyrus Fife, Drum & Bugle Corps, standing at attention.

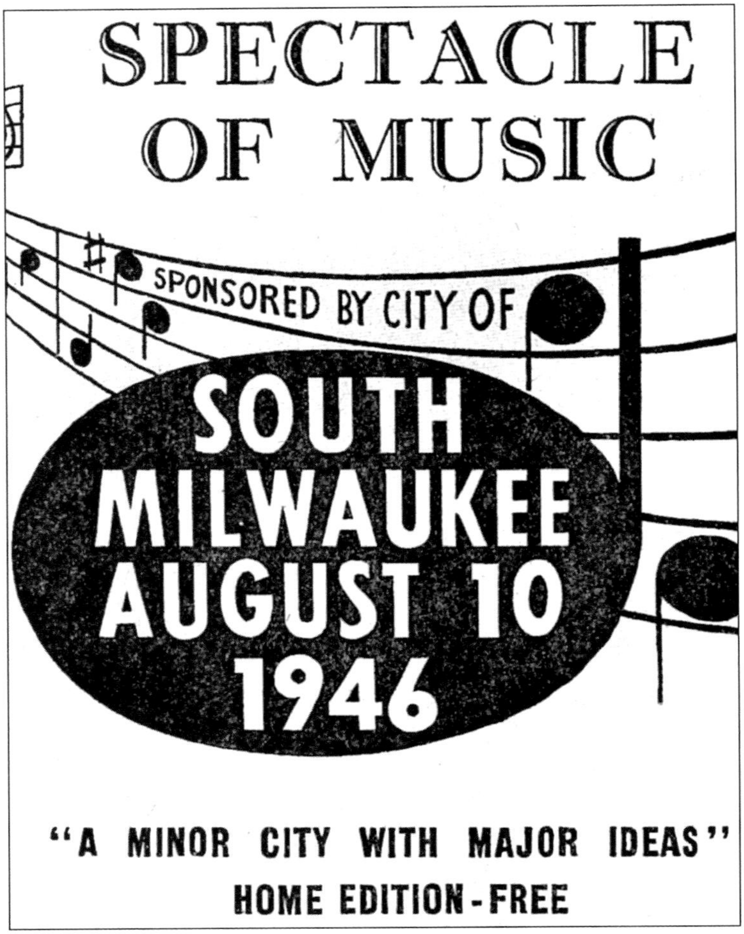
SPECTACLE OF MUSIC

SPONSORED BY CITY OF

SOUTH MILWAUKEE
AUGUST 10
1946

"A MINOR CITY WITH MAJOR IDEAS"

HOME EDITION-FREE

This program cover from the first Spectacle of Music, in 1946, featured the city's motto: "A Minor City with Major Ideas." How true it was, for the Spectacle would become a nationally known event, as marching bands, drill teams, and drum and bugle corps from across the country competed for prize money. The Spectacle of Music lasted until 1978, though there are current efforts to revive it.

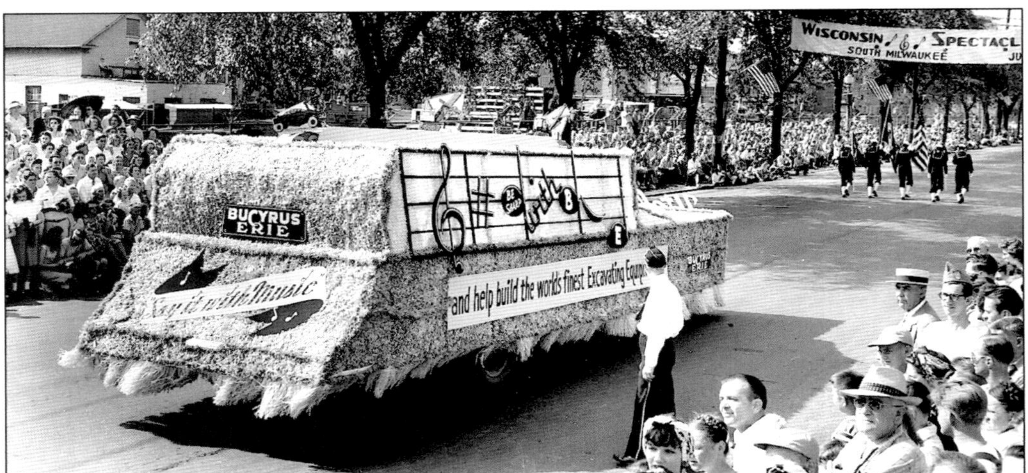

The Bucyrus-Erie Float is near the head of this c. 1950 Spectacle parade. This shot was taken in front of city hall and looks northwest along Tenth Avenue.

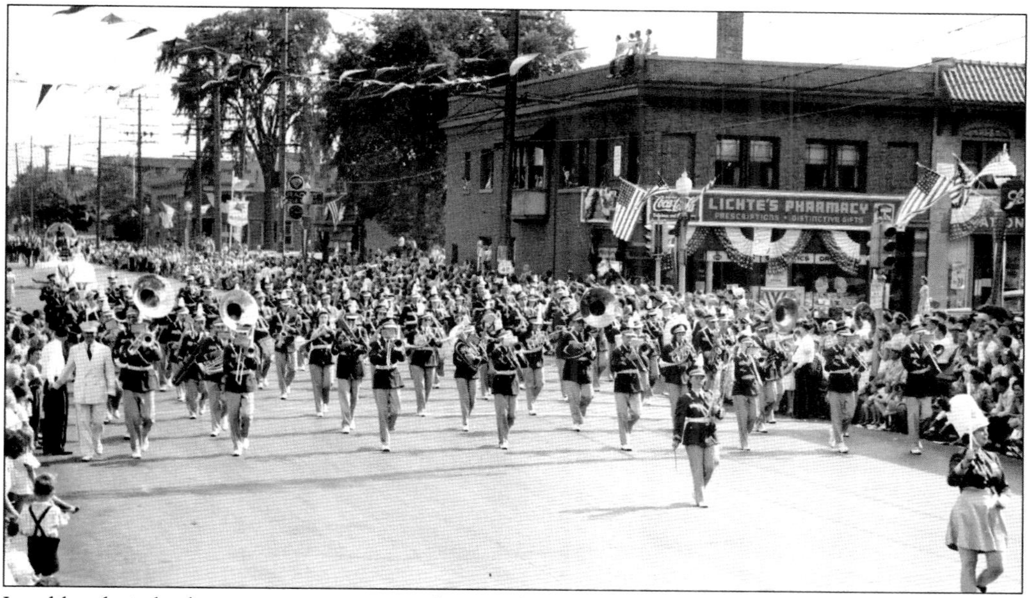

Lead by their high-stepping majorette, the South Milwaukee Municipal Band wows 'em at the 1947 Spectacle parade. Taken from an upper floor of the old Dretzcka Building (the former Hotel Blatz) at Tenth and Milwaukee, this thrilling image makes it almost possible to "hear" this photograph. Note the daring lads perched precariously atop Lichte's Pharmacy building.

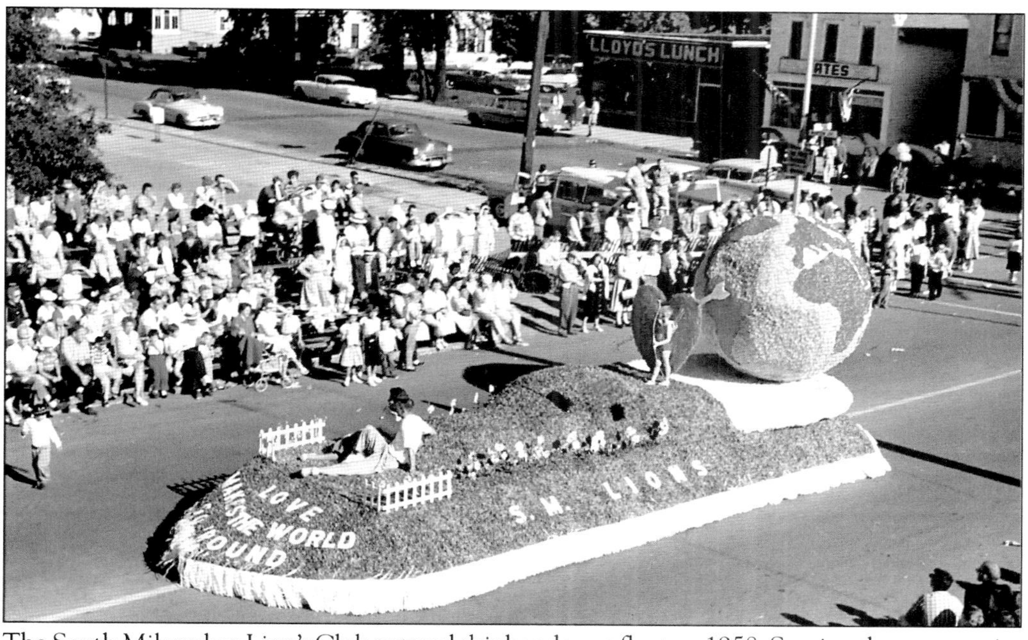

The South Milwaukee Lion's Club entered this handsome float, *c*. 1958. Serving the community since 1937, the Lion's Club has long been an active supporter of many of the city's charitable ventures. In the background, Leo Gates' electrical shop can be seen. On the right is Captain Wexstaff's old tavern on the southeast corner of Tenth and Madison Avenues. Another South Milwaukee landmark, Lloyd's Lunch, is also seen here.

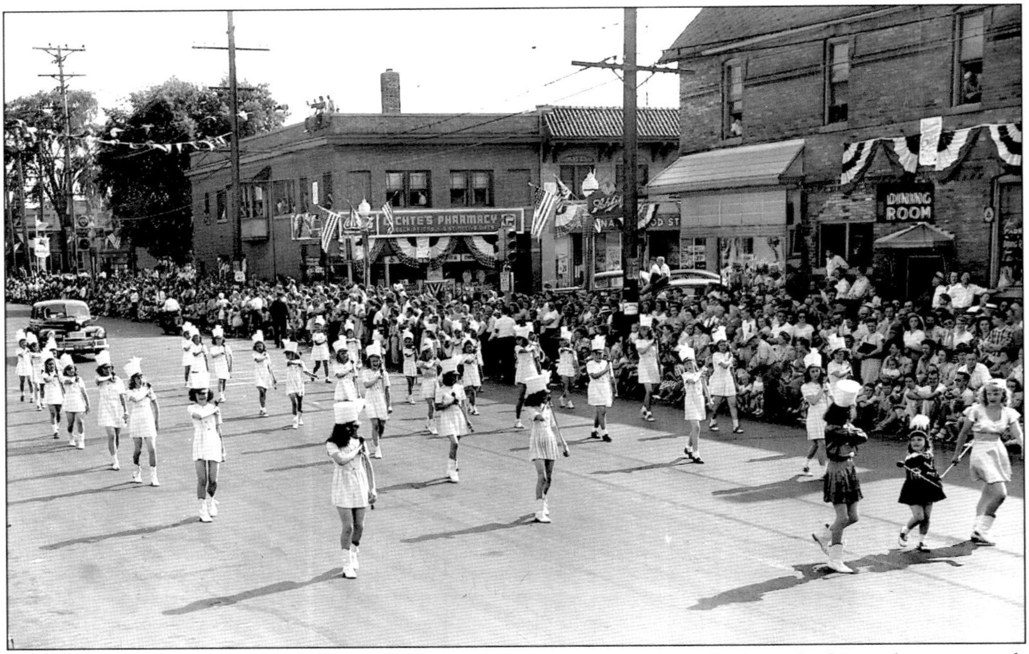

A local Twirling Corps, known as "Ginnie's Twirlers", steps to the beat before a large crowd. Nice hats!

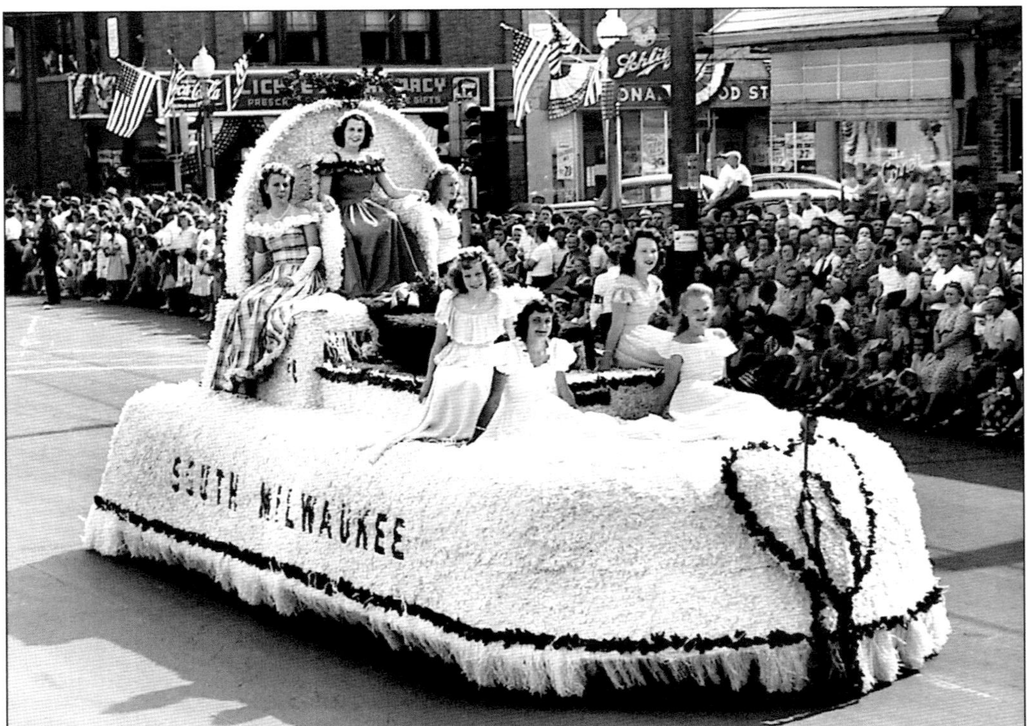

Ardis Haldemann, the 1947 Spectacle Queen, glides past an admiring audience with her court.

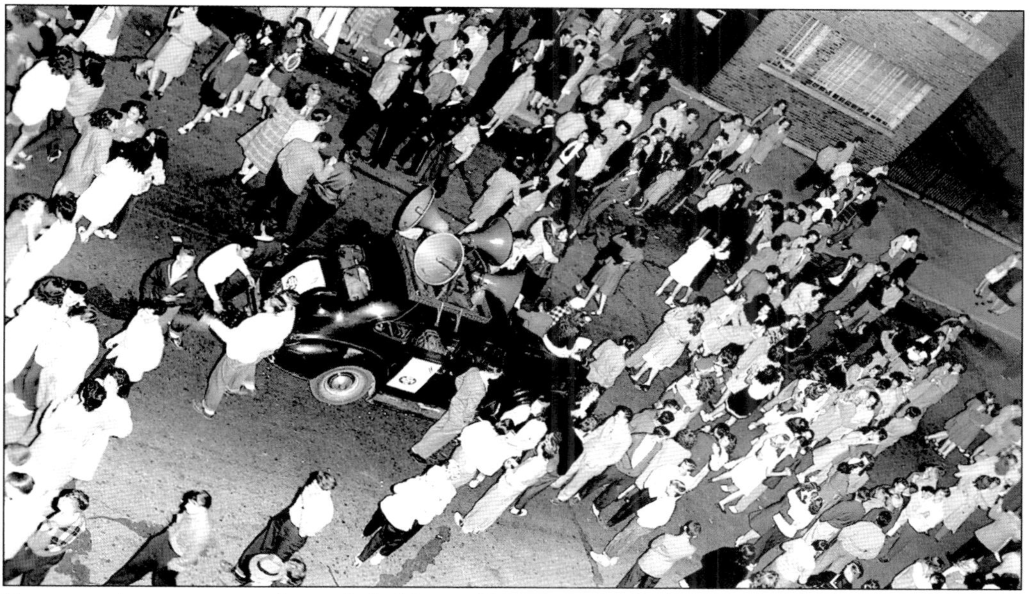

Barnstorming, a street festival held on Friday night before Saturday's big parade and competition, was always an annual highlight. Milwaukee Avenue would be crowded with thousands of revelers, with the sound of music filling the air, guaranteeing a wonderful time for all. This photograph was taken from atop Fitzgerald's Hardware store.

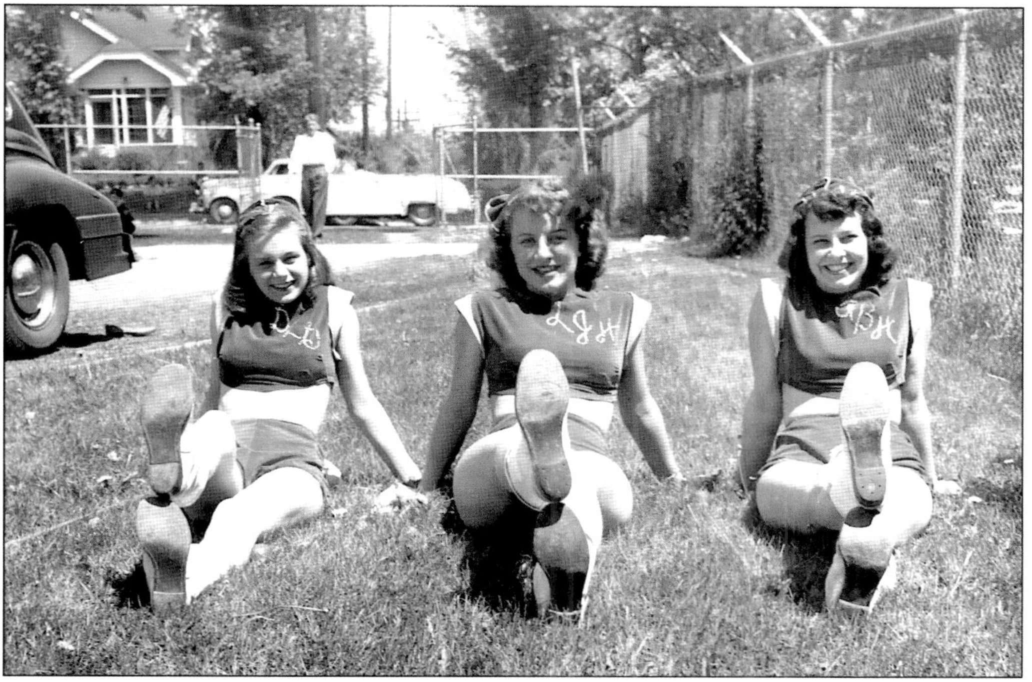

A trio of Twirlers limber up before the big competition at the high school athletic field. Saturday evening's Grand Spectacle program was the climax of the entire event. During its heyday, crowds of over 10,000 spectators would routinely pack the stadium.

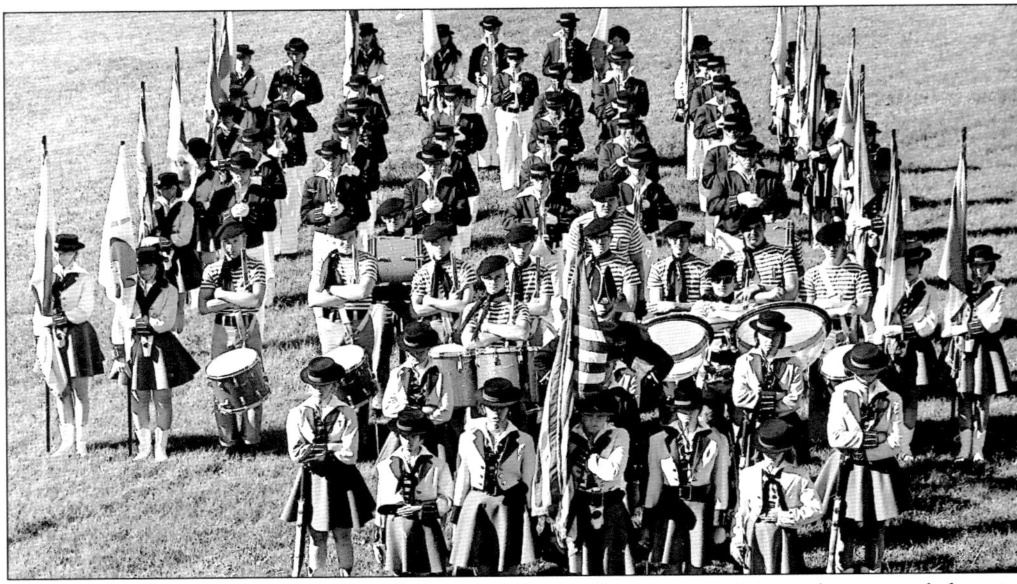

South Milwaukee's own Mariners Drum and Bugle Corps were always the natural favorite during the weekend competitions. Under the tutelage of Dr. H.R. Patin, a local dentist, the Spectacle City Mariners had won national renown for their on-field performances. The drum major, barely seen behind the flag in this 1965 photograph, was always a sight to behold. He was known informally as "Captain Crunch."

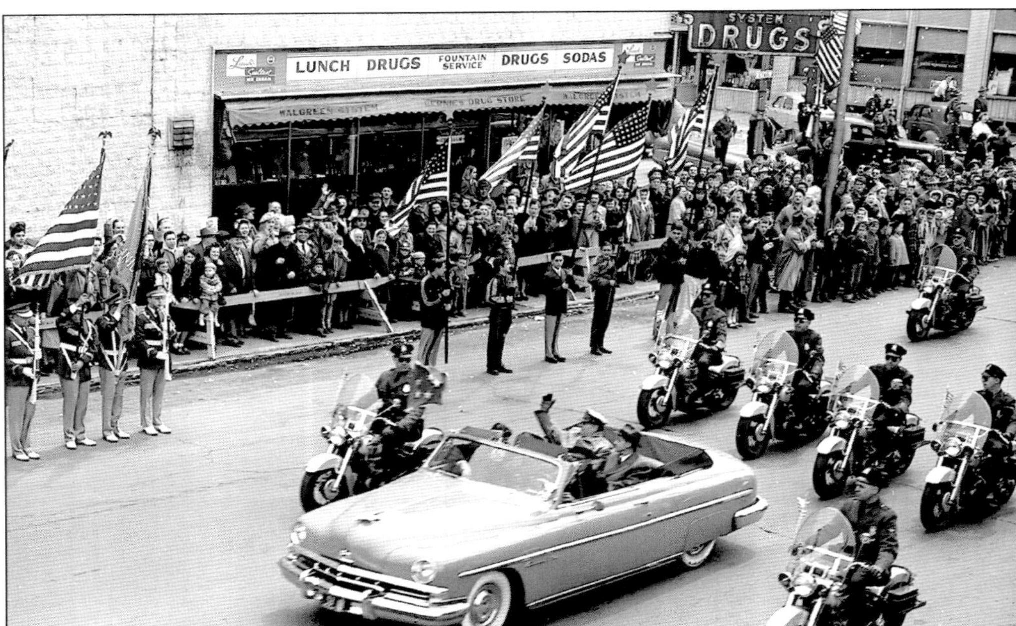

Having spent a portion of his youth growing up in Milwaukee, General Douglas MacArthur was a frequent visitor to the area. During these visits, he liked to take driving tours of the surrounding communities. MacArthur's motorcade passed through South Milwaukee on several occasions, one of which was documented here on April 27, 1951, at Tenth and Milwaukee Avenues.

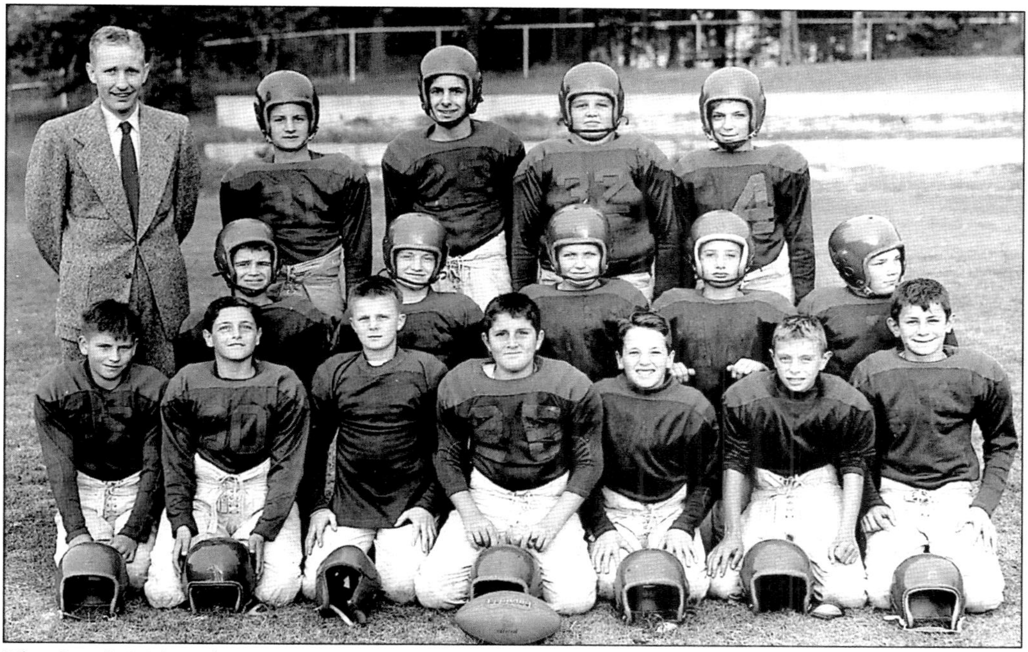

The South Milwaukee Recreation Department sponsored a seventh and eighth grade football program for many years. The games were played at Rawson Field. Here, we see Coach James Solum with his team, Wisconsin, *c.* 1955. (Courtesy of Pete Brunner)

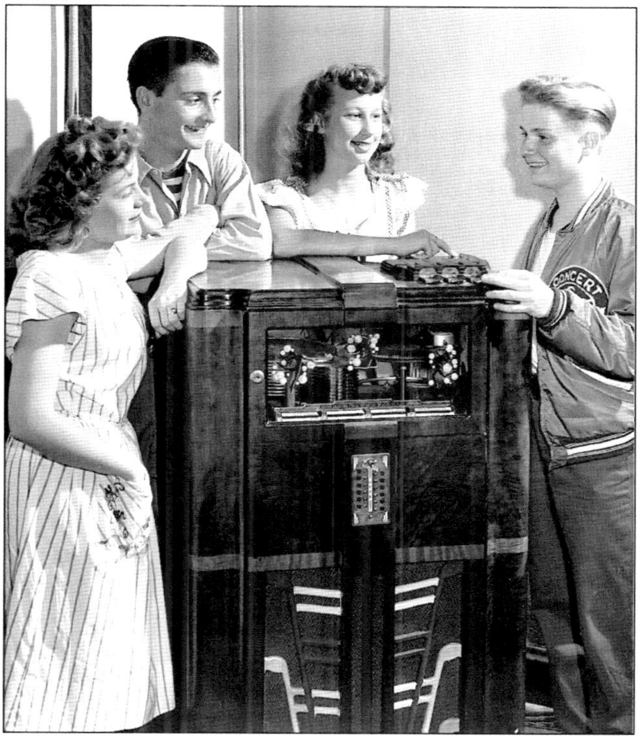

In a scene straight out of *Happy Days*, local teenagers gather around the jukebox at the Bucyrus-Erie Club in this *c.* 1958 photograph. The former Schutz Brothers Furniture Company building, the B-E Club would become the South Milwaukee Community Center in 1996.

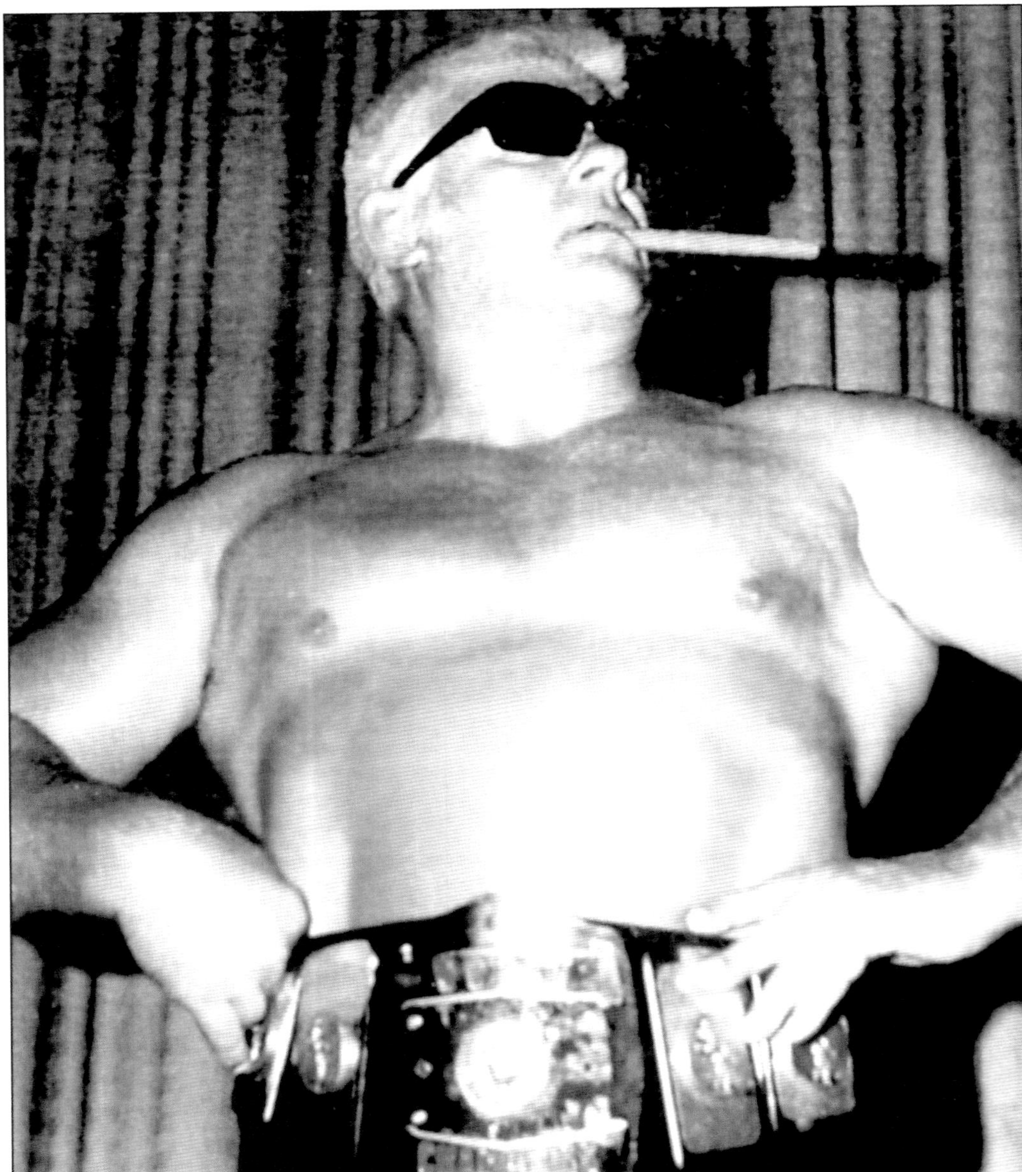

Any real chronicle of South Milwaukee's history would be incomplete without mention of the world famous professional wrestler, Reggie "The Crusher" Lisowski. A 1944 graduate of South Milwaukee High School, Lisowski was the starting fullback on the school's football team. He began his professional wrestling career in 1949. By 1966, The Crusher, a perennial fan favorite, was a three-time American Wrestling Association (AWA) World Heavyweight Champion. Together with Dick "The Bruiser" Afflis, these two would become one of the most popular and successful tag teams in the history of professional wrestling.

The Crusher's last match was held in 1989, capping a career that spanned 40 years. Despite his worldwide fame and genuine folk hero status, Reggie Lisowski never lost touch with his hometown roots. Together with his beloved wife Faye (nee Radomski), Lisowski would raise a family and spend his life calling South Milwaukee home. (Courtesy of Reggie Lisowski.)